AF478147

Traces and Their Antecedents

TRACES AND THEIR ANTECEDENTS

Samuel David Epstein

New York   Oxford
OXFORD UNIVERSITY PRESS
1991

Oxford University Press

Oxford   New York   Toronto
Delhi   Bombay   Calcutta   Madras   Karachi
Petaling Jaya   Singapore   Hong Kong   Tokyo
Nairobi   Dar es Salaam   Cape Town
Melbourne   Auckland

and associated companies in
Berlin   Ibadan

Published by Oxford University Press, Inc.
200 Madison Avenue, New York, New York 10016

Oxford is a registered trademark of Oxford University Press

Library of Congress Cataloging-in-Publication Data
Epstein, Samuel David.
Traces and their antecedents / Samuel David Epstein.
p. cm. Revision of author's thesis
(Ph. D.—University of Connecticut at Storrs, 1987).
Includes bibliographical references and index.
ISBN 0-19-506485-2 (acid-free paper)
1. Grammar, Comparative and general—Syntax.
2. Government-binding theory (Linguistics)
I. Title. P291.E67 1991
415—dc20 90-37801

9 8 7 6 5 4 3 2 1

Printed in the United States of America
on acid-free paper

*This book is dedicated
to my mother Lucy,
my father Joe,
and to Josh, my brother*

Preface

This book is a revised version of Epstein (1987). It is primarily concerned with determining those principles of Universal Grammar that directly govern the distribution of traces. Throughout, I use the term "trace" in its standard sense to mean an empty category created by movement. (For a detailed discussion of the concept "trace" see Chomsky, 1981, 2.4.5.) The book consists of four chapters. The first is introductory in which the fundamental concepts of the Government and Binding theory are presented. Chapter 2 concerns the Empty Category Principle (ECP), Chapter 3 explores conditions on A-chains, and Chapter 4 discusses Case requirements on traces. The first chapter is intended for those not completely familiar with the Government and Binding framework. The intent is to provide enough background to enable the reader to understand the ensuing discussion. It should be noted that some of the rudimentary definitions presented in this chapter may be slightly modified in subsequent chapters. Throughout, I will indicate the particular definitions being assumed. Those familiar with the theory can, of course, omit this introductory chapter. The investigation of the ECP conducted in Chapter 2 assumes, in large part, the formulation of this principle proposed in Lasnik and Saito (1984) (L&S); it also investigates certain modifications of this analysis advocated in Chomsky (1986b). The chapter concerning the ECP is entitled "Deriving Asymmetries in Gamma Assignment." Gamma assignment, as it is proposed by L&S, is simply the assignment of an abstract feature, arbitrarily called "gamma," to traces occurring in syntactic representations. Under the application of the gamma assignment algorithm, traces are assigned either $[+g]$ of $[-g]$, with the particular value depending entirely on the configuration in which the trace occurs. If a trace is assigned $[-g]$, the representation containing it is excluded; that is, there is a filter starring a representation containing a trace bearing the feature $[-g]$. If a trace is assigned $[+g]$, no violation results. Hence, the gamma-assignment algorithm is the theoretical object directly expressing the distinction between well formed and ill formed occurrences of traces.

Our concern in Chapter 2 is with the fact that this gamma-assignment algorithm displays two asymmetries. We attempt to eliminate both of them. The first is an argument–nonargument asymmetry, under which

(1) Only an argument receives a gamma feature at S-structure

Given (1), the gamma-assignment algorithm states that, at S-structure, each argument trace is assigned a gamma feature, but neither adjunct traces nor traces in Comp are assigned a gamma feature at this level. We argue that this need not be stipulated as part of the gamma-assignment algorithm, but, rather, can be reduced to independent principles. In particular, we argue that (1) can be eliminated by reordering the level at which the ECP filter applies while concurrently adopting the independently motivated theories of indexing and movement proposed in Chomsky (1982). We show that it is an entailment of these theories that a wh-adjunct and its traces (in direct contrast to an argument and its traces) have no indices until the level of LF. From this independently motivated difference in indexing, the argument–adjunct asymmetry in large part follows.

After eliminating this asymmetry by appeal to the particular theories of indexing and movement we adopt, entailments of these theories, beyond the derivability of the asymmetry, are investigated. We suggest that the indexing algorithm proposed can itself be simplified if D-structure is assumed to be both wholly X'-consistent and a representation of only argument structure. Under this conception of D-structure, adjuncts are, by definition, absent at this level of representation. We suggest that adjuncts are inserted in the syntactic component and that the insertion of such meaning-bearing categories is nonproblematic, given that such insertion is restricted to the noninterpretive (i.e., syntactic) component. We also note that this adjunct-insertion analysis entails the existence of generalized transformations that, as Kevin

Kearney (personal communication) has pointed out, are also required under Chomsky's (1981) insertion-analysis of "tough"-constructions. This concludes our investigation of the asymmetry (1).

The second asymmetry in *g*-assignment with which we are concerned is the asymmetry expressed by the existence of two formally unrelated forms of proper government, namely, antecedent government and lexical proper government. Following Chomsky (1986b), we suggest that lexical proper government is reducible to antecedent government (at least for verb–complement traces) provided the application of Affect-alpha and *g*-assignment are freely ordered with respect to one another in the LF component. We refer to this ordering as *successive cyclic* g-*assignment* in the LF component. This ordering is in fact entertained by L&S, but they reject it, since it overgenerates certain cases of long-distance adjunct movement. To prevent this kind of overgeneration, resulting from successive cyclic *g*-assignment at LF, Chomsky (class lectures, Fall 1986) has proposed a number of principles specifically mentioning adjuncts. These principles thus represent additional stipulated argument–adjunct asymmetries. Thus, although successive cyclic gamma assignment at LF may indeed allow for the elimination of lexical proper government, thereby eliminating one kind of asymmetry in gamma assignment, it appears to do so only at the expense of incorporating different, new argument–adjunct asymmetries. However, we argue that these asymmetries can also be eliminated under natural assumptions concerning the nature of the indexing algorithm under which the first asymmetry, namely (1), is eliminated.

In summary, both asymmetries appear to be eliminable without appealing to any stipulated distinction between argument and adjunct categories.

Following this, we investigate the consequences of successive cyclic *g*-assignment in the syntactic component. We suggest that there is no principled means by which to exclude such *g*-assignment in the syntax, given that it is permitted in the LF component. We show that, under syntactic successive cyclic *g*-assignment, "that"–trace configurations are overgenerated. (When a wh-phrase occupies Comp, the phrase itself can assign $[+g]$ to its trace and can then vacate Comp, which can subsequently become occupied by "that.") To prevent such derivations, we assume, following Lasnik and Saito (forthcoming), Davis (1984, 1987), and Rizzi (1986), that only a head can properly govern. This prevents assignment of $[+g]$ by phrases and thereby allows a number of ways of excluding "that"–trace configurations. Given that only a head can properly govern, we return to Chomsky's (1986b) elimination of lexical proper government discussed earlier. We note that successive cyclic g-assignment cannot be the result of successive cyclic adjunction of phrases, since phrases cannot assign gamma. Instead, we propose that what was thought to be successive cyclic phrasal adjunction is, in fact, successive cyclic movement through Specifier position accompanied by intermediate level Specifier–Head coindexing. (A similar analysis is independently proposed in Tiedeman [1987].) This Specifier–Head indexing can produce an indexed head that can properly govern in conformity with the restriction that only a head can properly govern.

We then reveal a need, within the framework of Chomsky (1986b), for the restriction that only a head can properly govern. We show that the theories of adjunction and government assumed there, including the assumption that phrases can antecedent-govern, is overly permissive, allowing overgeneration in a number of cases. If only heads can properly govern, such overgeneration is correctly blocked. If it is true that only a head can properly govern, then the theory of phrasal adjunction, as given in May (1985), plays no direct role within the subtheory ECP. We argue further that certain facts regarding pronominal variable binding also fail to provide support for this theory of adjunction.

Chapter 3 is entitled "Determining Properties of A-Chains." The purpose throughout is to eliminate, or at least simplify, chain-specific conditions, thereby demonstrating that, to a large extent, the properties of A-chains follow from independent principles of grammar. This chapter begins with analyses of Super-Raising and Improper Movement, arguing that the representations derived by such movement are excluded by an interaction of the ECP and the Local Binding Condition. Throughout this section a detailed formulation of the Local Binding Condition is motivated. Following this, we attempt to simplify this Condition. In its original form, as proposed by Chomsky (1981), this constraint on links of an A-chain requires that one member of a chain-link (call this member X) must locally A-bind the other member of the chain-link (call this member Y). This local A-binding requirement in fact amounts to three distinct requirements. First, X (the link head) must occupy an A-position. Second, X must bind Y (the link tail). Finally, if some category C binds Y (the link tail), then C must bind X (the link head). We argue that the first and second of these requirements imposed by the Local A-binding Condition are eliminable: Each can be derived from independent principles. Thus, it need not be stipulated that a link head occupies an A-position, nor does it have to be stated that members of an A-chain link are in a Binding relation. We suggest that the former property follows from Chomsky's (1986a) proposal that a theta chain is the abstract representation of an argument, whereas the latter property is derivable from (among other things) our proposal that the Theta Criterion applies cyclically. If our arguments are correct, then the Local Binding Condition is reducible to the single requirement that "if some category C binds the link tail, then C must bind the link head."

The final chapter investigates Case requirements on traces. We argue that, contrary to standard assumption, wh-trace need not be Case marked. This constitutes evidence, in addition to other evidence reviewed, against the Visibility Principle, while also permitting a simplification of the Case Filter, a filter we adopt. Finally, we investigate the commonly assumed requirement that NP-trace cannot be Case marked. This requirement is shown to be inadequate. Alternative requirements are therefore proposed.

Cambridge, Mass.   S.D.E.
June 1990

Acknowledgments

I am grateful to a number of people for their generous assistance with this project. First and foremost I thank Howard Lasnik, whose input has been an invaluable help. I am also grateful to David Michaels, who was a great source of support over the entire course of this undertaking. To Esther Torrego, too, I am indebted. She has been very helpful with all the things that have gone into writing this book and I thank her for her insight. In addition, I am grateful to Andy Barss, Maggie Browning, Lori Davis, and Juan Uriagereka. They have listened to many of my ideas and I thank them as well for their comments on my work and for the many enjoyable conversations about syntax we have had.

I would also like to thank the following people for their various contributions: Jim Gee, Mike Flynn, Chris Allen, Hyon Sook Choe, Paul Gorrell, Mark Hale, Sung Shim Hong, Kevin Kearney, T. Daniel Seely, Johan Seynnaeve, and Ewa Willim.

Finally, I am most indebted to Elaine McNulty. She has listened (at least once) to most ideas, if not every idea, in this book. I thank her for her patience and for her invaluable comments and criticisms that have made this a much better book than it would otherwise have been.

Contents

Traces and Their Antecedents

1

Introduction

This study is conducted within the Government-Binding theory of syntax presented originally in Chomsky (1981) and elaborated further in Chomsky (1982, 1986a). This theory of syntax, a modular one, consists of the following subtheories, the essential properties of which are briefly reviewed in this chapter:

1. X' theory
2. Government theory
3. Binding theory
4. Control theory
5. Bounding theory
6. Case theory
7. Theta theory
8. The Empty Category Principle

1. X' Theory

Within an X' theory of phrase structure, each lexical category X (= noun, verb, adjective, preposition) is immediately dominated by a category X' that is, in turn, immediately dominated by a category X''. We refer to X as the "head" of the "projections" X' and X''. The X' projection of the head X consists of X and its complements. The X'' projection, the "maximal projection" of X, consists of X' and the Specifier of X'. This schema thus defines the dominance relations of phrase structure representations. The order of constituents can be assumed to follow from properly formulated specifications of certain principles and parameters, including those governing Case assignment and theta assignment, and perhaps also from a principle that independently determines head–complement order.

By analogy with the lexical categories, we assume that the distribution of the nonlexical category INFL(ection), consisting of (at least) tense and agreement, also conforms to X′ theory. That is, INFL heads a projection INFL′ consisting of INFL and a complement V″. INFL′ is immediately dominated by INFL″, the maximal projection of INFL, consisting of INFL′ and a Specifier, namely, the subject N″ of INFL″.

As with the other nonlexical category, Comp(lementizer), we assume that this category is "defective." Although Comp heads a projection C′, consisting of Comp and INFL″, we assume that C′ = C″, that is, Comp heads only a single projection.[1] (Here we follow Chomsky 1986a, but see Chomsky 1986b for an analysis within which Comp is assumed to project categories in conformity with the X′ schema.) This X′ theory of constituent structure constrains D-structure, a level of representation that is, among other things, a direct representation of lexical structure. At levels of representation other than D-structure, X′ theory may not be satisfied, a result of the structural changes effected by certain transformational operations. Each of the remaining subtheories to be reviewed here consists of principles defined (at least in part) in terms of the X′ theory of constituent structure just outlined.

2. Government Theory

A unifying concept of the theory of syntax under discussion here is that of "government." A recent definition of this term is

(9) Government: A governs B if A = X^0 (in the sense of X′ Theory) A c-commands B and B is not protected by a maximal projection, where we say that B is protected by a maximal projection if there is a maximal projection including B but not A (see Chomsky 1982).

"Government," so defined, is a relation holding between two categories within a phrase structure representation. For a category

A to govern a category B, three conditions must be met. First, there is a restriction on the class of governors, such that only a head (as defined within X′ Theory) can be a governor. Second, for a head to govern a category B, the head must c-command B. The relation "c-command" also plays a unifying role throughout the theory. This relation can be defined as

(10) C-command: A c-commands B if neither A nor B dominates the other and the first branching node dominating A dominates B (Reinhart, 1979).

The third and final prerequisite to government is that there be no maximal projection that includes B, the governee, and that fails to include A, the governor.

The relation "government" plays a unifying role in that a number of distinct subtheories consist of principles incorporating this term. In particular, principles of Binding theory, Case theory, Theta theory, the Empty-Category Principle (and perhaps Bounding theory and control theory as well) are defined in terms of government.

3. Binding Theory

The theory of Binding imposes certain distributional requirements on anaphors, pronominals, and R-expressions ("names"), thereby providing a ready means for accounting for the interpretive properties of these three types of categories. There are three principles of binding, one for each category type:

(11) Principle A: An anaphor must be bound in its governing category

(12) Principle B: A pronominal must be free in its governing category

(13) Principle C: An R-expression must be free

The terms "bound," "free," and "governing category" are defined as follows. First, "bound" (or "binds") is defined in terms of "c-command":

(14) Binds: A binds B if and only if A and B are coindexed and A c-commands B

"Free" is defined simply as:

(15) Free: A is free if and only if A is not bound

Finally, "governing category" may be defined as:

(16) Governing category: The governing category of a category C is the minimal NP or S containing C and a governor of C (see Chomsky, 1981)

As a brief illustration of the content of this subtheory, consider a sentence such as

(17) John likes himself

We wish to explain the fact that the object anaphor "himself" is obligatorily interpreted as coreferential with "John." Consider the following representation of this sentence, one in which "himself" and "John" are not coindexed:

(18) $[_{S'} [_S \text{John}_i \text{ likes himself}_j]]$

This representation is excluded by Principle A of the Binding theory, since the anaphor "himself" (which is not coindexed with any category) is not bound in this representation. By contrast, consider the following representation in which the anaphor "himself" is coindexed with the subject NP "John":

(19) $[_{S'} [_S \text{John}_i \text{ likes himself}_i]]$

This representation satisfies Principle A of the Binding theory. The governing category of the anaphor "himself" is S. Principle A is satisfied, since "himself" is bound in S by virtue of the fact that it is coindexed with and c-commanded by the subject NP "John." Thus, we see that Principle A requires that (in a simple sentential structure) a direct object anaphor must be coindexed with the subject NP. Given this, suppose the following principle of interpretation is also assumed:

(20) Coindexed categories are obligatorily interpreted as coreferential

This principle interprets the coindexed NPs in (19) as coreferential. In this way, the Binding theory, operating in conjunction with principles of interpretation such as (20), provides an account of interpretive facts such as the one with which we began, namely, the fact that "himself" in sentence (17) obligatorily corefers with "John." This fact is accounted for; in the representation of this sentence the Binding theory requires coindexation of "John" and "himself," which is, in turn, obligatorily interpreted as expressing a coreferential relation between these two categories.

Consider next pronouns such as the one in direct object position in

(21) John likes him

The interpretive fact to be explained in this case is that "him" (in direct contrast to "himself") is obligatorily interpreted as noncoreferential with "John." Consider the following representation of this sentence:

(22) $[_{s'} [_s$ John$_i$ likes him$_i]]$

If this structure were allowed, then principle (20) applying to it would analyze the two NPs as obligatorily coreferential, since they are coindexed. Thus, if this representation of sentence (21) were generated, it would wrongly be predicted that this sentence permits a coreferential interpretation of the subject and object NPs. Correctly, such structures are excluded, specifically, by Principle B of the Binding theory. In (22) the governing category of the pronominal "him" is S, and "him" is bound by "John" within its governing category, thereby violating Principle B. To satisfy this principle of Binding, "him" must be contraindexed with "John," as in

(23) $[_{s'} [_s$ John$_i$ likes him$_j]]$

The interpretive facts can then be explained by adopting the following principle of interpretation:

(24) Contraindexed categories are obligatorily interpreted as noncoreferential

Finally, consider R-expressions, such as the NP "John," occurring in the following sentence:

(25) He likes John

The interpretive fact to be explained in this case is that "John" cannot corefer with "he." In the following representation these two categories are coindexed:

(26) $[_{s'} [_s$ he$_i$ likes John$_i]]$

However, this structure is ruled out by Principle C of the Binding theory. The only well formed representation of this sentence is one in which the two *NP*s are contraindexed

(27) $[_{S'} [_S$ he$_i$ likes John$_j]]$

Under the Principle of Interpretation (24), the relevant interpretive fact regarding sentence (25) is explained.

4. Control Theory

PRO, a category that is both a pronominal and an anaphor, is, by definition, subject to both Principles A and B of the Binding theory. Since these two principles impose contradictory requirements on any occurrence of PRO having a governing category, it follows that the only way for PRO to satisfy both principles simultaneously is for this category to lack a governing category. Consider the following representation:

(28) $[_{S'}[_S$ John$_i$ tried $[_{S'}[_S$ PRO to go]]]]$

Binding theory is satisfied, since PRO, being ungoverned, has no governing category in this representation. Thus, in contrast to pure anaphors, pure pronominals, and R-expressions, the Binding theory requires of PRO only that it occur in a particular type of position (namely, an ungoverned one). Crucially, the Binding theory imposes no requirement concerning the indexation of PRO. Consequently, to account for the fact that "John" and "PRO" obligatorily corefer, as is clear from the interpretation of the sentence represented, some subtheory of grammar must ensure that these two categories are coindexed. The module of grammar that governs the indexation of PRO, and thereby accounts for the interpretive properties of this element, is Control theory.

5. Bounding Theory

The theory of Bounding imposes locality conditions on the syntactic application of movement rules. The central tenet of this subtheory is the Subjacency Principle, formulated as follows:

(29) The Subjacency Principle: in the configuration:

$$\ldots X \ldots [_A \ldots [_B \ldots Y \ldots] \ldots] \ldots X \ldots$$

no rule may apply so as to move a category from the position Y to position X or conversely, where A and B are bounding nodes.

In English, the bounding nodes are NP and S. Thus, the Subjacency Principle accounts for the ungrammaticality of such sentences as the following:

(30) *Who do you believe the claim that John likes?

(*meaning:* Who is the person x such that you believe the claim that John likes x?)

The *S*-structure representation of this sentence is

(31) $[_{S'}$ Who$_i$ $[_S$ do you believe $[_{NP}$ the claim that John likes $t_i]]]$

In the derivation of such a structure, a single application of syntactic movement extracts the NP "Who" from both NP and S, each of which are bounding nodes. As a result, the Subjacency Principle is violated.

6. Case Theory

The theory of Case concerns the assignment of a formal feature, called the "Case feature," to certain categories occurring in syntactic representations. The Case feature is an abstract one (i.e., its presence has no morphological realization in a large class of constructions). Central to this subtheory is the Case filter, a principle requiring that each lexical NP be assigned a Case feature. The assignment of Case features to lexical NPs is constrained in at least three ways. First, there are restrictions on the class of Case assigners; only verbs, prepositions, and INFL containing AGR(eement) are capable of assigning a Case feature.[2] Second, government plays a role within Case theory too, in that a Case feature can be assigned only if the Case assigner governs the Case recipient (i.e., the lexical NP). Finally, there is a further, perhaps parameterized, constraint on Case assignment under which a Case assigner and a Case recipient must be adjacent to one another. This is called "The Case Adjacency Condition" (see Stowell, 1981). Given these principles of Case assignment, the

NP "John" lacks Case and therefore violates the Case filter in each of the following examples:

(32) [$_{S'}$[$_S$I am proud John]]

(33) [$_{NP}$ the indictment John]

(34) [$_{S'}$[$_S$I tried [$_{S'}$[$_S$ John to go]]]]

(35) [$_{S'}$[$_S$ I like very much John]]

Example (32) is excluded since "proud," the only category adjacent to "John," is an adjective and therefore has no Case feature to assign. "John" is thus Caseless and the Case filter is consequently violated. Example (33) is similarly excluded, since nouns, like adjectives, are simply not Case assigners. Notice, if "of" appears in the position immediately preceding "John," both examples become grammatical. This follows because "of" is a preposition, hence a Case assigner that, if it were to appear immediately before "John," would both govern and be adjacent to this NP, with the result that Case assignment could apply, thereby satisfying the Case filter. The structure in (34) is excluded, since the NP "John" is not governed by a Case assigner. The verb "tried" fails to govern "John," and "to," the realization of INFL lacking agreement, is not a Case assigner. The Case filter is consequently violated. Finally, in example (35), "John" is governed by a Case assigner, namely, the verb "like." Nevertheless, "John" is not assigned Case, since "like" is not adjacent to this NP. Again, the Case filter is violated.

In Chapter 4 we examine certain constraints on the distribution of traces that are often assumed to be imposed by the theory of Case.

7. Theta Theory

The principles of Theta theory constrain the co-occurrence of predicates and arguments (while also expressing the thematic relations between the two). These co-occurrence restrictions are established by first assuming that each predicate possesses at least one "thematic," or "theta," role, which the predicate assigns to an argument. (The class of arguments includes, among other categories, "referential" NPs [e.g., "John," "the problem," etc.] and sentential complements.) Given that each predicate has at least one theta role to assign, the relative distribution of predicates and arguments is established by the Theta Criterion, the most fundamental principle of Theta theory:

(36) The Theta Criterion: Each argument bears one and only one theta role and each theta role is assigned to one and only one argument (see Chomsky, 1981)

Theta role assignment (as constrained by the Theta Criterion) occurs only under government (i.e., for a predicate to assign its theta role to an argument, the former must govern the latter). Thus, government plays a significant role within this subsystem as well.

Different predicates have distinct theta-assigning properties. For example, predicates differ as to the number of theta roles they assign. A predicate such as "solve" has two theta roles, what we might call a "subject theta role" and an "object theta role." Accordingly, the following structure is allowed:

(37) $[_{S'}[_S$ John solved the problem]]

This representation satisfies the Theta Criterion, since each argument bears one and only one theta role. ("John" is assigned only the subject theta role and "the problem" is assigned only the object theta role). Furthermore, each theta role is assigned to one and only one argument. (The subject theta role is assigned to only "John" and the object theta role is assigned to only "the problem.") By contrast, the following structure is ill formed:

(38) $*[_{S'}[_S$ John solved]]

This violates the second conjunct of the Theta Criterion, since there is no object present to receive the object theta role assigned by "solve." However, unlike "solve," there are verbs that assign only a subject theta role. The verb "sleep" is an example. Consequently, in contrast to (38), the following satisfies the Theta Criterion:

(39) $[_{S'}[_S$ John sleeps]]

Like the verb "sleep," the verb "seem" assigns only one theta role. However, in direct contrast to "sleep," "seem" assigns its only theta role to a (sentential) direct object while assigning no theta role whatsoever to subject position. These particular theta-assigning properties of the verb "seem" are evidenced in the following structures:

(40) $[_{S'}[_S$ It seems $[_{S'}$ that $[_S$ John left]]

(41) *$[_{S'}$ $[_S$ Fred seems $[_{S'}$ that $[_S$ John left]]

Example (40) is well formed (i.e., this structure satisfies the Theta Criterion). The single (object) theta role assigned by "seem" is assigned to the complement argument S'. Since "seem" assigns no subject theta role, the subject position cannot be occupied by an argument. Hence, the nonargument, nonreferential "it" occurs in this position. By contrast, (41) violates the Theta Criterion, since the argument "Fred" fails to bear a theta role, thereby violating the first conjunct of this principle.

Given that (41) is ill formed, the following generalization might be advanced: "The Theta Criterion dictates that an argument, such as 'Fred,' can never occur as the subject of 'seem,' since the argument would always fail to receive a theta role in this position, thereby violating the Theta Criterion." There is, however, one exception. An argument can, in fact, occur as a subject of "seem" in the following type of structure:

(42) $[_{S'}[_S$ Fred$_i$ seems $[_S$ t_i to sleep]]

This structure satisfies the Theta Criterion by virtue of the fact that the argument "Fred" binds its trace (t), which is assigned a theta role, namely, the subject theta role assigned by "sleep." The two *NP*s "Fred" and t are said to constitute a "chain" in such structures. The properties of such chains and the principles determining these properties are investigated in Chapter 3.

8. The Empty Category Principle

The Empty Category Principle (ECP) accounts for distributional distinctions between traces, for example, subject and object traces. One such subject–object asymmetry is illustrated by the following contrast:

(43) *$[_{S'}$ Who$_i$ $[_S$ do you think $[_{S'}$ that $[_S$ t_i left]]]]

(44) $[_{S'}$ What$_i$ $[_S$ do you think $[_{S'}$ that $[_S$ John bought t_i]]]]

Descriptively, a subject trace is disallowed when a complementizer (e.g., "that") is present, as in (43), whereas an object trace can licitly co-occur with a complementizer, as shown in (44). The ECP accounts for this kind of contrast, among others, by requiring that all traces be properly governed. Roughly speaking, the object trace in (44) is properly governed by virtue of being a complement to a lexical category, namely, the verb "bought." The trace in (44) is thus said to be "lexically properly governed," and it therefore satisfies the ECP. By contrast, the subject trace in (43) is not lexically properly governed, since, by definition, a subject is not the complement of a lexical head (i.e., no subject trace is lexically properly governed). If the ECP were to require that all traces be lexically properly governed, then (43) would be excluded, as desired. But this requirement excludes subject traces in general. Of course, this is an incorrect result; a subject trace is allowed, provided the complementizer "that" is absent, as in the following structure:

(45) $[_{S'}$ Who$_i$ $[_S$ do you think $[_{S'}$ t_i $[_S$ t_i left]]]]

Thus, the ill-formedness of (43) cannot be due to some requirement that all traces must be lexically properly governed, since this requirement wrongly excludes (45). The ECP excludes (43) while allowing (45) by recognizing another form of proper government, in addition to lexical proper government, called "antecedent government." Thus, the ECP requires that a trace be properly governed in at least one of the two following ways, lexically or by an antecedent. Example (43) is excluded by the ECP because the subject trace is not lexically properly governed (as noted earlier), nor is it antecedent-governed. The subject trace is not antecedent-governed, since its antecedent, namely, "who," is "too far away" from the trace, in particular, an S' separates the trace from its antecedent, thereby preventing antecedent government. Hence, this trace is neither antecedent-governed nor lexically properly governed (i.e., the ECP is violated and the structure is correctly excluded). Structure (45), however, satisfies the ECP. Again, the subject trace, like all subject traces, is not lexically properly governed. However, in contrast to the subject trace in (43), the subject trace in (45) does have a very close antecedent, namely, the trace in Comp. Since no S' separates the subject trace from its antecedent in Comp, the former is antecedent governed (i.e., the ECP is satisfied and (45) is correctly allowed).

Beyond accounting for such distributional distinctions between subject and object traces created by syntactic movement, the ECP also accounts for subject–object asymmetries exhibited by traces of LF movement. Moreover, the particular formulation of the ECP we investigate accounts for the distribution of traces in Comp as well as adjunct traces. In the following chapter, the formulation of the Empty Category Principle is examined in detail.

Notes

1. Throughout, we often use standard notation while intending X′ interpretation. Thus, the reader should assume NP = N″, VP = V″, AP = A″, PP = P″, S = I″, S′ = C″, and so on.

2. But see Chomsky (1986a) for arguments that adjectives and nouns may assign Case too.

2

Deriving Asymmetries in Gamma Assignment*

Introduction: An Argument–Nonargument Asymmetry

Lasnik and Saito (1984) (L&S) propose the following principle governing gamma (g) assignment:

(1) Only an argument receives a g-feature at S-structure

In this section we will eliminate (1), deriving its effects from independently motivated principles of grammar. In the resulting system there is no asymmetry with respect to the level at which argument and nonargument traces are g-assigned. Rather, at every level of representation each trace present is g-assigned.

Before deriving (1), we will review the general features of the ECP as proposed by L&S, including the motivation for principle (1).

Lasnik and Saito's ECP

As formulated by L&S, the ECP has two parts. First, it indicates the configurations in which proper government of a trace obtains. Second, it filters representations containing traces that are not

---

*The analysis of argument-adjunct asymmetries presented in this chapter was given in Chapter 2 of Epstein (1987). See Rizzi (1990, Chapter 3) for a similar analysis of argument–adjunct asymmetries.

properly governed. They regard the first part as the assignment of a feature $[+g]$ in certain configurations, and the assignment of $[-g]$ otherwise

(2) $t \rightarrow [+g]$ when lexically or antecedent governed
$t \rightarrow [-g]$ otherwise

The second part of the ECP is construed as a filter

(3) $*t$
     $[-g]$

Under this formulation of the ECP, three purely empirical questions emerge:

(4) At what level does filter (3) apply?

(5) What is the definition of "proper government"?

(6) At what point in a derivation does g-assignment occur?

L&S (n. 63) assume that

(7) Filter (3) applies at S-structure and at LF

With regard to question (5), "proper government" is defined by L&S as follows:

(8)   A properly governs B iff
     A properly lexically governs B or
     A antecedent-governs B

(9)   A properly lexically governs B iff
     A governs B, and
     A is an X^0 lexical category, and
     A Case-marks or Theta-marks B

(10) A antecedent-governs B iff
     A c-commands B, and
     A and B are coindexed, and
     There is no X, X an NP or S' such that
     A c-commands X, and X dominates B,
     unless B is the head of X

(11) C-command: A c-commands B if
     neither A nor B dominates the other
     and the first branching node dominating
     A dominates B (from Reinhart, 1979)

With regard to question (6), L&S propose that *g*-assignment occurs at the output of each component and only there. Principle (1) is, of course, also assumed. These assumptions are formally expressed in the following model:

(12) Syntactic Component:

    a. D-structure

    b. Affect-alpha

    c. Index Comp

    d. Assign $[+g]$ to any properly governed argument

    e. Obligatorily assign $[-g]$ to any argument that is not properly governed

    f. $*t$
       $[-g]$

(13) LF Component:

    a. Affect-alpha

    b. Index Comp

    c. Assign $[+g]$ to any properly governed category

    d. Obligatorily assign $[-g]$ to any category that is not properly governed

    e. $*t$
       $[-g]$

With this much background we may now begin to determine the motivation for principle (1).

The Motivation for Principle (1)

To see the motivation for principle (1), we will examine a number of "that"–trace configurations (i.e., configurations in which antecedent government of a trace fails to obtain because of the presence of "that"). The fact that antecedent government fails to obtain in such configurations follows both from L&S's definition of antecedent government and from their assumptions regarding the structure of Comp. L&S tentatively propose that Comp universally consists of one and only one base-generated position, which they call the "head of Comp." It is also assumed that adjunction to Comp is possible only in LF. As L&S note, under this analysis it is predicted that a Comp can never contain multiple categories at S-structure (i.e., the doubly filled Comp filter is eliminable).[1] L&S further assume that

(14) Comp obligatorily receives the index of its head at each syntactic level

Following Aoun, Hornstein, and Sportiche (1981), it is assumed that an indexed Comp can be an antecedent governor.

Argument Traces

Assuming the ECP and the structure of Comp as proposed by L&S, consider the following data:

(15) What do you think John likes

(16) What do you think that John likes

(17) Who do you think likes John

(18) *Who do you think that likes John

The S-structure representations of (15) and (16) are as follows:

(19) $[_{S'} [_{C_i}$ What$_i]$ $[_S$ do you think $[_{S'} [_{C_i} (t_i)]$ [John likes $t_i]]]]$

(20) $[_{S'} [_{C_i}$ What$_i][_S$ do you think $[_{S'} [_C$ that]$[_S$ John likes $t_i]]]]$

Given that Comp consists of only one position, the S-structure of (16), namely (20), does not contain a trace in Comp, since Comp is occupied by "that." Consequently, Subjacency as a constraint on representation would be violated, where Subjacency as a constraint on representation is defined as

(21) In the configuration:
$. . .X. . .[_A. . .[_B. . .Y. . .]. . .]. . .X. . .$
if X and Y are successive links in a A–A′ chain then either A or B is not a bounding node

For this reason as well as others, L&S assume that Subjacency is a constraint on syntactic movement:

(22) In the configuration:

$$\ldots X\ldots[_A\ldots[_B\ldots Y\ldots]\ldots]\ldots X\ldots$$

no rule may apply so as to move an element from the position Y to position X or conversely, where A and B are bounding nodes

The derivation of (20) satisfies (22); the lexical item "that," having no semantic content, need not be present at D-structure. Since "that" is absent, syntactic movement of "what" can proceed from Comp to Comp, thereby satisfying (22). Provided the movement of "what" from the embedded Comp leaves no trace, an available option, "that" can be inserted after "what" is moved to the matrix Comp and prior to S-structure. Given that Subjacency is a constraint on movement, notice that the following derivation satisfies this principle:

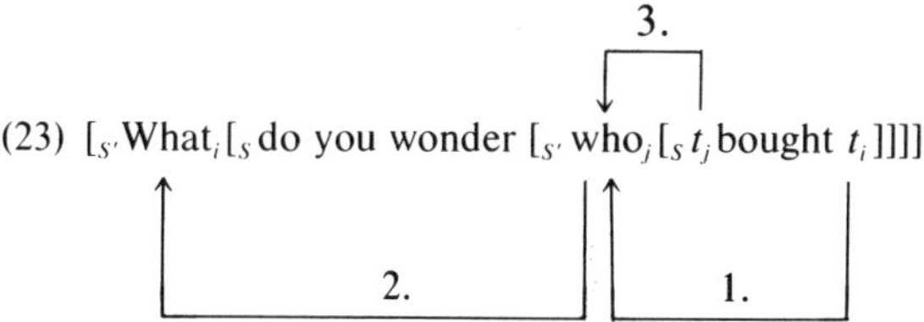

$$(23)\ [_{S'} \text{What}_i [_S \text{do you wonder } [_{S'} \text{who}_j [_S t_j \text{ bought } t_i]]]]$$

To rule out such derivations, L&S assume the principle of the Strict Cycle. Notice, however, that the preceding derivation of the S-structure (20) apparently violates this principle. After "what" is raised out of the embedded Comp into the matrix Comp (a matrix-S' operation), "that" is inserted in the embedded Comp, an operation affecting only positions in a previously cycled domain, namely, the embedded S'. To avoid this unwanted result, we might assume that the insertion of "that" is not really an instance of Affect-alpha; hence, it is an operation not constrained by the Strict Cycle. This result follows from the analysis of Chomsky (1973) under which "that"-insertion is simply the spelling out of the features of a [-wh] Comp.

With regard to the ECP, notice that in (20), the trace of "what" is not antecedent governed. This is thus one type of structure motivating the existence of lexical proper government. The trace in (20), although not antecedent-governed, is lexically properly governed by the verb "likes." Therefore, this trace is assigned

$[+g]$ and the ECP (i.e., filter (3) is satisfied at both S-structure and LF. Since Subjacency constrains only movement, and since movement only optionally creates a trace, a trace can, but need not, occur in Comp in the S-structure (19). Regardless, the ECP is satisfied, since t_i is lexically properly governed by "likes." Thus, in the case of a direct object trace of wh-movement, the presence or absence of "that" in Comp has no effect on grammaticality. By contrast, as is well known, in the case of a subject trace of wh-movement the presence or absence of "that" in an adjacent Comp determines grammaticality. The S-structure representations of (17) and (18) are

(24) $[_{S'}[_{C_i}\text{Who}_i][_S \text{ do you think } [_{S'}[_{C_i} t_i][_S t_i \textit{ likes John}]]]]$
$$[+g]$$

(25) $*[_{S'}[_{C_i}\text{Who}_i][_S \text{ do you think}[_{S'}[_C \text{that}][_S t_i \text{ likes John}]]]]$
$$[-g]$$

In (25), t_i is neither antecedent-governed nor lexically properly governed. Thus, t_i is assigned $[-g]$ and the ECP is violated at S-structure. Similarly, in (24) if the trace in Comp is absent, with the result that Comp is unindexed, the ECP is violated at S-structure, just as it is in (25). However, if the trace in Comp is present and Comp is therefore indexed Comp_i, then t_i is antecedent-governed and the ECP is satisfied both at S-structure and at LF. The contrast in grammaticality between sentences (17) and (18) is thus predicted by L&S's ECP.

Adjunct Traces

Huang (1982) notes that adjunct wh-phrases (e.g., "on which day") do not exhibit "that"–trace effects. This phenomenon is equally well illustrated with adjuncts such as "why." Thus, the following is perfectly grammatical with "why" construed as a modifier of the embedded sentence (or VP):

(26) Why do you think that John left

Examples such as (26) are, in fact, ambiguous, in that "why" can also be construed as a modifier of the matrix sentence. The fact that "why" can be construed as a matrix modifier is unsurprising. The S-structure corresponding to this matrix-modifier reading is[2]

(27) $[_{S'}[_{C_i}$ Why$_i][_S$ do you think$[_{S'}[_S$ John left $]]t_i]]$

Given that adjunct traces are subject to the ECP and are, by definition, not lexically properly governed, t_i must be antecedent-governed and is, under definition (10), of antecedent government. Hence, the ECP is satisfied. Indeed, if antecedent government failed to obtain in such configurations, matrix modification by an adjunct would be impossible, and it would then be incorrectly predicted that, for example, "Why did John leave" is ungrammatical. More interesting than the availability of a matrix modifier reading is the fact that (26) can also be interpreted with "why" as a modifier of the embedded sentence. The S-structure representation of such a reading is apparently

(28) $[_{S'}[_{C_i}$ Why$_i][_S$ do you think$[_{S'}[_C$ that$][_S$ John left $t_i]]]]$
$$[-g]$$

In the S-structure (28), t_i is neither antecedent-governed nor lexically properly governed; that is, t_i is not properly governed and is therefore assigned $[-g]$. Thus, the ECP (filter (3)) applying at S-structure is violated exactly as it is in the S-structure (25). We now confront the following problem: We must somehow allow an S-structure representation (such as (28)) containing a trace bearing $[-g]$, but at the same time we must rule out an S-structure (such as (25)) precisely because it contains a trace bearing $[-g]$. L&S solve this problem by first observing a distinction between the traces occurring in (28) and (25). In (28), which we want to generate, the trace that is not properly governed is an adjunct trace, whereas in (25), which we want to rule out, the offending trace is an argument. To allow the S-structure (28), despite the application of filter (3) (the ECP) at this level, L&S propose principle (1):

(1) Only an argument receives a g-feature at S-structure

Given (1), the S-structure (25) is unchanged; the subject trace is assigned $[-g]$, and the ECP is violated at S-structure. However, (28) is no longer generated. Rather, in the S-structure representation, the adjunct trace receives no g-feature whatsoever, as in

(29) $[_{S'}[_{C_i}$why$_i][_S$ do you think $[_{S'}[_C$that$][_S$ John left $t_i]]]]$

Since the trace is not g-assigned, filter (3) applying at S-structure is satisfied. Now, recalling that g-assignment occurs at the output of each component, it follows that if the S-structure (29) is mapped into an LF representation in which "that" occurs in Comp, the ECP will be violated at LF as in the following LF representation:

(30) $[_{S'}[_{Ci}$Why$_i][_S$ do you think$[_{S'}[_C$that$][_S$ John left $t_i]]]]$
$$[-g]$$

The trace is assigned $[-g]$ and the ECP is violated at LF. Thus, while principle (1) allowed the S-structure representation to "escape" the S-structure application of the filter (3) (the ECP), by withholding g-assignment at this level, we now require a way to generate a well-formed LF representation (i.e., one in which the trace is assigned $[+g]$). L&S argue that such a well-formed LF representation can be generated in the following way: In the LF component, "that" can be deleted, a licit operation, since the deleted element has no semantic content. Next, "why" is moved down to the embedded Comp and is subsequently raised back up to the matrix Comp, this latter operation leaving a trace in Comp. After movement applies, Comp indexing applies, with the result that Comp and the trace in Comp are coindexed. Thus, the following LF representation is generated:

(31) $[_{S'}[_{C_i}$Why$_i][_S$ do you think$[_{S'}[_{C_i}t_i][_S$ John left $t_i]]]]$
$$[+g]$$

The ECP (i.e., filter (3)) is satisfied at LF, since t_i is antecedent-governed and therefore assigned $[+g]$.

Notice no LF operation can similarly "rescue" an S-structure such as (25). Under principle (1), in such an S-structure the argument trace is assigned $[-g]$, and therefore filter (3) is violated at S-structure.

We have now seen how, under principle (1), the ECP accounts for "that"–trace effects with subject traces in English and for the suppression of such effects with adjuncts.

Traces in Comp

Thus far we have discussed g-assignment of argument traces and adjunct traces but have ignored traces in Comp. L&S present evidence that traces in Comp, like argument and adjunct traces, are subject to the ECP. Consider, for example, the following contrast:

(32) ?What do you believe the claim that John said Bill bought

(33) *Why do you believe the claim that John said that Bill bought a car

An interpretation of (33) in which "why" modifies the most deeply embedded sentence is strongly unavailable (hence less available than the only reading of (32)). Under the analysis proposed in L&S, this contrast follows; (32) violates only Subjacency, whereas (33) violates both Subjacency and the ECP. Consider first (33), which has two possible S-structure representations, depending on whether a trace appears in Comp at this level

(34) $[_{S'}[_{C_i}\text{Why}_i][_S\text{do you believe}[_{NP}\text{the claim }[_{S'}\text{that}$
$[_S\text{John said }[_{S'}[_{C(i)}(t_i)][_S\text{Bill bought a car }t_i]]]]]]]$

Even if the movement of "why" proceeded through the two embedded Comps, Subjacency is violated, since one instance of movement applied to "why" in such a way as to move this category from the position of "that" to the matrix Comp. Subjacency is violated, since two bounding nodes, NP and S, dominate "that" yet fail to dominate the matrix Comp.

As concerns the ECP, under principle (1), t_i is not g-assigned at S-structure. Notice that such S-structure configurations provide further motivation for (1). Given that an S-structure such as (34) including the trace in Comp is generable, notice that without principle (1), the trace in Comp would assign $[+g]$ to the adjunct trace at S-structure. In the LF component, the trace in Comp could delete. Incorrectly, the ECP would be satisfied and it would thereby be incorrectly predicted that an unavailable interpretation of (33) is possible. As noted, under principle (1), the adjunct trace is not g-assigned at S-structure. Now, in the LF component, a representation such as (34), with the trace appearing in Comp, can be generated in two different ways. First, the trace in Comp could have been created by syntactic movement of "why." Alternatively, a trace in Comp might not have been created by syntactic movement yet could be created in the LF component by down and back movement of "why." Regardless, if the trace in Comp is absent at LF, the ECP is certainly violated; t_i is neither lexically properly governed nor antecedent-governed at this level (i.e., this trace is assigned $[-g]$ and filter (3), the ECP, is violated). But suppose the trace in Comp is present. If so, it antecedent-governs the adjunct trace, as in

(35) $[_{S'}$ Why$_i[_S$ do you believe$[_{NP}$ the claim$[_{S'}$ that
$[_S$ John said$[_{S'}$ $t_i[_S$ Bill bought a car $t_i]]]]]]]$
$$[+g]$$

The ECP is satisfied, since no trace bearing the feature $[-g]$ occurs. Thus, it is wrongly predicted that sentence (33) allows an interpretation in which "why" modifies the most deeply embedded sentence. To avoid this result, L&S assume that traces in Comp, like other traces, are subject to g-marking. Under principle (1), traces in Comp, being nonarguments, are not g-assigned until the output of LF. Thus, under (1), in the LF representation of (33), there must be a trace in the lowest Comp to g-assign the adjunct trace. However, the trace in Comp is itself assigned $[-g]$, since it is neither antecedent-governed nor lexically properly governed. Thus, the ECP is violated. By contrast, notice that the derivation of sentence (32) satisfies the ECP. At no level of representation is a trace in Comp required, since the direct object trace is lexically properly governed. Consequently, the ECP is satisfied, provided no trace in Comp appears at LF. We have just seen the motivation for L&S's proposal that a trace in Comp is subject to the ECP. As noted, under principle (1) such traces are not g-assigned until LF. This is yet another empirically correct effect of principle (1), since, as L&S note, there is a contrast in grammaticality between the (a) and (b) examples in both (36) and (37):

(36) a. ?Who do you think that John said left?

    b. *Who do you think that John said that left?

(37) a. ?Who do you wonder whether John said left?

    b. *Who do you wonder whether John said that left?

The S-structure representation of (36a) is

(38) $[_{S'}[_{C_i}\text{Who}_i][_S \text{do you think } [_{S'}[_C \text{that}][_S \text{John said } [_{S'}[_{C_i} t_i][_S t_i \text{ left}]]]]]]$
$$[+g]$$

Under principle (1), the subject trace is g-assigned at S-structure. Since the subject trace is not lexically properly governed, it receives $[+g]$ at S-structure only if the trace in Comp is present so as to antecedent-govern the subject. Thus, to satisfy the ECP applying at S-structure, the trace in Comp must be present to g-assign the subject. But now, in the absence of (1), the trace in Comp would be g-assigned at S-structure. Were this the case, the trace in Comp would be assigned $[-g]$. Filter (3) (the ECP) applying at S-structure would then be violated, just as it is violated in the S-structure representation of (36b) (which is identical in relevant respects to (25)). Hence, (36a) would be wrongly analyzed as an ECP violation, with the result that the contrast between (36a) and (36b) is lost. However, under (1), the trace in Comp, being a nonargument, is not g-assigned at S-structure. Hence, filter (3), applying at S-structure, is satisfied. In the LF component, two alternative options can be exploited, each resulting in a well-formed LF representation. The trace in Comp could simply be deleted, or "that" could be deleted followed by down and back movement of "who," creating a trace in the Comp formerly occupied by "that." Under either option, the ECP is satisfied at LF. The only well-formed S-structure of (37a) is

(39) $[_{S'}[_{C_i}\text{Who}_i][_S \text{do you wonder}[_{S'}[_C \text{whether}][_S \text{John said } [_{S'}[_{C_i} t_i][t_i \text{ left}]]]]]]$
$$[+g]$$

Again, the trace in Comp must be present to g-assign the subject. Under principle (1), the trace in Comp is not g-assigned at S-structure. An LF representation satisfying the ECP is derived only if the trace in Comp deletes. Retention of the trace in Comp leads to a violation of the ECP at LF. Since "whether" has semantic content, it cannot delete. Consequently, if a trace occurs in the lowest Comp, it will be assigned $[-g]$ at LF.

In this section we have seen that traces in Comp are subject to g-assignment; furthermore, under principle (1), such g-assignment occurs only in the LF component.

Summary of the Motivation for Principle (1)

To demonstrate the motivation for principle (1), as proposed in L&S, we have discussed their analyses of "that"–trace effects with arguments, adjuncts, and traces in Comp. As noted, L&S propose that the following filter (i.e., the ECP) applies at S-structure and at LF:

(40) *t
     $[-g]$

Principle (1) was then motivated for the purposes of ruling out S-structures such as (25) while allowing those such as (29):

(25) $[_{S'}[_{C_i} \text{Who}_i][_S \text{do you think}[_{S'}[_C \text{that}][_S t_i \text{ likes John}]]]]$
                                      $[-g]$

(29) $[_{S'}[_{C_i} \text{Why}_i][_S \text{do you think}[_{S'}[_C \text{that}][_S \text{John left } t_i]]]]$

In (25) the subject trace is assigned $[-g]$. Consequently, filter (3) (the ECP) is violated at S-structure. In (29), under (1), the adjunct trace is assigned no g-feature whatsoever. Hence, the ECP applying at S-structure is satisfied. In the LF component, Affect-alpha can apply in such a way that a trace of "why" occurs in the embedded Comp, with the result that the ECP is satisifed at LF.

The correctness of principle (1) was also evidenced by the fact that S-structure to LF mappings such as the following do not occur:

(34a) $[_{S'} \text{Why}_i[_S \text{do you believe}[_{NP} \text{the claim}[_{S'} \text{that}[_S \text{John}$
        $\text{said } [_{S'} t_i[_S \text{Bill bought a car } t_i]]]]]$
                        $[+g]$

(34b) $[_{S'} \text{Why}_i[_S \text{do you believe}[_{NP} \text{the claim}[_{S'} \text{that}[_S \text{John}$
        $\text{said } [_{S'}[_S \text{Bill bought a car } t_i]]]]]]$
                        $[+g]$

Under (1), the adjunct trace is not g-assigned until LF. For this trace to acquire the feature $[+g]$, the trace in Comp must be present at LF as in

(35) *$[_{S'} \text{Why}_i[_S \text{do you believe}[_{NP} \text{the claim}[_S \text{that}[_S \text{John}$
        $\text{said } [_{S'} t_i[_S \text{Bill bought a car } t_i]]]]]]]$
          $[-g]$ $[+g]$

The ECP is violated at LF because the trace in Comp is not properly governed. Of course, deriving this result entails that traces in Comp are subject to g-assignment. Given this, principle (1) is again motivated by the fact that S-structures such as (38), necessitated by the ECP, do not violate this principle.

(38) $[_{S'}$ Who$_i[_S$ do you think$[_{S'}$ that $[_S$ John said $[_{S'} t_i [_S t_i$ left$]]]]]]$
$$[+g]$$

Under (1), the trace in Comp is not g-assigned at S-structure. Hence, the ECP is satisfied at this level. At LF, the trace in Comp can delete.

In short, we have seen that principle (1) has three distinct effects:

(41a) An argument trace is g-assigned at S-structure

(41b) An adjunct trace (i.e., a trace in adjoined position) is g-assigned only at LF

(41c) A trace in Comp is g-assigned only at LF

Deriving Principle (1)

L&S raise the question of whether (1) is an independent principle or follows from other principles. With regard to this issue they write:

> Since [(1)] distinguishes arguments from nonarguments, it must in some sense be related to the Extended Projection Principle, which requires that arguments be present at every level, in particular, at S-structure. That is, the Extended Projection Principle requires the trace of an argument, but not the trace of a nonargument, to be present at S-structure. Thus it appears that [(1)] follows straightforwardly from the Extended Projection Principle. An argument trace receives the g-feature at S-structure since it is present at this level. An adjunct trace receives the g-feature at LF since it is required to be present only at LF. However, this argument is sound only if an adjunct trace *cannot* be present at S-structure. And the Extended Projection Principle entails only that such a trace *need not* be present at that level. If an adjunct trace can be present at S-structure (and we do not see

how to exclude this possibility in general), we lose the contrast between (121) and the totally impossible (128)

(121) ?*[$_{S'}$ Who$_i$ [$_S$do you believe[$_{NP}$the claim[$_{S'}$that [$_S$ John said[$_{S'}$t'$_i$ [$_S$t$_i$ came]]]]]]]

(128) *Why$_i$ do you believe the claim that John said [Bill left t$_i$]

(128) can have the following S-structure representation

(129) Why$_i$ do you believe[$_{NP}$ the claim that John said[$_{S'}$t'$_i$ [$_S$Bill left t$_i$]]]

If t$_i$ can be present at S-structure, it can receive $[+g]$ from t'$_i$ at this level, and t'$_i$ can then delete at LF. Consequently, (129) violates only Subjacency and must have the same grammatical status as (121), an incorrect result. Thus at least one useful effect of [(1)] cannot be deduced from the Extended Projection Principle. Apparently, [(1)] must, at least in part, remain a principle. [L&S, p. 269]

Thus, to derive the fact that adjuncts are not g-assigned at S-structure, without appealing to (1), it must be the case that some principle (or principles) P ensure that an adjunct trace cannot be present at S-structure. Under P we need not appeal to (1) to derive the fact that adjunct traces are not g-assigned at S-structure. Rather, under P, this fact follows, since adjunct traces are necessarily absent at this level of representation, and hence unavailable for g-assignment. As L&S note, P is not equivalent to the Extended Projection Principle, which requires only that an adjunct trace need not be present at S-structure.

Later we will follow L&S's suggestion that principle (1) is related to the Extended Projection Principle. In particular, it is argued that an independently motivated theory of movement entails that adjuncts, as well as traces created by syntactic movement of an adjunct, have no indices at S-structure. Given that any trace created by adjunct movement must be antecedent-governed, it follows that any trace left by syntactic adjunct movement cannot be assigned $[+g]$ at S-structure precisely because adjuncts and their traces, being indexless, cannot antecedent-govern. (It may be that indexless traces are prohibited altogether at S-structure. If so, there are no adjunct traces at this level.) From this independently motivated theory, it also follows that adjuncts and their traces *are* indexed in the LF component; hence, at this level, and only at this level, adjunct traces can be assigned $[+g]$. We shall see that the theory of movement adopted here subsumes the effects of principle (1) for traces of adjuncts.

Notice, however, that this result does not allow us to eliminate (1) completely. Recall that this principle has two crucial effects with respect to nonarguments. Not only does (1) dictate that adjunct traces are not *g*-assigned at S-structure, but, as discussed earlier, it also dictates that traces in Comp are not *g*-assigned at this level. Recall this effect of (1) was needed to generate S-structures such as the following:

(38) $[_{S'}$ who$_i$ $[_S$ do you think $[_{S'}$ that $[_S$ John said $[_{S'}$ t_i $[_S$ t_i left$]]]]]$
$$[+g]$$

As L&S note, the ungrammaticality of the sentence represented in (38) is not as severe as an ECP violation. However, if (1) is simply eliminated, the trace in Comp (required at S-structure to *g*-assign the subject trace) would be assigned $[-g]$ with the result that filter (3) (the ECP) would be violated at S-structure, an incorrect result. With this in mind, recall that we will derive the effects of (1) on adjunct traces by showing that such traces are indexless or absent at S-structure. Notice that this approach will not work for traces in Comp. That is, we *cannot* assume that traces in Comp fail to be *g*-assigned at S-structure, because they are indexless or absent at this level. Such an approach will not work, since, as we have seen, the ECP itself requires that certain traces in Comp (e.g., see (38)) are present and bear an index at S-structure; these conditions are prerequisite to *g*-assignment of a subject trace in English.

This indicates that (1) is to be derived from at least two independent sources, one ensuring that adjunct traces are indexless (or absent) at S-structure and another, which either prevents *g*-assignment of traces in Comp at S-structure or allows such *g*-assignment to occur without violating the ECP.

Traces in Comp

To begin, notice that the system of principles proposed in L&S contains a potential redundancy. Following L&S, we have assumed that the filter (3) applies at both S-structure and LF. With respect to this organization of grammar they write

> all that we require is that filter [(3)] be *permitted* to apply at [LF]. There is no need to restrict it to LF by stipulation. No problems arise

if the filter applies at S-structure as well, since any t marked $[-g]$ at
S-structure will still be present, and still be marked $[-g]$ at LF. No
LF principle can ever salvage a derivation in which $[-g]$ appears at
S-structure [L&S, n. 63].

The assumption that the filter (3) applies also at S-structure appears to create a redundancy when taken in conjunction with the
independent proposal that g-marking is indelible, a notion formally stated by L&S as

(42) g-marking may not apply to a g-marked trace

Under (42), once a trace receives a value for g, it never receives
another value. (Notice that (42), like (1), is a principle stating an
asymmetry in g-assignment.) Principle (42) is motivated by L&S
to rule out the following derivation in which a trace is marked
$[-g]$ at S-structure and is subsequently marked $[+g]$ at LF, the
latter feature assignment resulting from LF deletion of "that" followed by down and back movement of "who," creating a trace
in Comp

(43a) SS: $[_{s'}\text{Who}_i[_s\text{do you think}[_{s'}\text{that}[_st_i\text{ left}]]]]$
$$[-g]$$
(43b) LF: $[_{s'}\text{Who}_i[_s\text{do you think}[_{s'}t_i[_st_i\text{ left}]]]]$
$$[+g][+g]$$

Under (42), such a derivation is precluded. But notice that this
derivation is independently precluded if filter (3) (the ECP) applies at S-structure. Thus, if filter (3) applies at S-structure, it
filters S-structure representations such as (43a). Hence, there is
no need to appeal to (42) to preclude "g-changing" operations
from applying in the LF component. Conversely, if (42) precludes
"g-changing" operations in the LF component, there is apparently no need to apply filter (3) at S-structure. In short, there is
an apparent redundancy between the S-structure application of
filter (3) and principle (42). To eliminate the redundancy (while
also ruling out (43)) we have two clear options.[3]

First, we could simply eliminate (42) and assume filter (3) applies at S-structure (as well as LF). Alternatively, (42) could be
retained while filter (3) is assumed to apply only at LF.

These two alternative analyses would appear to be empirically
equivalent. If filter (3) applies both at S-structure and at LF, any

S-structure containing a trace bearing $[-g]$ will be ruled out, as will any LF representation containing a trace marked $[-g]$. Similarly, if filter (3) applies only at LF yet principle (42) is assumed, then any trace marked $[-g]$ at S-structure must remain $[-g]$ throughout the derivation, including the level of LF representation at which level filter (3) applies.

Notice, however, that the two analyses are, in fact, distinct. If the filter (3) applies at S-structure then

(44) There are no well-formed derivations that include an S-structure representation containing a trace bearing $[-g]$

However, if filter (3) applies only at LF while (42) is also assumed, then

(45) There are well-formed derivations that include an S-structure representation containing a trace bearing $[-g]$

To see this distinction, consider again the following S-structure:

(46) $[_{S'} \text{who}_i [_S \text{do you think}[_{S'} \text{that } [_S \text{John said}[_{S'} t_i [_S t_i \text{ left}]]]]]]$
$$[+g]$$

(Recall that the ungrammaticality of the sentence represented is not as severe as that of an ECP violation.) Now assume that principle (1) is simply eliminated with the result that the nonargument trace is obligatorily g-assigned at S-structure, as is the subject trace. The following S-structure is then generated:

(47) $[_{S'} \text{Who}_i [_S \text{do you think}[_{S'} \text{that}[_S \text{John said } [_{S'} t_i [_S t_i \text{left}]]]]]]$
$$[-g][+g]$$

The trace in Comp is assigned $[-g]$, since it is neither lexically properly governed nor antecedent-governed. Now if the filter (3) applies at S-structure, (47) is filtered. Incorrectly, the ECP is violated at S-structure. However, if filter (3) applies only at LF (while (42) is also assumed), the S-structure (47), like any S-structure, satisfies the ECP, since this principle (i.e., filter) does not constrain S-structure. Further, a well-formed LF representation is derivable, which is precisely the result we want. Filter (3) applying at LF can be satisfied, provided the trace in Comp, marked $[-g]$, deletes in the LF component, an available option.

Thus, by assuming that filter (3) (the ECP) applies only at LF, while also assuming (42), the effect of principle (1) on traces in Comp is derivable. Instead of appealing to (1) to prevent S-structure g-assignment of traces in Comp, we allow (in fact, by analogy with argument traces, we force) such traces to be g-assigned at this level, including the assignment of $[-g]$, as in (47). However, S-structures containing traces bearing $[-g]$ never violate the ECP, since this principle (i.e., filter (3)) applies only at LF. In the LF component, a syntactic trace in Comp bearing $[-g]$ can always delete, since it has no semantic content. Consequently, filter (3), applying at LF, is satisfied. Similar LF deletion of an argument trace is precluded; an argument trace assigned $[-g]$ in the syntax cannot delete in the LF component, since arguments, by definition, bear theta roles, a type of semantic content. Nor can their g-value be changed in the LF component, since (42) explicitly precludes this.

In summary, we have derived the effects of (1) for traces in Comp by eliminating a potential redundancy in the L&S analysis. In the analysis adopted here, filter (3) applies only at LF.[4] As a result, it appears that (42), as proposed by L&S, must be assumed so as to prevent the application of "g-changing" operations as depicted in (43). However, in the next section we shall attempt to derive (42) from a more basic principle of grammar. Following this, the effects of principle (1) for adjunct traces will be derived, thereby allowing us to eliminate (1) altogether.

The Elimination of Principle (42)

We have crucially assumed that the filter (3) applies not at S-structure but at LF. Under this assumption, principle (42) is required to preclude derivations such as (43) in which a trace bears $[-g]$ at S-structure yet bears $[+g]$ at LF.

Notice, however, that in addition to ruling out such unwanted derivations, (42) has another effect; it prevents derivations in which a category is g-assigned at S-structure and then is additionally assigned a second g-feature (alongside the first) at LF. Thus, (42) prohibits a g-assigned category from acquiring a second, additional g-feature at LF. Such assignment of a second g-feature is exemplified by the following derivation in which a subject trace is assigned $[-g]$ at S-structure and the additional feature $[+g]$ at LF:

(48a) SS: $[_{s'}$ Who$_i[_s$ do you think $[_{s'}$that $[_s t_i$ left]]]]
$$[-g]$$

(48b) LF: $[_{s'}$ Who$_i[_s$ do you think $[_{s'} t_i$ $[_s t_i$ left]]]]
$$[+g]\ [-g]$$
$$[+g]$$

This type of double g-assignment is the null hypothesis, given that g-assignment applies obligatorily at the output of both the syntactic and LF components.[5] Such additional LF g-assignment is prevented by (42), but this seems unnecessary, since filter (3) applying at LF is nonetheless violated because of the presence of a trace bearing $[-g]$.

As discussed earlier, another effect of (42) is a necessary one: to prevent derivations such as (43), in which the subject trace is assigned $[-g]$ at S-structure yet bears $[+g]$ and only $[+g]$ at LF. Notice that in such derivations a feature that is present at S-structure, namely, $[-g]$, is absent at LF. Equivalently, such derivations include the deletion of a feature in the LF component. Thus, to generate the S-structure (43a) and then map it into the LF representation (43b), the following operations (ordered as given) must apply

(49) a. The subject trace that is not properly governed is assigned $[-g]$ at the output of the syntactic component

 b. In the LF component, the feature $[-g]$ is deleted from the feature matrix of the subject

 c. At the output of the LF component, the subject trace is assigned $[+g]$, since it is properly governed

Clearly, (49a) and (49c) are licit operations. It is (49b) that must be prevented. If (42) prevents this, we might suppose that this effect is an instance of a more general prohibition on deletion. Consider the following deletion prohibition proposed in Davis (1984)[6]:

(50) Syntactic features may not be deleted

Under the reasonable assumption that $[\pm g]$ is a syntactic feature, (50) appears to be exactly what we require, since it would subsume (42) and thus prevent the LF deletion of $[-g]$ from the feature matrix of the subject trace. However, under our assumption that $[\pm g]$ is a syntactic feature, (50) is overly restrictive in that it would also prevent an LF operation that we require, namely, the LF deletion of a trace in Comp bearing the feature $[-g]$ (such as the trace in Comp in (47)). Thus, whereas (50) has the desired effect of disallowing $[-g]$ from being deleted from the feature matrix of the subject trace in (43a), it also prevents the requisite deletion of a trace in Comp bearing $[-g]$, since this too entails deleting the syntactic feature $[-g]$. The distinction we need to make is this: To prevent LF deletion of the feature $[-g]$ from the feature matrix of the subject trace in (43a), we could assume that *features cannot be deleted from a feature matrix*. Yet to allow the required LF deletion of the trace marked $[-g]$ occurring in Comp in (47) we could assume that *entire feature matrices (i.e., categories) can be deleted*. The following "all or nothing" constraint on deletion captures this:

(51) Only entire feature matrices are subject to deletion

Under (51) deletion is a category-level operation, and only a category-level operation.[7]

Consequently, the only way to delete a given feature f is to delete the entire feature matrix of which f is a member. Equivalently, the only way to delete a feature is to delete a category.

Under (51), (42) is eliminable. In subsuming (42) under (51) we retain the desired effect of (42); any g-feature g that is assigned to a category C at S-structure will appear at LF in the feature matrix of C, unless C (i.e., the entire feature matrix including g) is deleted in the LF component.

The elimination of (42) rested on the assumption that (51) holds of deletion. Following L&S we also assume that categories with semantic content cannot be deleted. As a result, the following type of derivation is correctly excluded. Consider again an S-structure such as (43a):

(43a) $[_{S'} \text{Who}_i [_S \text{ do you think } [_{S'} \text{ that } [_S t_i \text{ left}]]]]$
$$[-g]$$

Recall that the original motivation for (42) is to prevent the deletion of the feature $[-g]$ from the feature matrix of the trace. If this feature could be deleted, this deletion could be followed by the application of "that"-deletion and down and back movement, which could then result in the assignment of $[+g]$ (and only $[+g]$) at LF (see (43b)). (51) prevents the deletion of $[-g]$ from the matrix of the trace. Under (51), the only way to eliminate the feature $[-g]$ is to delete the subject trace (i.e., the entire category) bearing $[-g]$. If this entire category could be deleted, that"-deletion followed by down and back movement into Comp *and into the subject position* could then incorrectly result in a well-formed LF representation, hence derivation. However, deletion of the subject trace is precluded, since categories with semantic content cannot delete.

Thus far we have seen derivations in which a trace in Comp is assigned $[-g]$ at S-structure and is deleted in the LF component. We have also seen derivations in which a subject trace is assigned $[-g]$ at S-structure and is additionally assigned $[+g]$ at LF. In such derivations the additional assignment of $[+g]$ is without effect; the LF representation violates the ECP. There is one other type of derivation that should be examined (if it exists), one in which a trace is assigned $[+g]$ at S-structure and $[-g]$ at LF. The possibility of such multiple g-assignment as proposed here apparently results in misanalyzing the following sentence as an ECP violation:

(37a)　?Who do you wonder whether John said left?

Recall, under the elimination of (1), (37a) has the following S-structure representation:

(39)　$[_{S'}$Who$_i[_S$ do you wonder$[_{S'}$ whether$[_S$ John said $[_{S'}$ $t_i[_S$ t_i left]]]]]]$
　　　　　　　　　　　　　　　　　　　　　$[-g]$ $[+g]$

This S-structure, like any S-structure, satisfies the ECP, since filter (3) applies only at LF. At LF, then, to satisfy the ECP, the trace in Comp must delete. However, given that there is additional g-assignment of the subject trace at LF, the following LF representation is apparently generated:

(52)　$[_{S'}$ Who$_i[_S$do you wonder$[_{S'}$ whether $[_S$ John said $[_{S'}[_S t_i$ left]]]]]]$
　　　　　　　　　　　　　　　　　　　　$[+g]$
　　　　　　　　　　　　　　　　　　　　$[-g]$

Because of the necessary deletion of the trace in Comp, the subject trace is assigned $[-g]$ at the output of the LF component.

(Recall that Affect-alpha [including Deletion] precedes g-assignment.) Thus, it appears that the ECP is violated, an incorrect result. The preceding violation is, however, only apparent. In fact, (52) is not generated. Recall that L&S assume

(14) Comp obligatorily receives the index of its head at each syntactic
       level

Thus, to be more precise, the S-structure representation in question is not (39) but

(53) $[_{S'} [_{C_i} \text{Who}_i][_S \text{do you wonder}[_{S'} [_C \text{whether}][_S \text{John said}$
       $[_{S'} [_{C_i} t_i][_S t_i \text{left}]]]]]]$
           $[-g] [+g]$

In the LF component the trace in Comp deletes yet the index on Comp remains. Given that an indexed Comp can be an antecedent governor (an assumption L&S adopt from AHS [1981]), at LF, the subject trace is additionally assigned $[+g]$. In the LF representation, then, the subject trace appears as

(54) t_i
       $[+g]$
       $[+g]$

The ECP is therefore satisfied.

To summarize, we have derived the effect of principle (1) on traces in Comp. Whereas (1) dictates that a trace in Comp is not g-assigned at S-structure, we have eliminated (1) with the result that a trace in Comp at S-structure *is* g-assigned at this level. If a trace in Comp at S-structure is assigned $[-g]$, the ECP is satisfied at S-structure, since filter (3) (i.e., the ECP) does not apply at this level. Since any trace in Comp at S-structure can be deleted in the LF component, the central descriptive fact regarding traces in Comp at S-structure is explained; the S-structure occurrence of a trace in Comp that is not properly governed (i.e., bears $[-g]$) does not constitute a violation of the ECP. Thus, it is not necessary to appeal to (1) to prevent g-assignment of traces in Comp at S-structure.

Since we have crucially assumed that filter (3) applies only at LF, it appeared that we must also assume the following principle stating another asymmetry in g-assignment:

(42) *g*-marking may not apply to a *g*-marked trace

(42) had to be assumed so as to prevent certain illicit derivations, such as (43), in which a trace bears $[-g]$ at S-structure yet bears $[+g]$, and only $[+g]$, at LF. Nonetheless, we have proposed that (42) is derivable from the following more general constraint on deletion:

(51) Only entire feature matrices are subject to deletion

Under (51), if a trace bears $[-g]$ at S-structure and the trace is not deleted in the LF component, then the trace bears $[-g]$ at LF as well. Hence, (42) is eliminable. Given that (42) is eliminated, a simpler *g*-assignment algorithm results. At the output of both the syntactic and LF components, *g*-assignment applies to any trace that is present, regardless of whether the trace already bears a *g*-feature.

Adjunct Traces

As discussed earlier, L&S note that in the absence of principle (1), S-structure to LF mappings of the following type are over-generated:

(34a) $[_{S'}$Why$_i[_S$do you believe$[_{NP}$ the claim$[_{S'}$ that
$[_S$John said $[_{S'}$ $t_i[_S$ Bill bought a car $t_i]]]]]]]]$
$[+g]$

(34b) $[_{S'}$ Why$_i[_S$do you believe $[_{NP}$ the claim$[_{S'}$that
$[_S$John said $[_{S'}$ $[_S$ Bill bought a car $t_i]]]]]]]]$
$[+g]$

Under (1), the adjunct trace is not *g*-assigned at S-structure, so such derivations are prevented. Nonetheless, even with principle (1), a derivation satisfying the ECP is generable. Principle (1) dictates that in the S-structure representation, neither trace in (34a) is *g*-assigned. However, under (14), recall that Comp is indexed at S-structure. Thus, the following S-structure is generated:

(55) $[_{S'}[_{C_i}$Why$_i$ $[_S$do you believe$[_{NP}$ the claim $[_{S'}$ that
$[_S$John said $[_{S'}[_{C_i}$ $t_i[_S$ Bill bought a car $t_i]]]]]]]]$

In the LF component the trace in Comp can delete. The adjunct trace is nonetheless assigned $[+g]$ at this level, since the indexed

Comp is an antecedent governor. Thus, even with principle (1), the S-structure (55) can be mapped into the following LF representation:

(56) $[_{S'}$ Why$_i[_S$ do you believe $[_{NP}$ the claim $[_{S'}$ that
$[_S$ John said $[_{S'}[_{C_i}]$ $[_S$ Bill bought a car $t_i]]]]$
$$[+g]$$

Incorrectly, the ECP is satisfied.

The analysis proposed here eliminating (1) allows similar cases of overgeneration. Without (1) the following S-structure is generated in which each trace is g-assigned:

(57) $[_{S'}$ Why$_i[_S$ do you believe $[_{NP}$ the claim $[_{S'}$ that
$[_S$ John said $[_{S'}[_{C_i} t_i]$ $[_S$ Bill bought a car $t_i]]]]$
$$[-g] \qquad\qquad\qquad [+g]$$

In the LF component, the trace in Comp can delete. Further, the adjunct trace is assigned a second $[+g]$ feature, since this trace is still antecedent-governed by the indexed Comp:

(58) $[_{S'}$ why$_i[_S$ do you believe the claim that John said
$[_{S'}[_{C_i}]$ $[_S$ Bill bought a car $t_i]]]]$
$$[+g]$$
$$[+g]$$

To prevent such derivations one might filter an LF representation containing an indexed Comp that is empty, as in (58). However, this proposal is problematic. Recall that the following derivation must be generable under the simplified "double" g-marking algorithm:

(59a) $[_{S'}$ who$_i[_S$ do you wonder$[_{S'}$ whether$[_S$ John said
$[_{S'}[_{C_i} t_i]$ $[_S t_i$ left]]]]]]$
$$[+g]$$

(59b) $[_{S'}$ who$_i[_S$ do you wonder$[_{S'}$ whether$[_S$ John said
$[_{S'}[_{C_i}]$ $[_S t_i$ left]]]]]]$
$$[+g]$$
$$[+g]$$

Thus, if empty indexed Comps were prohibited at LF, we would wrongly filter (59b) alongside (58), thereby losing the contrast in grammaticality between the sentences represented. (Similarly, the stipulation that "empty indexed Comps cannot antecedent-govern" fails to properly distinguish (58) and (59b); that is, both would be characterized as ECP violations.) We require some other way of preventing S-structures such as (57) from being mapped into LF representations such as (58). Apparently, one way to prevent the generation of S-structures such as (57) is *somehow* to prevent the adjunct trace (i.e., the trace in adjoined position) from appearing at S-structure, thereby preventing it from being assigned $[+g]$ at this level. Notice, however, that even if we were to somehow prevent the adjunct trace from appearing at S-structure, a derivation satisfying the ECP could still be generated. Suppose the adjunct "why" were base-generated in its adjoined position. In the syntax, this category could move from its D-structure position to the most deeply embedded Comp, leaving no trace in its D-structure position. Next, "why" could move from the most deeply embedded Comp to the matrix Comp, leaving a trace in the embedded Comp. Subsequent application of Comp indexing yields the following S-structure:

(60) $[_{S'}$Why$_i$[do you believe the claim that John said
$[_{S'} [_{C_i} t_i] [_S$ Bill bought a car]]]]
$[-g]$

In the LF component, the trace in Comp can delete. Further, "why" can be moved down, adjoining to the lowest S (or VP). Next, "why" can be raised back up to the matrix Comp, leaving a trace in the position in which "why" was base-generated. Thus, the following LF representation is derived from the S-structure (60):

(61) $[_{S'} Why_i [_S$ do you believe the claim that John said
$[_{S'} [_{C_i}] [_S$ Bill bought a car t_i]]]]
$[+g]$

The ECP is satisfied, since each trace present at LF bears only $[+g]$. Thus, even if some principle P were to ensure that adjoined traces are absent at S-structure, such derivations would still satisfy the ECP. What we see is that at least two types of derivations must be precluded, a derivation like that from (57) to (58) (in which the adjoined trace is present at S-structure) and a derivation like that from (60) to (61) (in which the adjoined trace is absent at S-structure). The possibility of the latter derivation indicates that even if we could somehow prevent the S-structure presence of adjoined traces, LF representations such as (61) are still incorrectly generable.

Notice, the culprit in each unwanted derivation is the trace in Comp at S-structure. It is this trace that is triggering Comp-indexing. Once the Comp is indexed, it antecedent-governs the adjoined position at both S-structure and LF. As we have seen, the trace in Comp triggering such Comp-indexing can simply delete in the LF component, thereby avoiding a violation of the ECP. To prevent such derivations we must somehow prevent the trace in Comp from appearing at S-structure. More precisely, the minimal result we require is this: If a trace of the adjunct does occur in Comp at S-structure, the trace does not trigger Comp-indexing. This result follows if an adjunct trace occurring in Comp at S-structure has no index (and hence S-structure Comp-indexing fails to occur). This in turn follows if it is more generally the case that

(62) Any trace created by syntactic movement of an adjunct has no in-dex at S-structure

In the next section, we shall derive (62) from independently mo-tivated theories of movement and indexing. From these theories it follows that adjuncts and their traces have no indices at S-structure. This then explains why the trace of an adjunct cannot be assigned $[+g]$ at S-structure as in (57), as well as explaining why LF representations such as (61) cannot be derived from S-structures such as (60) in which the adjunct trace is absent.

MOVEMENT AND THE THEORY OF INDEXING

Chomsky (1981, 1982) assumes that movement definitionally re-sults in the creation of a trace that is coindexed with the moved element. Thus, movement has two defining characteristics:

(63) Movement of a category C from position P results in the creation of a trace in position P

(64) Movement of a category C from position P to position P′ creates coindexation of C and the trace occupying P

Pesetsky (1982) notes that (63) creates a certain amount of re-dundancy in that, to a large extent, independent principles re-quire that (63) hold. Thus, for example, movement from an A-position must leave a trace under the Projection Principle, whereas the ECP requires that certain traces be left in Comp, as does Subjacency, if this principle constrains representation (contra L&S). An additional example is the principle prohibiting vacuous quantification which (in at least some languages) requires that operator movement create at least one trace determinable as a variable. Thus, (63) is to a large extent redundant.[8]

To the extent that it is not redundant, it appears to be overly restrictive. As L&S argue, certain instances of Polish LF movement from A′-position must be allowed to leave no trace. Under (63) this option is unavailable, incorrectly resulting in a problem of undergeneration (see L&S, p. 253). Following L&S, we assume here, as we have earlier, that

(65) Movement optionally creates a trace

Of course, this less restrictive conception of movement still allows traces to be created as they are in the unwanted S-structures (57) and (60). However, (65) says nothing regarding the indexation of such traces. Rather, it is (64)—the assumption that movement definitionally creates coindexation—that is responsible for the distribution of *indexed* traces in (57) and (60). More precisely, (64) determines that an indexed trace can occur in Comp in (57) and (60). As noted, it is precisely because this trace is indexed (a result of (64)) that S-structure Comp-indexing is triggered with the incorrect result that the ECP can be satisfied. Thus, (64) is really responsible for the overgeneration we seek to prevent.

Interestingly, Chomsky (1982) notes a certain problem confronting the assumption that (64), in part, defines movement. We shall see that this problem and ours have one and the same solution (involving the elimination of (64) and a reformulation of the defining characteristics of movement).

REDEFINING MOVEMENT

In this section we discuss a problem, noted in Chomsky (1982), confronting (64): the assumption that movement definitionally creates coindexation. To reveal this problem we must first briefly review certain aspects of the framework proposed in Chomsky (1982). In particular, we will be concerned with the proposed properties of UG from which the distribution of parasitic gaps is assumed to follow.

To begin, Chomsky (1982) assumes that parasitic gaps are base-generated empty pronominal categories.[9] From the Binding theory of Chomsky (1981) and a proper specification of the Null Subject Parameter it follows that such categories are permitted at S-structure in non-null subject languages only if they can be determined as variables at this level of representation. The determination of empty categories is performed by the Functional Determination algorithm, which applies at S-structure.[10]

As proposed by Chomsky (1982, p. 35), "An empty category is a variable if it is in an A-position and is locally A'-bound." Thus, Chomsky (1982) proposes (66) and (67), whereas (68) follows from the theory of Binding:

(66) A parasitic gap is a base-generated empty pronominal

(67) Under Functional Determination, an empty category is a variable if it is in an A-position and is locally A'-bound

(68) A parasitic gap is permitted at S-structure only if it can be determined as a variable under Functional Determination

By introducing one more feature of the analysis of Chomsky (1982), we will be able to determine the problem confronting (64).

Chomsky (1982) formalizes what has been called "The Resumptive Pronoun Parameter" as follows:

(69) [±]Operators can be base-generated in Comp

In languages with resumptive pronouns, (69) is specified for the positive value, whereas in languages disallowing resumptive pronouns, (69) is specified for the negative value (see Chomsky, 1982, for further discussion). Notice that under the negative specification of (69), an operator can occur in Comp only if it is moved to this position. Given that movement does not create pronominals, it follows that resumptive pronouns cannot be generated. Under the positive setting, an operator can be base-generated in Comp, thereby allowing a resumptive pronominal to be base-generated in an A-position.

In summary, Chomsky (1982) proposes (66)–(68); he also proposes that, in certain languages, operators may be base-generated in Comp. As noted by Chomsky (1982, p. 59), one unwanted consequence of these assumptions is that a wh-operator could be base-generated in Comp, while a parasitic gap could be generated in *any* position c-commanded by the operator. Such a D-structure could then be mapped into an S-structure, provided that the parasitic gap is locally A'-bound by the operator at this level, since then the parasitic gap would be determined as a licit category (i.e., a variable, under Functional Determination). As Chomsky notes, given that Subjacency constrains only movement, this possibility must be excluded; otherwise constructions violating island conditions would be freely generable. To avoid this result, Chomsky (1982) proposes the following:

(70) Free syntactic indexing applies only to A-positions

Under (70), the problem of base-generating island violations disappears. An operator base-generated in Comp can bear no index at S-structure. Therefore, the parasitic gap cannot be bound (hence, it cannot be locally A'-bound) by the operator at this level. Consequently, the parasitic gap is not determinable as a variable at S-structure, with the result that the Binding theory is violated. As Chomsky notes, (70) not only prevents the base generation of island violations, but also correctly accounts for the fact that resumptive pronouns do not license parasitic gaps (see Chomsky, 1982, p. 61). The prediction is obtained as follows: Recall that, in generating structures containing resumptive pronouns, an operator is base-generated in Comp. Now if an operator that is base-generated in Comp could bear an index at S-structure, then, provided the parasitic gap is coindexed with the operator, the parasitic gap would be determined as a licit category (i.e., a variable) at S-structure. Consequently, it would be wrongly predicted that resumptive pronouns license parasitic gaps. The correct result, that resumptive pronouns do not license parasitic gaps, is obtained under (70). This principle dictates that an operator base-generated in Comp can bear no index at S-structure. As a result, a parasitic gap cannot be coindexed with the operator at this level. This then precludes determining the parasitic gap as a variable, with the result that such structures are filtered by the Binding theory. Thus, (70) is needed to prevent both base generation of island violations and parasitic gap licensing by resumptive pronouns.[11]

However, given (70), we require some way for an operator base-generated in Comp to acquire an index in the LF component. If there were no way for such an operator to acquire an index in LF, then any derivation in which an operator is base-generated in Comp would be ill formed, since the resulting LF representation would violate the following principle:

(71) No vacuous quantification

To avoid this result, Chomsky (1982) proposes

(72) Free LF A'-indexing

Under (70) and (72), then, an operator base-generated in Comp bears no index at S-structure yet it is freely indexed at LF.

With this much background we are now in a position to determine the problem confronting the assumption that movement definitionally creates coindexation.

As we have seen, to prevent parasitic gap licensing by resumptive pronouns as well as free base generation of island violations, it must be ensured that operators base-generated in Comp have no index at S-structure. With the intent of ensuring this, Chomsky (1982, p. 59) proposes (70). However, Chomsky (1982, p. 68) notes that (70) alone does not, in fact, ensure that an operator base-generated in Comp has no index at S-structure. As he notes:

> it is necessary to exclude the possibility that base-generated operators in Comp may pick up an index by Comp-to-Comp movement in the syntax, thus binding a base-generated EC at S-structure causing island violations [as well as illicit parasitic gap licensing (S.D.E.)]. The natural proposal for this case is that movement cannot "create" indices it can only carry over indices already assigned, excluding the unwanted possibility since the base-generated operator is only assigned an index at LF [Chomsky, 1982, p. 68].

Thus, to prevent the unwanted cases, Chomsky (1982) rejects (64)—the assumption that movement, by definition, creates coindexation—and he assumes instead that movement can only carry over indices that have already been assigned.

A theory of movement with precisely these properties is independently motivated and proposed in Davis (1982, 1984). She argues that movement does not definitionally create coindexation. Rather, she analyzes movement as an instance of what she calls "feature copy." Under her feature copy analysis:

(73) If a category C moves from position X to position Y then,

    a. if C had an index prior to movement, it retains the index after movement, and

    b. C leaves a copy of a certain set of its features in position X

Davis assumes that an index is one kind of feature that is copied under movement. Extending Davis' analysis, we propose the following (partial) indexing algorithm, which supplants (70):

(74) A-positions, and only A-positions, are freely indexed at D-structure

Notice that under (74), Chomsky's problem is immediately solved. An operator that is base-generated in Comp is not indexed at D-structure, since it does not occupy an A-position. Now, even if it moves from Comp-to-Comp in the syntax, it still will have no index at S-structure, since movement does not create coindexation but rather can only copy over indices already assigned. Hence, (74), and Davis' feature copy analysis, provides precisely the result Chomsky (1982) desires; the problem of base-generating island violations is solved; an operator base-generated in Comp bears no index at S-structure.

Now we will show that the feature copy analysis provides a similar solution to the problem of adjunct movement noted earlier. Recall that the derivations from (57) to (58) and from (60) to (61) can be overgenerated because of the fact that an *indexed* trace of "why" can occur in the embedded Comp at S-structure, thereby triggering syntactic Comp indexing, which in turn incorrectly allows for the satisfaction of the ECP. With this in mind, consider the D-structure underlying the S-structures (57) and (60):

(75) $[_{S'} [_{S} \text{you}_i \text{ believe } [_{NP_j} \text{ the claim } [_{S'} \text{that}$
    $[_{S} \text{John}_k \text{ said } [_{S'} [_{S} \text{Bill}_i \text{ bought a car}_m \text{ why }]]]]]]]]$

Under (74), "why" has exactly the status of an operator base-generated in Comp (i.e., since "why" does not occupy an A-position at D-structure, it is asigned no index). Now suppose syntactic movement of "why" proceeds through the most deeply embedded Comp, leaving a trace in this position. The resulting S-structure representation is as follows (we assume, as earlier, that creation of a trace in the D-structure position of "why" is optional):

(76) $[_{S'}$ Why$[_S$ do you$_i$ believe$[_{NP_j}$ the claim$[_{S'}$ that
$[_S$ John$_k$ said$[_{S'}[_C t][_S$ Bill$_i$ bought a car$_m (t)]]]]]]]$

Since "why" was assigned no index at D-structure, syntactic movement of this category cannot create indexed traces under the feature copy analysis. Thus, the trace in Comp has no index. Consequently, S-structure Comp indexing does not apply. As a result, if any traces are created by syntactic movement of an adjunct, they are necessarily assigned $[-g]$ at S-structure, since they cannot be antecedent-governed. Thus, our original problem is solved: S-structures such as (57) and (60) are not generable. Rather, S-structures of the following type are generated:

(77) $[_{S'}$ Why $[_S$ do you$_i$ believe$[_{NP_j}$ the claim$[_{S'}$ that
$[_S$ John$_k$ said$[_{S'}[_C (t)][_S$ Bill$_i$ bought a car$_m (t)]]]]]]]$

Thus, if syntactic adjunct movement creates traces, they are indexless (as is the adjunct) at S-structure. Hence, antecedent government at S-structure is impossible. Thus, from an independently motivated theory of movement and indexing, we have now derived that any trace left by syntactic movement of an adjunct is necessarily marked $[-g]$ at S-structure. Recall that one needed effect of principle (1) was to prevent the assignment of $[+g]$ to an adjunct trace at S-structure (as in (57)). We have now derived this effect without appealing to (1). Further, as shown by (60), even with (1), cases of long distance adjunct movement were overgenerated. However, the indexing theory under which (1) is subsumed has the desired result of preventing this, as we have seen.[12]

Recall another effect of principle (1) was to prevent the assignment of $[-g]$ to an adjunct trace in the S-structure representation of

(26) Why do you think that John left?

Notice, however, that under the analysis assumed here there is no reason to prevent such S-structure assignment of $[-g]$. Neither "why" nor its trace has an index at S-structure; hence, the trace is assigned $[-g]$ at this level.

(78) $[_{S'}[_C$ Why $] [_S$ do you think $[_{S'}$ that $[_S$ John left t]]]]$
$$[-g]$$

This is of no consequence, since the ECP (filter (3)) does not apply at S-structure. Alternatively, since no S-structure principle seems to require the presence of the adjunct trace at this level, we might assume that it is allowed to be absent at this level (i.e., its presence is optional). Under either derivation it is not necessary to appeal to principle (1) to generate a well-formed S-structure representation of sentences such as (26).[13]

We have now apparently derived the effects of principle (1) from independently motivated principles. In the resulting analysis, any trace present at S-structure is obligatorily g-assigned at this level, regardless of whether it is an argument or a nonargument.

However, to derive (1) completely we still must provide an analysis of the LF operations allowing for the generation of a well-formed LF representation of (26) yet precluding the generation of an LF representation of the unavailable interpretation of

(33) *Why do you believe the claim that John said that Bill bought a car?

Beginning with (26), there are two possible S-structure representations of this sentence, depending on whether the adjunct trace appears at this level:

(79) $[_{S'}$ Why $[_S$ do you think $[_{S'}$ that $[_S$ John left (t)]]]]
$$([-g])$$

Consider first the S-structure in which the trace is present. To derive a well-formed LF representation, this trace must delete in the LF component. This operation is licit; in particular, deletion of the trace does not constitute deletion of semantic content. The trace bears no theta role, nor is it in any semantic sense a variable, since the trace, being unindexed, just like "why," is unbound. Given deletion of the trace, we now confront two salient problems. First, to satisfy the LF principle prohibiting vacuous quantification, "why" will have to bind a variable in the LF representation. Second, any trace created in the LF component must, of course, satisfy the ECP. To begin, recall that Free LF A′-indexing applies in the LF component. Suppose this rule applies (or can apply) prior to movement (i.e., prior to the application of Affect-alpha). Then "why" can be indexed and, under Davis' feature copy analysis, subsequent movement of "why" could create a trace coindexed with this operator (i.e., a variable), thereby satisfying the principle prohibiting vacuous quantification. To achieve this result, "why" can move down adjoining to the lowest S (or VP). "Why" could then move back up into the matrix Comp, leaving a trace (bearing the same index as "why") in adjoined position. If no other instances of Affect-alpha apply, the following LF representation is generated:

(80) $*[_{S'}[_{C_i}$ Why$_i][_S$ do you think$[_{S'}$ that$[_S$ John left $t_i]]]]$
$$[-g]$$

The ECP is violated. To avoid this, suppose that (in addition to moving "why" down into the adjoined position and back to the matrix Comp) "that" is also deleted and, in addition, "why" is also moved down into the embedded Comp and back up to the matrix Comp, leaving an indexed trace in the embedded Comp. These operations followed by Comp indexing and g-assignment yield the following LF representation, satisfying the ECP:

(81) $[_{S'}[_{C_i}$Why$_i][_S$ do you think$[_{S'}[_{C_i} t_i][_S$ John left $t_i]]]]$
$$[+g] \qquad\qquad [+g]$$

Thus, (81) is derivable by applying the following operations (as ordered) in the LF component:

(82) a. Affect-alpha; if present, delete the adjunct trace bearing $[-g]$

     b. Affect-alpha; delete "that"

     c. Free LF A'-indexing; "why" is indexed

     d. Affect-alpha; Under the feature copy analysis, movement of "why" down from the matrix Comp to adjoined position and back to the matrix Comp can create a trace in adjoined position that is coindexed with "why"

     e. Affect-alpha; Movement of "why" down from the matrix Comp to the embedded Comp and back up to the matrix Comp creates a trace in the embedded Comp that is coindexed with "why"

     f. Comp-indexing

     g. g-assignment

A few characteristsics of such LF rule application should be noted. First, if the principle of the Strict Cycle constrains LF movement (the null hypothesis, given that this principle constrains syntactic movement), it is satisfied by the derivation indicated. (82a) and (82b) apply on the embedded S' cycle. On the matrix S' cycle, (82d) and (82e) apply. Notice that each movement of "why" from the matrix Comp is, by definition, an operation applying on the matrix S' cycle. Hence, any movement of "why" down from the matrix Comp must be immediately followed by movement of "why" back to the matrix Comp as in (82d) and (82e). Notice also that under L&S's crucial assumption that Affect-alpha precedes Comp-indexing and g-assignment, it follows that these latter two operations are not instances of Affect-alpha. We assume that Affect-alpha consists of movement, deletion and insertion, while the affected element must be a category (i.e., an entire feature matrix). Comp-indexing and g-assignment are therefore not instances of Affect-alpha. Consequently, if the Strict Cycle constrains LF, it is of no consequence that Comp-indexing and g-assignment apply solely within previously cycled domains. In this regard, Free A'-indexing is like Comp-indexing and g-assignment (i.e., it is not an instance of Affect-alpha, but is rather a feature-adding rule). For this reason, we might assume that Free A'-indexing (like Comp-indexing and g-assignment) is ordered after Affect-alpha. Thus, in contrast to (82), we might assume the following (ordered) organization of LF:

(83) a. Affect-alpha

    b. Free LF A'-indexing

    c. Comp-indexing

    d. g-assignment

Notice under (83), in deriving an LF representation of (79), Affect-alpha applies first in the LF component (i.e., "why," which has no index, moves down and back, creating traces that have no indices under the feature copy analysis). Next, (83b) applies and can coindex "why" and any traces created by movement of "why." (83c) and (83d) can then yield the well-formed LF representation of (79).[14]

Finally, we must rule out the LF representation of (84) in which "why" binds a variable within the most deeply embedded S. The S-structure representation is as follows:

(84) $[_{S'}$ Why $[_S$ do you believe$[_{NP}$ the claim$[_{S'}$ that$[_S$ John said
    $[_{S'}[_C(t')]$ $[_S$ Bill bought a car (t)]]]]]]]]
        $([-g])$ $([-g])$

If any traces are present at S-structure, they are necessarily assigned $[-g]$ and must therefore delete in the LF component; otherwise the ECP will be violated. In attempting to overgenerate an
LF representation of the unavailable interpretation, suppose
down and back movement of "why" creates a trace in the position of t. For this trace to be assigned $[+g]$, a trace must also be
created in the position of t'. For the trace in the position of t' to
be properly governed, "that" must delete and a third trace must
occur in this position as well. This results in the following intermediate representation:

(85) $[_{S'}[_C$ Why$][_S$ do you believe$[_{NP}$ the claim$[_{S'}[_C t'']][_S$ John said$[_{S'}[_C t'][_S$ Bill
    bought a car t]]]]]]]]

Free LF A'-indexing could then coindex "why" and all three
traces. Comp indexing and g-assignment then apply, producing
an LF representation. The ECP is violated, since t'' is assigned
$[-g]$. If t'' were absent, t' would be $[-g]$. If t'' and t' were absent,
t would be $[-g]$. If all three traces were absent, the principle
barring vacuous quantification would be violated. Hence, correctly, there is no well-formed LF representation of the unavailable interpretation.

Summary and Discussion

In this section we have eliminated Principle (1), deriving those of
its effects that are necessary from independently motivated principles of grammar. Lasnik and Saito's general framework, including the motivation for principle (1), was reviewed first; then this
principle was derived as follows. First, we noted that principle
(1) has effects on two types of nonargument traces. It dictates
that a trace in Comp is not g-assigned at S-structure while also
ensuring that the same is true of an adjunct trace (i.e., a trace in
adjoined position). Following L&S, we assume that this latter result follows if adjunct traces are (in some sense) absent at S-
structure. However, we then noted that this approach cannot be

extended to traces in Comp, since the ECP itself dictates that in languages such as English, traces must be present in Comp at S-structure. Hence, we assumed that (1) was to be derived from at least two sources; one (somehow) ensuring that adjunct traces are (in some sense) absent at S-structure and another (somehow) allowing S-structure g-assignment of traces in Comp to occur without ever violating the ECP.

To derive the effects of principle (1) on traces in Comp, we began by noting a potential redundancy in the analysis of L&S. They assume that filter (3) (i.e., the ECP) applies at both S-structure and LF while also proposing (42) ($=$ g-marking may not apply to a g-marked trace). It was argued that the inclusion of both S-structure application of filter (3) and (42) is redundant. We then proposed that filter (3) does not apply at S-structure (which in turn appeared to necessitate inclusion of (42)). Since the filter (3) does not apply at S-structure, principle (1) is no longer needed to prevent g-assignment of traces in Comp at S-structure. Rather, (1) can be eliminated and traces in Comp (like argument traces) can be g-assigned at S-structure. The assignment of $[-g]$ to a trace in Comp at S-structure does not violate the ECP, since this principle (i.e., filter (3)) does not apply at S-structure. Further, since any traces in Comp can delete in the LF component, no derivation including an S-structure containing a trace in Comp marked $[-g]$, violates the ECP because of the presence of such a trace. Thus, the descriptive facts regarding traces in Comp are derived without appeal to principle (1): At S-structure a trace in Comp that is not properly governed (i.e., bears $[-g]$) does not induce an ECP violation, whereas at LF such traces violate the ECP.

Because we proposed that filter (3) does not apply at S-structure, it then appeared that (42) was necessary to rule out S-structure "that"–t effects. (42) was apparently required to prevent a trace at S-structure bearing $[-g]$ from bearing $[+g]$ (and only $[+g]$) at LF. Were this allowed, the ECP would be satisfied incorrectly. Although preventing such derivations appeared to require (42), we argued that this constraint was derivable from deeper principles. It was noted first that such g-changing operations in fact entail the deletion of a feature, namely, $[-g]$. We proposed that such feature deletion is unavailable, given (51)

($=$ Only entire feature matrices are subject to deletion). Thus, (42) was eliminated under the more general syntactic principle (51), the latter, like (42), precluding g-changing operations. We then noted that the elimination of (42) also results in a simpler g-assignment algorithm: At the output of each component every trace that is present is g-assigned, regardless of whether it bears a g-feature.

Next, without appealing to (1), the facts regarding g-assignment of adjunct traces were derived. We began by noting that even with (1), cases of long-distance adjunct movement were incorrectly overgenerated. As noted, a trace in Comp, created by syntactic movement of an adjunct, can trigger Comp-indexing at S-structure. At LF, the trace in Comp can delete and the ECP can be incorrectly satisfied, given that the indexed Comp antecedent-governs the adjoined trace at LF. We then showed that this kind of overgeneration occurs even if the adjoined trace is absent at S-structure (see (60)). Thus, even if some principle P were to subsume (1) by ensuring that adjoined traces are absent at S-structure (hence, unavailable for g-assignment at this level), such cases of long-distance adjunct movement can still be overgenerated. We argued that such overgeneration is a direct result of S-structure Comp-indexing being triggered by the S-structure appearance of an indexed trace of adjunct movement in Comp. To prevent such Comp-indexing, we assumed it must be the case that traces created by syntactic movement of adjuncts have no indices at S-structure (hence, they cannot trigger Comp-indexing at this level). From a theory of movement and indexing (the motivation for which was completely independent of the ECP) we then derived the fact that syntactic traces of wh-adjuncts (as well as wh-adjuncts themselves) have no indices at S-structure. It then follows that traces of wh-adjuncts cannot be antecedent-governed (i.e., cannot be assigned $[+g]$ in the syntax). Therefore, we no longer have to appeal to principle (1) to obtain this result. Rather, just like argument traces and traces in Comp, we assume adjoined traces are g-assigned in the syntax. No trace created by syntactic adjunct movement can be assigned $[+g]$ in the syntax, since adjuncts and their traces, being indexless, cannot antecedent-govern. The obligatory assignment of $[-g]$ to such traces (if present) at S-structure has no consequences with respect to the ECP, since this principle (i.e., filter (3)) applies only to LF representation. Thus, principle (1) is eliminated.

The Simplification of the Indexing Algorithm

The crucial aspects of the indexing algorithm subsuming (1) (= Only an argument is g-assigned at S-structure) are expressed as follows:

(86) A-positions and only A-positions are indexed at D-structure

(87) Movement does not create coindexation; movement is feature copy

(88) There is no indexing at S-structure

(89) Free LF A'-indexing

A number of aspects of this theory of indexing demand explanation. First, as concerns (86), we should ask, "Why is it that A-positions and only A-positions are indexed at D-structure?" We suspect that the answer is closely related to the fact that D-structure, as conceived by Chomsky (1981), is a "pure representation of GF-Theta." Extending this conception of D-structure, suppose we assume that A-positions are the only positions present at D-structure. This assumption would immediately explain why it is that only A-positions are indexed at this level. However, the assumption from which the explanation follows cannot be maintained; there can be no A-positions in the absence of non–A-positions. Equivalently, there can be no positions to which theta roles are assigned in the absence of a theta role assigner, the latter of which, by definition, occupies a nonargument position. Suppose, then, that we assume that being a pure representation of GF-theta entails that

(90) D-structure is a categorical representation of argument structure and only argument structure

We interpret (90) to mean D-structure contains only (i) theta role assigners, (ii) theta role recipients, and (iii) the categories they project and/or the categories they are projected from (consistent with X' theory). From this it does not follow that only A-positions are indexed at D-structure. For example, heads such as V, or single-bar categories such as V', being present at D-structure, are, in principle, subject to indexing. (Whether or not such categories are indexed at D-structure, I leave open.) However, the minimal result we desire does in fact follow. That is, under (90), we now explain why adjunct categories such as "why" are not indexed at D-structure. Since they are not part of argument structure, they are absent at this level and are hence unavailable for indexing. Notice also that our assumption that adjuncts are absent at D-structure is a necessary one if X' consistency is to be construed as a defining characteristic of D-structure. Although this account provides a true explanation for the failure of adjunct indexing at D-structure, it has consequences that directly contradict previous assumptions. Given a trivial S-structure to PF mapping, we assume that adjuncts are present at S-structure. The analysis proposed thus far therefore entails that

(91) Adjuncts are inserted in the syntactic component

But this is incompatible with a principle we have assumed throughout, namely:

(92) Categories with semantic content cannot be inserted (or deleted)

If insertion (and deletion) of categories bearing semantic content is prohibited, then adjuncts like "why," which clearly have semantic content, must be present at D-structure. If these categories must be present at D-structure, we are forced to stipulate (as in (86)) that they are not indexed at this level (i.e., we can no longer derive their failure to be indexed at D-structure from their absence at this level). Thus, it is principle (92) that precludes syntactic insertion of "why." Under (92), such categories must be present at D-structure, which in turn forces the stipulation that they are not indexed at this level. But before adopting (92), and the stipulation it entails, we should determine the motivation for this principle. We know of two possible kinds of motivation, one interpretive, the other formal. First, given that a grammar defines an abstract association of sound and meaning, the prohibition is presumably motivated by interpretive facts of the following kind, to take but one example:

(93) A PF representation of the form [$_{PF}$ John saw Bill] cannot be interpreted in the same way as a PF representation of the form [$_{PF}$ John hit Bill] (where "PF" is intended to indicate that everything enclosed in brackets should be in phonetic form)

One seemingly necessary aspect of an account of such facts is the assumption that (92) holds in the PF component. This dictates that, given the S-structure of "John hit Bill," the verb "hit" cannot be deleted and replaced by the verb "saw." Notice that if such operations could apply in the PF component, it would be wrongly predicted that a sentence/PF such as "John saw Bill" has an interpretation synonymous with "John hit Bill." The prediction is made because, in the absence of (92), mappings such as the following would presumably be allowed:

(94) D-structure: John hit Bill
     S-structure: John hit Bill
     PF: John saw Bill
     LF: John hit Bill

Given that (92) precludes such derivations, the relevant interpretive facts are accounted for. Notice, however, that such sound–meaning associations (i.e., interpretive facts of the form *PF$_x$ is associated with LF$_x$* do not, in fact, motivate (92). Rather, such evidence provides motivation only for a prohibition somewhat weaker than (92), namely:

(95) Categories with semantic content cannot be inserted or deleted *in the interpretive components, PF and LF*

Of course, (95) is compatible with the following, which is precisely the result we desire:

(96) Categories with semantic content (e.g., "why") can be freely inserted and deleted in the syntactic component

In short, there can be no interpretive arguments against (96). Now before we can adopt (95), and (96), we must ask, "Is there any noninterpretive evidence against doing this?" L&S argue that there is evidence against (96). Recall that they assume Subjacency is a constraint on movement. Consequently, the following derivation satisfies this principle:

(97) a. D-structure:
    [$_{S'}$[$_S$ You wonder[$_{S'}$[$_S$ John bought what$_i$]]]]

   b. Move 1:
      [$_{S'}$[$_S$ You wonder[$_{S'}$ what$_i$[$_S$ John bought t_i]]]]

   c. Move 2:
      [$_{S'}$ What$_i$ [$_S$ do you wonder [$_{S'}$[$_S$ John bought t_i]]]]

   d. Insertion:
      [$_{S'}$ What$_i$[$_S$ do you wonder[$_{S'}$ whether [$_S$ John bought t_i]]]]

As discussed earlier, L&S prevent such derivations by adopting (92); that is, they assume categories with semantic content cannot be inserted anywhere (hence, they cannot be inserted in the syntactic component). Thus, such derivations appear to constitute formal (i.e., noninterpretive) motivation for (92), a principle prohibiting syntactic insertion of categories bearing semantic content. Notice, however, that such derivations are also excluded by the principle of the Strict Cycle, a principle independently motivated if Subjacency constrains only movement.[15] If such derivations can be excluded, without appeal to (92), then we are apparently left with no formal or interpretive motivation for a principle as strong as (92). In the absence of motivation for (92), we assume the weaker, interpretively motivated (95), which prohibits only insertion and deletion of categories with semantic content in the interpretive components. Thus, we tentatively assume (96) holds (i.e., categories bearing semantic content can be inserted and deleted in the syntactic component). Given this, we can now tentatively maintain the following analysis: D-structure is a pure representation of argument structure and only argument structure (as in (90)). Consequently, adjuncts such as "why" are necessarily absent at this level of representation. This explains immediately (and without a stipulation like (86), restricting D-structure indexing to A-positions) why it is that adjuncts are not indexed at this level. (The analysis also entails that D-structure is a strictly X'-consistent level of representation.) Under (95) syntactic insertion of categories with semantic content is allowed. Therefore, "why" can be inserted in the syntax, thereby accounting for its presence at S-structure and at PF. If this analysis is tenable, the stipulation that D-structure indexing is restricted to A-positions is eliminable. Consequently, (86) could be replaced with the following, simpler D-structure indexing algorithm:

(86′) D-structure: INDEX

Although this analysis has no doubt other consequences, we will note just one before leaving this topic. Given the existence of phrasal adjuncts such as "because John left" (a non-wh analog of "why"), the analysis proposed here entails the existence of generalized transformations (i.e., transformations taking more than one phrase marker as input and yielding one phrase marker as output). Since such phrasal adjuncts exhibit theta relations (i.e., there are theta relations within such phrases), they must be present at D-structure. But since adjoined structures are prohibited at this level, it must be the case that phrases like "because John left" are generated independently (hence as nonadjuncts) at D-structure and are then syntactically concatenated, by application of generalized transformation, with the structure to which they are adjoined in derived, S-structure representation.

Interestingly, the analysis presented here is not the only contemporary analysis concerning generation in nonargument position that entails the existence of generalized transformations. Chomsky's (1981) analysis of "tough"-constructions is similar in this regard. Chomsky (1981) proposes that the S-structure representation of "tough" complements, containing no direct object, are derived by A′-movement of an empty category (*ec*) from direct object position to Comp. Thus, under this analysis, D-structure to S-structure mappings of the following kind are assumed:

(98) a. D-structure:

$[_{S'}[_{S} \text{NP is tough}[_{S'}[_{S} \text{PRO to please } ec_i]]]]$

     b. S-structure:

$[_{S'}[_{S} \text{NP is tough}[_{S'} ec_i [_{S} \text{PRO to please } t_i]]]]$

Given this analysis of the complement structure of "tough," consider now a sentence such as the following:

(99) John is tough to please

The question that immediately emerges is this: "What is the D-structure representation of (99)?" As Chomsky notes, the D-structure cannot be of the following form, in which the N″ "John" occupies matrix subject position at this level:

(100) D-structure:

$*[_{S'}[_{S}[_{N''} \text{John}] \text{is tough}[_{S'}[_{S} \text{PRO to please } ec_i]]]]$

(100) is a direct violation of the Theta Criterion of Chomsky (1981), the argument N″ "John" occupies a nonargument position at D-structure. (The fact that matrix subject position is a non-argument position is evidenced by its ability to accommodate nonarguments such as the expletive "it" in, for example, *It is tough to please John.*) Hence, (100) cannot be the D-structure. But if the N″ "John" is not base-generated in matrix subject position, yet appears there at S-structure, it would seem that this argument must move to matrix subject position. This, however, is also problematic, because there is no obvious position in the D-structure representation from which the N″ argument "John" could be moved to matrix subject position. Thus, Chomsky (1981, p. 313) writes:

> It therefore follows that the matrix subject is not inserted at D-structure, but is also not moved to the matrix subject position. The only resolution to this paradox in our terms, is to assume that lexical insertion of the matrix subject is at S-structure in this case.

Now to see why this analysis entails the existence of generalized transformations we need only consider the slightly more complex example, the importance of which was noted by K. Kearney (personal communication):

(101)　The man who left is tough PRO to please

As Kearney notes, the subject N″, "the man who left," is not listed in the lexicon. But if it is syntactically inserted, as dictated by Chomsky's analysis of "tough" constructions, appeal to generalized transformations is presumably necessitated. Thus, our analysis entailing syntactic insertion of nonarguments (including, e.g., "because John left") is similar to Chomsky's (1981) analysis of "tough" constructions entailing syntactic insertion of arguments into nonargument position. Both analyses must recognize generalized transformations. Further, notice that both analyses assume that categories with semantic content can indeed be inserted in the Syntax.

As a final note regarding this analysis entailing adjunct insertion, notice that if it is tenable, it can perhaps be interpreted as providing the following indirect argument for the existence of D-structure. Prior to S-structure, the introduction of categories into phrase markers can be viewed as occurring in two distinct ways. First, there is insertion of all and only GF-related categories. Indexing then applies, deriving what we call "D-structure." This type of representation is then mapped into a different type of representation via the introduction of categories that are not part of argument structure. These categories are not indexed. If, by contrast, both classes were simultaneously generated as either "D-structure" or "S-structure," we would require a stipulation distinguishing the two subclasses of categories, those that are indexed (arguments) and those that are not (nonarguments). Under the present analysis, the stipulation is not necessary; the distinction follows by recognizing a level of representation containing only argument structure, namely, D-structure, to which indexing applies.

We will now summarize our discussion of (86) (= A-positions and only A-positions are indexed at D-structure). We have tentatively assumed that adjuncts like "why" are syntactically inserted, a result of the fact that they are, by definition, absent at D-structure, which is a level representing only argument structure. Their absence at D-structure explains their failure to be indexed at this level while also allowing the D-structure indexing algorithm (86) to be simplified as follows, thereby eliminating the stipulation that only A-positions are indexed at D-structure:

(86′) D-structure: INDEX

Finally, the absence of adjuncts at D-structure allows us to maintain the X′-consistency of this level of representation.

Turning now to (87), the feature copy analysis of movement, we would like to argue that the copying of features under movement is entirely free. Recall first that, following Pesetsky (1982), we assume that the creation of traces under movement is optional, as was discussed earlier. Notice, under the feature copy analysis of movement, failure to leave a trace is simply the extreme case of copying no features at all under movement. Given that independent principles ensure the correct output for this extreme case in which no features are copied, we suggest that the result holds in general (i.e., independent principles ensure the correct output is properly distinguished from all other possible cases). That is, we assume that feature copying under movement is entirely free; any feature f within the feature matrix of the moved category can be freely copied or not copied under movement. Independent principles ensure the correct output. To take but a few examples, the Projection Principle requires that traces be left in movement from an A-position. Further, the prohibitions against free variables and vacuous quantification ensure that indices are copied in the case of LF A′-movement, whereas conditions on A-chains (e.g., the Theta Criterion) ensure index copy under A-movement. The fact that gender and number features are also copied under movement (cf. *Which man do you think are satisfied with herself*) can be seen to follow from a feature-matching requirement imposed on categories in a binding relation. This requirement is independently needed to rule out binding compatible representations such as *John$_i$ likes herself$_i$*. As discussed in Brody (1984, p. 377) the fact that the + wh feature is not copied under wh-movement (see also L&S) arguably follows from the principle prohibiting vacuous quantification, given that any category bearing a + wh feature is an operator. I assume this argument can be extended to account for the fact that quantifier movement similarly fails to leave a category bearing the + Q(uantifier) P(hrase) feature. Thus, we tentatively assume feature copy is free. If so, (87) can be simplified as follows:

(87′) Movement: Optionally copy features

Next, consider (88) (= "There is no indexing at S-structure"). With respect to this aspect of the indexing algorithm, we note only that it is perhaps conceptually preferable to the S-structure indexing algorithm proposed in Chomsky (1982). To see this, recall that Free A′-Indexing must be precluded at S-structure (as proposed in Chomsky (1982)). Recall that Chomsky (1982) achieves this result by simply stipulating that Free S-structure indexing is restricted to A-positions. By contrast, no such A–A′ distinction in the S-structure indexing algorithm is necessary here. As noted earlier, the D-structure indexing algorithm proposed here, operating in conjunction with the feature copy analysis, renders the Free S-structure A-position indexing algorithm, proposed in Chomsky (1982), unnecessary. Consequently, to account for the fact that there is no free S-structure A′-indexing, we can simply say that there is no indexing whatsoever at S-structure (i.e., the failure of S-structure A'-indexing follows, without reference to an A–A' distinction, from the nonexistence of all indexing at S-structure). Nonetheless, notice we are still forced to stipulate that there is no indexing at S-structure. The optimal assumption, that indexing is free at this level, cannot be assumed, since this would allow Free A'-indexing at this level, an operation that must be excluded.

The only aspect of the indexing algorithm yet to be considered is (89) (= Free LF A'-indexing). We tentatively suggest that this part of the indexing procedure can be formally restated as

(89') LF: INDEX

If so, the LF and D-structure indexing algorithms are the same. But if the LF indexing algorithm is simply "INDEX," what restricts its application to A'-positions? We assume the correct answer is "Nothing" (i.e., LF indexing is free to apply to A-positions). If LF indexing assigns an index to an A-position, it either assigns the A-position its first index (given the optionality of D-structure indexing and of feature copy, an A-position might not be indexed at D-structure and at S-structure) or it assigns it an additional index, in which case the category in this position would bear more than one index. We assume the former case is allowed (i.e., an A-position is, in principle, allowed to have no index until LF). (When an index is necessary prior to LF [e.g., when an A-position must bind an anaphor at S-structure] if no index is present, independent principles, such as the Binding theory, preclude the representation.)

As far as the second case is concerned (i.e., additional index assignment to an A-position at LF), we leave open whether representations containing categories bearing set indices are filtered or allowed at LF. Given that indices are categorical features, the question amounts to the proper characterization of "Category" at LF. Once given, any purported restriction on the application of INDEX is presumably eliminable. (For an analysis postulating set indices, motivated by certain coreference facts, see Epstein [1983]; for a set-index analysis, motivated by certain disjoint reference facts, see Sportiche [1983, 1985].)

In summary, we tentatively assume that (86)–(89) can be simplified as follows:

(86′) D-structure: INDEX, (Optional)

(87′) Movement = FEATURE-COPY, (Optional)

(88′) S-structure: NO INDEXING

(89′) LF: INDEX, (Optional)

This concludes our discussion of the simplification of the indexing algorithm as well as our discussion of the elimination of principle (1) (= Only an argument receives a g-feature at S-structure). In the following section we consider another asymmetry in g-assignment.

Toward the Elimination of Lexical Proper Government

In this section we shall show that the same indexing algorithm allowing for the elimination of (1) also allows us to go some distance toward eliminating yet another asymmetry in g-assignment, namely, the asymmetry expressesd by the existence of two formally unrelated forms of proper government: antecedent government and lexical proper government. By modifying analyses proposed in Chomsky (Fall 1986, lectures), we will argue that lexical proper government is indeed eliminable, at least for verb–complement traces. We shall begin by noting serious empirical and conceptual problems confronting Chomsky's analysis eliminating lexical proper government. First (following Epstein, 1986b), it is suggested that under the analysis presented in Chomsky (1986b), lexical proper government of verb–complement traces is not, in fact, eliminable. Next, we shall show that (following Chomsky, Fall 1986, lectures) lexical proper government seems to be eliminable by assuming a less restrictive rule ordering than that motivated by L&S. However, under this less restrictive rule ordering allowing for the elimination of lexical proper government, the facts motivating the more restrictive L&S rule order cannot be explained. Consequently, for the purpose of accounting for these facts, it seems that another argument–adjunct asymmetry in g-assignment must be stipulated. Thus, although the less restrictive rule ordering does indeed allow for the elimination of lexical proper government (thus, it allows for the elimination of the asymmetry in g-assignment expressed by the existence of both lexical and antecedent government), it does so only at the expense of incorporating a new stipulation stating another argument–adjunct asymmetry in g-assignment. We shall argue that this stipulation, apparently necessitated by the less restrictive rule order, is eliminable; the stipulated fact can be straightforwardly explained by making explicit certain properties of the indexing algorithm independently motivated earlier.

To begin, consider again the following:

(102) I wonder who bought what

(103) *I wonder who left why

Within most ECP accounts, this kind of contrast is accounted for by assuming that trace complements (as distinct from noncomplements) satisfy the ECP by virtue of being in a particular relation with a lexical category (i.e., complements are lexically properly governed and hence are not dependent on an antecedent to satisfy the ECP).[16]

The nature of the lexical relation constituting proper government differs from analysis to analysis. For example, Chomsky (1981) proposes that government by a lexical X^0 constitutes proper government. Stowell (1981) argues that theta assignment by a lexical category is a necessary condition for lexical proper government to obtain. L&S suggest that a category is lexically properly governed only if it is Case-marked or theta-marked by a lexical category. Epstein (1986b) argues that Exceptional Case-marking constructions (e.g., *Who believes who(m) to be intelligent?*) independently motivate the assumption that Case-marking by a lexical category constitutes proper government and that this in turn makes it unnecessary to recognize theta-marking by a lexical category as a form of proper government (a welcome result for other reasons). Of course, if lexical proper government exists, its formulation is an empirical issue. However, for the purpose of distinguishing sentences such as (102) from those such as (103), we could adopt any of the definitions of lexical proper government mentioned earlier. Under any of these formulations, an S-structure such as (102) can be mapped into a well-formed LF representation of the following form:

(104) $[_{S'}[_S \text{I wonder}[_{S'}[_{C_i} \text{what}_j [_{C_i} \text{who}_i]][_S t_i \text{bought } t_j]]]]$

The direct object trace satisfies the ECP by virtue of being lexically properly governed by the verb "bought." By contrast, (103) is mapped into an LF representation violating the ECP:

(105) *$[_{S'}[_S$ I wonder $[_{S'}[_{C_i}$ why$_j[_{C_i}$ who$_i]][_S t_i$ left $t_j]]]]$

The ECP is violated because the trace of "why" is not properly governed (i.e., it is neither lexically properly governed nor antecedent-governed). Notice that if the trace of "why" were antecedent-governed in (105), we would incorrectly predict that the ECP is satisfied. Crucially, then, the trace of "why" is not antecedent-governed in the LF representation (105). This trace is not antecedent-governed, because it is not bound, and binding is necessary for antecedent government to obtain. (For recent discussion of the binding requirement on antecedent government see, for example, Chomsky [1986b]; L&S [forthcoming]; and Barss [1985]. For less recent discussion see Chomsky [1981] and the references cited. We shall return to the binding requirement later.) Now, since "what" in the LF representation (104), occupies a position identical to the position "why" occupies in (105), "what" cannot antecedent-govern its trace in (104) (just as "why" cannot antecedent-govern its trace in (105)). To distinguish (104) from (105), then, lexical proper government is assumed to hold only of the object trace in (104).

Chomsky (1986b)—Verb Complements and Adjuncts: Another Asymmetry

Chomsky (1986b) provides an analysis of government and bounding suggesting that antecedent government may be the only form of proper government of verb–complement traces. Under this analysis, the trace complement of a passive verb must be antecedent-governed (i.e., theta-marking does not represent proper government of such traces). Our main concern here will be with his analysis of active verb complements. Chomsky argues that, given the option of adjunction to V″, such traces can be antecedent-governed. Hence theta-marking, Case-marking, government by an X^0, or any other conceivable form of lexical proper government can be eliminated as forms of proper government of such traces.

To see how lexical proper government is eliminable under this analysis, consider again the LF representation (104). As noted earlier, it is crucial to ruling out (105) that binding be prerequisite to antecedent government. Consequently, the trace of "what" is not antecedent-governed in this representation. In the absence of lexical proper government, then, (104), like (105), violates the ECP. However, by assuming that wh-phrases may adjoin to V'', the following LF representation of the S-structure (102) is also generable.[17]

(106) $[_{S'}[_S \text{I wonder } [_{S'}[_{C_i} \text{what}_j [_{C_i} \text{who}_i]][_S t_i [_{V''} t'_j [_{V''} \text{bought } t_j]]]]]]$

In this representation t'_j antecedent-governs t_j (see Chomsky, 1986b). Hence, it would seem that we no longer have to appeal to lexical proper government of the direct object trace. However, (106), in fact, violates the ECP, because t'_j (the antecedent governor of t_j) is itself not properly governed. Notice that it must be the case that t'_j violates the ECP. If a V''-adjoined trace such as t'_j did not violate the ECP, then LF representations such as (107b) would be overgenerated, thereby predicting wrongly that sentences such as (107a) are grammatical:

(107) a. *I wonder who said he left why

     b. $[_{S'}[_S \text{I wonder } [_{S'}[_{C_i} \text{why}_j [_{C_i} \text{who}_i]$
        $[_S t_i [_{V''} t''_j [_{V''} \text{said}[_{S'} t'_j [_S \text{he left } t_j]]]]]]]]]]$

In (107b), t_j and t'_j are properly governed. (107b) is ruled out because t''_j is $[-g]$. But notice that t''_j in (107b) and t'_j in (106) occupy identical positions (i.e., neither is properly governed). Therefore, (106), like (107b), violates the ECP. Thus, if lexical proper government is eliminated, (106), like (104), violates the ECP. Hence, it appears that exploiting the option of V'' adjunction does not, in fact, allow for the elimination of lexical proper government. Rather, what we see in LF representations such as (106) is that V'' adjunction does indeed allow the direct object trace to be antecedent-governed by the V''-adjoined trace, but the V''-adjoined trace (necessarily present to g-assign the direct object trace) itself violates the ECP. Hence, the option of V'' adjunction is without effect; lexical proper government of verb complements must apparently be retained. However, for the purposes of eliminating lexical proper government of such categories Chomsky suggests a modification of the rule ordering proposed in L&S. Recall that L&S propose the following ordering:

(108) Affect-alpha precedes (and only precedes) g-assignment

Under this rule ordering, all instances of Affect-alpha (i.e., all instances of movement, of deletion, and of insertion) must be completed before g-assignment can occur. This is precisely the ordering we assumed in the preceding derivations (i.e., in deriving each LF representation of the S-structure (102), namely, (104) and (106)) "what" occupied Comp (i.e., all instances of Affect-alpha were completed) before g-assignment occurred. Recall that in deriving the LF representation (104), "what" was moved directly to Comp. Then and only then could g-assignment apply. As noted, in the absence of lexical proper government of the direct object trace, the ECP was violated. In deriving the LF representation (106), "what" was moved to Comp via V'' adjunction, leaving a trace in V''-adjoined position. With all instances of Affect-alpha thus completed, g-assignment then occurred; as shown, the ECP was violated.

To eliminate lexical proper government, Chomsky proposes the following rule ordering, which is, of course, more permissive than (108):

(109) Affect-alpha and g-assignment are freely ordered [i.e., Affect-alpha can both precede and follow g-assignment]

Under (109), as opposed to (108), well-formed LF representations of the S-structure (102) can be derived without appealing to lexical proper government of the direct object trace. In deriving an LF representation of the S-structure (102), suppose that Affect-alpha applies so as first to adjoin "what" to V'', as in the following intermediate representation:

(110) $[_{S'}[_S$ I wonder$[_{S'}$ who$_i[_S t_i[_{V''}$ what$_j[_{V''}$ bought $t_j]]]]]]$

Under the L&S ordering (108), g-assignment of t_j cannot apply at this point in the derivation, since "what" has not yet been moved to Comp (i.e., it is not the case that all instances of Affect-alpha have been performed). By contrast, the more permissive ordering (109) does allow g-assignment to occur at this point in the derivation prior to Affect-alpha. Since the direct object t_j is anteced-ent-governed by "what," it can be assigned $[+g]$, yielding

(111) $[_{S'}[_S$ I wonder$[_{S'}$ who$_i[_St_i[_{V''}$ what$_j[_{V''}$ bought $t_j]]]]]]$
$$[+g]$$

Since Affect-alpha can follow g-assignment under (109), "what" can now move from V''-adjoined position to Comp. If a trace is left in V''-adjoined position, the LF representation (106) is de-rived. As we have seen, the ECP is violated because the V''-adjoined trace is not properly governed. However, no principle requires a trace to be left in V''-adjoined position. If no trace is left, the ECP is satisfied, *without appealing to lexical proper gov-ernment of the direct object trace*. Notice, under (109), another derivation is possible. First, Affect-alpha could apply so as to move "what" to Comp (via V'' adjunction), leaving a trace in V''-adjoined position. Next, g-assignment can apply and the V''-adjoined trace can assign $[+g]$ to the direct object trace. Follow-ing this, Affect-alpha can apply again and the V''-adjoined trace can delete. Again, the ECP is satisfied without appealing to lexi-cal proper government of the direct object trace.

Thus, as Chomsky argues, under the ordering expressed in (109), lexical proper government of active verb complements is eliminable. Clearly, the free ordering in (109) is more permissive than the strict ordering in (108). Although we have seen that the free ordering allows for the elimination of lexical proper govern-ment, we might ask whether the free ordering is too permissive (i.e., does it overgenerate?). L&S, in fact, consider the free or-dering (109), but they reject it in favor of the more restrictive order (108). The problem, they note, is precisely one of over-generation. To see how (109) overgenerates, consider again an S-structure such as

(112) $[_{S'}$ Who$_i[_S t_i$ said $[_{S'}[_S$ he left why$_j]]]]$

Given (109), in the LF component, "why" could first move to the embedded Comp. Second, $[+g]$ can be assigned to the adjunct trace of "why." Next, "why" could move Comp-to-Comp, leav-ing no trace in the embedded Comp. Incorrectly, the ECP is sat-isfied. Similarly, "why" could move Comp-to-Comp, leaving a trace in the embedded Comp. This trace could antecedent-govern the adjoined trace (i.e., assign $[+g]$ to it) and then delete. Again, the ECP is incorrectly satisfied. Thus, as L&S note, the more permissive ordering (109) incorrectly allows such cases of over-generation. Hence, they reject (109) and adopt instead (108).

For the purpose of eliminating lexical proper government, Chomsky retains the permissive order (109). To prevent such illicit adjunct movement allowed by (109), Chomsky proposes the following:

(113) An adjunct must be fully represented

Notice that (113) specifically mentions adjuncts and, in so doing, represents a stipulated argument–adjunct asymmetry. If the predictive content of (113) is correct, we wish to derive these predictions without incorporating stipulations such as (113). Thus, before attempting to eliminate (113), we should first determine its predictive content (i.e., the exact manner in which it prevents the illicit derivations discussed earlier). Recall, in the first derivation (proceeding from the S-structure (112)), the following LF operations apply (ordered as given):

(114) a. AFFECT-alpha: "why" moves to the embedded Comp

    b. g-ASSIGN: the adjunct trace is assigned $[+g]$

    c. AFFECT-alpha: "why" moves to the matrix Comp, leaving no trace in the embedded Comp

Principle (113) precludes such derivations by precluding (114c). Specifically, (113) forces Comp-to-Comp adjunct movement to leave a trace (i.e., "full representation of the adjunct" requires that a trace be left in the embedded Comp). Given that a trace must be left in the embedded Comp, the ECP is necessarily violated, as desired. Thus, with respect to this derivation we see that (113) is to be interpreted as follows:

(115) Every movement of an adjunct obligatorily leaves a trace

Recall now that a second derivation proceeding from (112) must also be prevented. In this derivation the following LF operations occur as ordered:

(116) a. AFFECT-alpha: "why" moves to the embedded Comp

    b. AFFECT-alpha: "why" moves to the matrix Comp, leaving a trace in the embedded Comp

    c. *g*-ASSIGN: [+ *g*] is assigned to the adjunct trace

    d. AFFECT-alpha: The trace in Comp deletes

Principle (113) prevents such derivations by disallowing (116d). To disallow (116d), (113) is to be interpreted as

(117) The trace of an adjunct cannot delete

Hence, to prevent both derivations, (113) must be interpreted as (at least) the conjunction of (115) and (117). In this respect, (113) is equivalent to (at least) two independent stipulations concerning adjuncts.

Summarizing to this point, we have seen that the more permissive rule ordering does indeed allow for the elimination of lexical proper government of verb-complement traces. However, the facts motivating the more restrictive L&S rule order are not accounted for under this (overgenerating) permissive order. Consequently, two stipulations, each specifically referring to adjuncts, must apparently be incorporated so as to prevent such overgeneration. Thus, lexical proper government is eliminated under the order (109) but only at the expense of incorporating the two preceding stipulations concerning adjuncts.

We shall now argue that the more permissive rule order (109) can be maintained (thereby allowing for the elimination of lexical proper government) and that such cases of overgeneration can be prevented without appealing to (113) or to any other stipulations regarding adjuncts.

To begin, recall the indexing algorithm for which much independent motivation was given earlier:

(86) A-positions, and only A-positions, are indexed at D-structure

(87) Movement does not create coindexation; movement is feature copy

(88) There is no indexing at S-structure

(89) Free LF A'-indexing

(Notice that under this indexing algorithm, the S-structure (112) is, in fact, not generable [i.e., "why" can have no index at S-structure].)

As argued earlier, the asymmetry in *g*-assignment expressed by (1) (= Only an argument is *g*-assigned at S-structure) can be eliminated under this indexing algorithm, from which it follows that adjuncts, as well as their traces, have no indices at S-structure. (Hence, it follows that they are incapable of being assigned $[+g]$ at this level.) Recall that since an adjunct and its traces have no indices at S-structure, they must acquire indices in the LF component for the purposes of satisfying the LF principle prohibiting vacuous quantification. Thus, following Chomsky (1982), we assume the existence of Free LF A'-indexing under which an adjunct and its traces can be indexed in the LF component. Given the existence of Free LF A'-indexing, the following is a purely empirical question regarding the organization of the LF component:

(118) At what point in the LF Component does Free LF A'-indexing apply?

Suppose the answer is

(119) Free LF A'-indexing applies only after Affect-alpha applies

((119) is, of course, an empirical proposal concerning LF rule ordering, which is precisely the issue with which we have been concerned throughout this section.) Given (119), we can now assume the permissive order (109) and no longer have any need for the stipulation(s), such as (113), to prevent illicit adjunct movement. Recall that under (109), *g*-assignment and Affect-alpha are freely ordered. Thus, *any category, be it an argument or an adjunct, is allowed to g-assign at any point in a derivation.* No stipulation regarding adjuncts is necessary to prevent the illicit adjunct movement derivations discussed earlier, since the ordering in (119) prevents all such derivations. Given (119) and the preceding indexing algorithm, Affect-alpha, when applied to an adjunct and its traces, is completed before these categories are indexed. (That is, Movement, Deletion, and Insertion of adjunct categories are completed before such categories are indexed.) Since such categories must have indices in order for *g*-assignment to occur, it follows from (119) that Affect-alpha, when applied to an adjunct and its traces, precedes and only precedes *g*-assignment. Hence, the overgeneration of illicit adjunct movement discussed earlier is prevented; *an adjunct and its traces have no indices and hence cannot g-assign, until after all applications of Affect-alpha are completed*. Crucially, this result now follows without any stipulation regarding adjuncts. Thus, we have now derived the (illicit adjunct movement) facts that motivated the strict L&S rule order (108), but we have done so without incorporating this strict rule order. Rather, under the permissive order (109), these facts are derived. Notice also that, as desired, (119) has no effect on arguments (i.e., under the preceding indexing algorithm and the permissive ordering (109), argument categories can undergo Affect-alpha, then they can *g*-assign, then they can undergo Affect-alpha again. As we have seen, this ordering allows for the elimination of lexical proper government of verb-complement traces.

To summarize this section, we have assumed, following Chomsky:

(120) Adjunction of wh-phrases to V″ is possible

(121) (= (109)) Affect-alpha and *g*-assignment are freely ordered

However, we have rejected the following:

(113) An adjunct must be fully represented

As noted, (113) is tantamount to at least two stipulations concerning adjuncts. We have derived the argument–adjunct asymmetry in (113) by supplanting it with the following:

(119) Free LF A′-indexing applies only after Affect-alpha applies [i.e., indexing applies only at levels]

Under this organization of grammar, lexical proper government of verb complements is eliminable, and this result is obtained without appealing to any stipulated distinction between *g*-assignment of arguments and adjuncts.

We have just seen that the elimination of lexical proper government of verb complements is derived by assuming the permissive ordering (109) obtains *in the LF component*. However, in the absence of any principled prohibition (and I know of none) we must assume the permissive ordering (109) also obtains in the syntactic component. In the next section we investigate the consequences of this assumption with respect to "that"–trace effects and improper NP-movement.

The Permissive Ordering in the Syntax

We now investigate potential problems of overgeneration resulting from the assumption that the permissive ordering (109) characterizes the Syntactic Component as it does the LF component.

ADJUNCTS

No problems concerning adjuncts emerge under the assumption that (109) obtains both in the syntax and in the LF component. As argued earlier, an adjunct and its traces have no indices (hence, assignment of $[+g]$ to adjunct traces is precluded) until after Affect-alpha has applied in the LF component.

"THAT"–t EFFECTS

Given that g-assignment and Affect-alpha are freely ordered in the syntax, we must ensure that S-structures of the following type are not overgenerated:

(122) $[_{S'}$ who$_i[_S$ do you think $[_{S'}$ that$[_S$ t_i left$]]]]$
$$[+g]$$

One derivation that must be excluded but is apparently allowed under the permissive ordering of (109) is the following:

(123) a. D-structure: $[_{S'}[_S$ you think$[_{S'}[_S$ who$_i$ left$]]]]$

     b. Affect-alpha: $[_{S'}[_S$ you think $[_{S'}$ who$_i[_S t_i$ left$]]]]$

     c. g-Assign: $[_{S'}[_S$ you think $[_{S'}$ who$_i[t_i$ left$]]]]$
$$[+g]$$

     d. Affect-alpha: $[_{S'}$ Who$_i[_S$ do you think $[_{S'}[_S t_i$ left$]]]]$
$$[+g]$$

     e. Introduction of "that" yields the S-structure:
       $[_{S'}$ who$_i[_S$ do you think$[_{S'}$ that $[_S t_i$ left$]]]]$
$$[+g]$$

With regard to (123e), recall that the insertion of "that" as applied in deriving well-formed S-structure representations of sentences such as *What do you think that John likes?* appeared to violate the principle of the Strict Cycle; movement had to proceed through Comp, followed by insertion of "that" into Comp. Consequently, we proposed that the insertion of "that" is not an instance of Affect-alpha, therefore, it is not subject to the principle of the Strict Cycle. Rather, following Chomsky (1973), we have assumed that introduction of "that" is the spelling out of the features of a [-wh] Comp. Notice, however, that this spell-out analysis does not prevent the unwanted derivation that included (123e); rather, it simply assumes "that" to be the spell-out of the [-wh] Comp (and thus not an element lexically inserted into Comp).

To prevent this unwanted derivation, let us begin by assuming that "who," when it occupies the embedded Comp, cannot itself antecedent-govern (i.e., cannot assign $[+g]$ to) the trace in subject position. Rather, let us assume, as we have throughout, that Comp indexing is required for antecedent government to obtain. Thus, the unwanted derivation begins with the D-structure (123a) and proceeds not as in (123b)–(123e) but, more specifically, as in (124) (where assignment of $[+g]$ could occur at either points c, e, or f).

(124) a. Affect-alpha: $[_{S'}[_S$ you think $[_{S'}[_C$ who$_i][_S t_i$ left]]]]

     b. Index Comp: $[_{S'}[_S$ you think $[_{S'}[_{C_i}$ who$_i][_S t_i$ left]]]]

     (c. Assign $[+g]$ to t)

     d. Affect-alpha: $[_{S'}$ who$_i[_S$ you think $[_{S'}[_{C_i}][_S t_i$ left]]]]

     (e. Assign $[+g]$ to t)

     f. Spell-out: $[_{S'}$ who$_i[_S$ you think$[_{S'}[_{Ci}$ that] $[_S t_i$ left]]]]

     (g. Assign $[+g]$ to t)

     h. S-structure: $[_{S'}$ who$_i[_S$ do you think$[_{S'}[_{C_i}$ that] $[_S t_i$ left]]]]
                                            $[+g]$

We will now present three approaches to ruling out such derivations.

Restricting Spell-out

To prevent the derivation (124), we can now exploit a distinction between the insertion and spell-out analyses. Clearly, if "that" is the spelling out of a [-wh] Comp, there are restrictions on the type of [-wh] Comp that can be spelled out in this way. For example, one restriction is that only a [-wh] Comp that selects Tense can

be spelled out as "that." We shall now argue that a further restriction governing the spell-out of Comp prevents the unwanted
overgeneration exemplified by (124).

To begin, there are two important aspects to derivations such
as (124). First, the only way for the ECP to be satisfied is if Comp
is indexed i prior to S-structure. (If this fails to occur, the subject
trace will be immutably marked $[-g]$ at S-structure, ultimately
violating the ECP at LF.) Second, once Comp is indexed i, it
follows from the Deletion Prohibition (51), proposed earlier, that
this index cannot be deleted from the feature matrix of Comp,
since only categories (i.e., entire feature matrices) are subject to
deletion. Thus, the only way to eliminate the index on Comp is
to delete the entire Comp node bearing this index. (In the absence
of evidence to the contrary, we presume that this is licit, provided
Comp contains nothing having semantic content.) Given this, the
"that"–t violation can now be prevented by making the following
morphological assumption regarding the feature bundle called
"Comp":

(125) "that" is the (optional) morphological realization of a feature bun-
       dle (Comp) consisting of no index

Under (125), (124f) is not a possible operation, since Comp can
be spelled out as "that" only when the feature matrix of Comp
contains no index. Hence, "that"–t violations are not generable.
In short, Comp-indexing is required to g-mark a subject trace.
The appearance of "that" is therefore precluded, because an indexed Comp is not realizable as "that" and the only way to eliminate the index on Comp is to delete the entire Comp node. Under
this analysis, "that"–t configurations either are violations of the
ECP (if Comp is not indexed when "who" occupies this position) or constitute morphologically unrealizable structures (when
Comp is indexed).

Notice that (125) is apparently necessary. Yet, as stated, it is
both a language-specific and a morphologically specific condition
concerning those feature matrices that are (and are not) realized
as "that." Although (125) is descriptively adequate, in the absence of more general explanatory morphological principles from
which it could be derived, an explanation is lacking. Alternative,

perhaps more explantory, accounts are provided in the following sections.

A Filter Approach

We continue to assume that only an indexed Comp can antecedent-govern subject position. But suppose we abandon (125) and assume instead that "that" can be freely spelled out (i.e., regardless of whether Comp is or is not indexed). Now S-structures of the following type are generated:

(126) $[_{S'}$ Who$_i$ $[_S$ do you think $[_{S'}[_{C_i}$ that$]$ $[_S t_i$ left$]]]]$
$$[+g]$$

Comp-indexing was triggered when "who" occupied Comp. In the absence of (125), the embedded indexed Comp was freely spelled out as "that" after "who" vacated this position. Under the permissive ordering (109), the subject trace could have been assigned $[+g]$ at any point following Comp-indexing. Thus, the ECP is satisfied. We shall now argue that representations such as (126) are filtered because the structure of the embedded Comp is ill formed. To derive this result, we modify a filter proposed in L&S precluding representations seemingly distinct from those such as (126) displaying the "that"–t effect. To motivate the filter that we will ultimately modify so that it rules out (126), let us begin by considering the following sentence due to Baker (1970):

(127) Who wonders where we bought what?

As Baker notes, the sentence is ambiguous, but only in a very restricted way. The sentence is obligatorily interpreted as a direct question of "who." Further, it is obligatorily interpreted as an indirect question of "where." The ambiguity concerns only the interpretation of "what," which can be either directly or indirectly questioned.

Given the obligatory application of Comp-indexing, the S-structure of (127) is

(128) $[_{S'}[_{C_i}$ Who$_i][_S t_i$ wonders $[_{S'}[_{C_j}$ where$_j][_S$ we bought what$_k t_j]]]]$

(Notice we assume, crucially, that "where" has an index at S-structure, thereby triggering Comp-indexing. Under the indexing algorithm motivated earlier, it follows that "where" must have been indexed at D-structure, which in turn entails that "where" occupied an A-position at this level. See Huang, 1982, for a way to derive this result.) Now it appears that principles of selection ensure that "where" is obligatorily interpreted as an indirectly questioned element. That is, if "where" were to move to the matrix Comp at LF, the selectional requirement of "wonder" would be violated. However, as L&S note, this isn't necessarily the case. Suppose "where" does move to the matrix Comp at LF. The selectional requirement of "wonder" can still be met by moving "what" to the embedded Comp (formerly occupied by "where"). Thus, principles of selection do not prohibit the illicit mapping from an S-structure such as (128) to an LF such as

(129) $[_{S'}[_{C_i} \text{where}_j [\text{who}_i]][_S t_i \text{ wonders } [_{S'}[_{C_j} \text{what}_k] [_S \text{we bought } t_k t_j]]]]$

To rule out LF representations like (129), L&S propose the following filter:

(130) $*[. . .\text{HEAD}_i. . .]_j$ where i and j are not the same index

Filter (130) rules out the LF representation (129); the embedded Comp is an illicit category by virtue of bearing the index j, which is not identical to the index k borne by the head of Comp, "what."

With this in mind, consider again the "that"–t configuration (126). Recall that the ECP is satisfied, because the indexed Comp dominating "that" antecedent-governs the subject. Furthermore, notice that (126) satisfies filter (130); in (126) the head of Comp, namely "that," is unindexed, hence the filter is inapplicable (i.e., its Structural Description is not met). Nevertheless, the S-structure (126) has something in common with the ill-formed (129), which motivated filter (130). Each contains an indexed Comp that immediately dominates a head that is not coindexed with Comp. A unified account of these phenomena (i.e., the ill-formedness of the S-structure (126) and the LF (129)) can be provided by modifying filter (130) as follows, so that it precludes both types of structures:

(131) $*[. . .\text{HEAD}. . .]_i$ unless HEAD is indexed i

Filter (131) subsumes filter (130). The former dictates that an indexed Comp containing a head must exhibit Comp–head coindexing. (It makes no predictions regarding unindexed Comps, nor does it impose requirements on headless Comps.) Assuming (131) applies at S-structure, "that"–*t* configurations such as (126) are excluded. Provided (131) also applies at LF, representations such as (129) are similarly ruled out.[18]

Rule Ordering Again

A third approach to the "that"–*t* effect is to assume the following rule ordering obtains in the syntax (as is, in fact, proposed by L&S):

(132) Comp-indexing follows, and only follows, Affect-alpha

Under this ordering, derivations such as (124) are excluded; specifically, (124b) cannot precede (124d). More generally, it follows that if a category triggers indexing of a given Comp in the syntax, the triggering category will necessarily appear in that Comp at S-structure (since it cannot be Affected [moved or deleted] after triggering Comp-indexing). Equivalently, if a Comp is indexed at S-structure, the category inducing Comp-indexing will be present in Comp at S-structure. The "that"–*t* effect now follows. If Comp is not indexed, the subject trace is assigned $[-g]$, ultimately violating the ECP at LF. If Comp is indexed, the ECP is satisfied. However, it follows from the ordering (132) that the category inducing Comp-indexing occurs in Comp, hence "that" cannot.

Notice that if the ordering (132) obtained at LF, it is perhaps the case that Free LF A′-indexing could precede Affect-alpha (contrary to the arguments presented earlier that the opposite order must obtain). Given (132), consider again an S-structure such as

(133) $[_{S'}$ who$_i$ $[_S$ t_i said $[_{S'}$ $[_S$ he$_j$ left why]]]]

"Why" has no index at S-structure. Suppose now that, at LF, Free A′-indexing can precede Affect-alpha. If so, "why" could be indexed and could then move to Comp. But under the order (132), "why" cannot trigger Comp-indexing and then move to the matrix Comp, leaving no trace. Rather, to produce Comp-indexing, a trace will have to be left in the embedded Comp. This necessarily results in a violation of the ECP. Thus, it appears that, under (132), we could assume that Free LF A′-indexing can precede Affect-alpha.

However, this argument depends crucially on the assumption that "why" must first move to Comp. Suppose, as may well be the case, that "why" could first move to V"-adjoined position and that V"-adjoined position properly governs the initial trace. If so, then the order (132) could not prevent overgeneration resulting from the assumption that Free A'-indexing can precede Affect-alpha. That is, "why" could be indexed; then it could move to V"-adjoined position and assign $[+g]$ to the initial trace. Following this, "why" could then move to the matrix Comp, leaving no trace. Incorrectly, the ECP would be satisfied. We shall return to this issue later. It will be argued that the ordering (132) cannot be maintained. If correct, Free LF A'-indexing must certainly follow Affect-alpha, as argued earlier:

Summary: An Asymmetry Revealed and Eliminated

We began the last section by noting the following problem: If the permissive ordering (109) ($= g$-assign and Affect-alpha are freely ordered) characterizes the syntax, as it does LF, derivations such as (123) are overgenerated (i.e., "that"–t configurations are generable). In the derivation (123), "who" moves to the embedded Comp and then "who" itself assigns $[+g]$ to the subject trace. As depicted in derivation (123), if this were allowed, "who" could subsequently move Comp-to-Comp, leaving no trace, and "that" could then be spelled out in the embedded Comp; the derived "that"–t configuration satisfies the ECP. To prevent such derivations we assumed that

(134) "who," when occupying Comp, cannot itself assign $[+g]$; rather, only the indexed Comp can assign $[+g]$

Once Comp-indexing was assumed to be prerequisite to satisfying the ECP, we were able to construct three approaches to the "that"–t effect. The first assumed that "that" was the spelling out of only unindexed Comps. The second recognized a filter precluding a headed, indexed category C when C and the head are not coindexed. The third approach assumed Comp-indexing is ordered only after Affect-alpha.

Notice that each approach depends *entirely* on the supposition that Comp-indexing is required to satisfy the ECP. Recall that if Comp-indexing is not required, derivation (123) would be overgenerated (i.e., none of the preceding three approaches would prevent "that"–*t* configurations). But now we must ask, "Why is Comp-indexing required?" More specifically, "Why can't 'who' (when occupying Comp) itself assign $[+g]$ to the subject trace?" The latter question is particularly bothersome given that the analysis eliminating lexical proper government of verb complements crucially assumed that a wh-phrase adjoined to V″ could itself assign $[+g]$ to a verb–complement trace. But if this is so, then why cannot a wh-phrase in Comp similarly assign $[+g]$ directly to a subject trace (i.e., why is Comp-indexing required?)? These questions reveal a serious asymmetry in the analysis presented thus far. To eliminate lexical proper government of verb complements, Affect-alpha and *g*-assignment are freely ordered in the LF component. Consequently, a direct object wh-phrase can adjoin to V″, then the wh-phrase adjoined to V″ can itself assign $[+g]$ to the direct object trace. But if Affect-alpha and *g*-assignment are also freely ordered in the syntax (and we see no principled way to exclude this), then we must prevent derivations such as (123). To prevent such derivations, we had to assume that a wh-phrase in Comp cannot itself assign $[+g]$ to a subject trace (rather, Comp-indexing is required). Now we must apparently explain this asymmetry. But since we have no explanation of this asymmetry, we shall assume it does not in fact exist (i.e., instead of attempting to explain this asymmetry, we will now eliminate it by modifying the analysis proposed thus far). For the purpose of ruling out derivations such as (123), we will continue to assume that a wh-phrase in Comp cannot itself assign $[+g]$; rather, Comp-indexing is required. Following Lasnik and Saito (forthcoming), Davis (1984, 1987), and Rizzi (1986), we adopt the following principle:

(135) Only a head can properly govern

Under (135) it follows that a wh-*phrase,* regardless of the position it occupies, cannot assign $[+g]$. Thus, it is (135) that entails that a wh-phrase in Comp cannot antecedent-govern a subject trace. Rather, under (135), the indexing of Comp, a head, is prerequisite to antecedent government of a subject trace. As noted earlier, given that Comp-indexing is required, any one of the preceding three approaches to the "that"–*t* effect (each making crucial reference to Comp-indexing) can now be successfully invoked to rule out derivations such as (123). Thus, the assumption that Affect-alpha and g-assignment are freely ordered in the syntax (as in LF) does not lead to the overgeneration of "that"–t configurations.

But now we confront a new problem arising from this solution. Under (135), a wh-phrase adjoined to V″ cannot assign $[+g]$ to a direct object (i.e., under (135), even if we freely order Affect-alpha and g-assignment in the LF component, the option of adjoining a wh-phrase to V″ no longer allows us to eliminate lexical proper government). Equivalently, under (135), derivations of the following kind are no longer generable:

(136) a. S-structure: $[_{S'}[_{C_i} \text{Who}_i] [_S t_i \text{ bought what}_j]]]]]$

    b. Affect-alpha: (V″-adjunction)
      $[_{S'}[_{C_i} \text{Who}_i[_S t_i [_{V''} \text{what}_j [_{V''} \text{bought } t_j]]]]]$

    c. g-Assign: ("what" assigns $[+g]$ to t_j)
      $[_{S'}[_{C_i} \text{who}_i][_S t_i [_{V''} \text{what}_j [_{V''} \text{bought } t_j]]]]$
                            $[+g]$

    d. Affect-alpha: $[_{S'}[_{C_i} \text{what}_j[_{Ci} \text{who}_i]][_S t_i ([_{V''})[_{V''} \text{bought } t_j]]]]$
                                      $[+g]$

(135) precludes (136c), since "what" is not a head. Thus, it seems that freely ordering Affect-alpha and g-assignment is now without effect (i.e., lexical proper government of the direct object trace must be assumed). To avoid this appeal to lexical proper government, while still assuming (135), we propose that movement of the direct object wh-phrase to Comp can proceed via movement through a Specifier (Spec) position of V″. (For extensive discussion of and motivation for a theta-less Specifier position of V″, see McNulty, 1988.) Given this, the S-structure (136a) can be mapped into an intermediate LF representation such as the following, in which "what" occupies Specifier of V″:

(137) $[_{S'}[_{C_i} \text{who}_i][_S t_i [_{V''} \text{what}_j[_{V'} \text{bought } t_j]]]]$

But now, under (135), it is still the case that t_j is not antecedent-governed; "what" is not a head. Thus, our assumption that movement is through Specifier of V″ seems no better in this regard than the assumption that movement proceeds via V″ adjunction. There is, however, an important distinction. Suppose, as proposed in Chomsky (1986b), that there is a Specifier–Head Agreement rule that coindexes a Specifier and its head (see Chomsky, 1986b for discussion of this rule). If Spec–Head coindexing may apply at intermediate points in a derivation, the intermediate representation (137) is mapped into the following intermediate representation:

(138) $[_{S'}[_{C_i}$ who$_i]$ $[_S t_i [_{V''}$ what$_j[_{V'}$ bought$_j t_j]]]]$

Since "what" occupies Spec position of V'', Spec–head coindexing results in the coindexation of "what" and "bought." Since "what" is coindexed with t_j, "bought" and t_j are also coindexed. Consequently, t_j is now antecedent-governed in conformity with (135) (i.e., t_j is now antecedent-governed by a head, namely, V.[19]
   Given the analysis proposed thus far, we must now assume

(139) Affect-alpha can precede and follow Spec–head coindexing

Under (139), "what" can now move to Comp, thereby satisfying the LF principle of scope assignment dictating that all wh-phrases occupy Comp in LF representation. Provided no trace is left in Spec of V'', all traces present in the derived representation bear $[+g]$ (i.e., the ECP is satisfied). In an alternative derivation, "what" moves to Comp, leaving a trace in Spec of V'' along the way. Again, provided Spec–head coindexing can precede Affect-alpha, the trace in Spec can trigger Spec–head coindexing and can subsequently delete. The ECP is satisfied. Thus, both of these derivations result in the following well-formed LF representation:

(140) $[_{S'}[_{C_i}$ What$_j[_{C_i}$ who$_i]]$ $[_S t_i [_{V''}$ bought$_j t_j]]]$
$$[+g] \qquad [+g]$$

Notice in this representation (i.e., after the application of Affect-alpha, the direct object trace is still properly governed by the head V. Given this, we see that the elimination of lexical proper government of verb complements does not require the permissive ordering (109) (= Affect and g-assignment are freely ordered). Rather, following L&S, we could now assume that g-assignment applies only after Affect-alpha. Lexical proper government of the direct object trace is still eliminable, since, in the derived representation, the direct object trace is antecedent-governed by the head V. This, of course, results from the assumption that Affect-alpha and Spec–head coindexing are freely ordered.[20]

Given that this approach requires that Spec–head coindexing applies at intermediate levels, we assume that the other head-indexing rule, namely, Comp-indexing, can similarly apply at intermediate levels. That is, we assume that Affect-alpha can both precede and follow Comp-indexing. We therefore allow such derivations as (124) in which "who" moves to Comp, triggers Comp-indexing, and then moves Comp-to-Comp. Thus, the subsequent introduction of "that" can no longer be ruled out by our ordering analysis proposed earlier dictating that Comp-indexing can only follow Affect-alpha. However, the "that"–t configurations resulting from such derivations can either be ruled out by the preceding filter approach or the derivations themselves can be precluded by the preceding approach morphologically restricting the spell-out of Comp as "that."

If Comp-indexing and Spec–head indexing can apply prior to Affect-alpha, notice that we must still assume that Free LF A′-indexing only follows Affect-alpha. Under this ordering, an adjunct has no index and therefore cannot trigger head indexing until after Affect-alpha has applied at LF. Without this ordering, LF representations such as the following would be overgenerated (because "why" could be indexed and could then move through Comp, triggering Comp-indexing):

(141) $[_{S'}[_{Ci}\,\text{Why}_j\,[_{Ci}\,\text{who}_i]][_{S'}[_S\,t_i\,\text{said}\,[_{S'}[_{C_j}][_S\,\text{he left}\,t_j]]]]$
$$[+g]$$

Under the ordering proposed here, such representations are not generable; an adjunct has no index until after Affect-alpha applies in LF.[21] However, LF representations such as the following are generable:

(142) $[_{S'}[_{Ci}\text{Why}_i][_S\,\text{do you wonder}[_{S'}\,\text{whether}[_S\,\text{John}$
$[_{V''}\,t''_i[_{V'}[_V\,\text{said}_i[_{S'}[_{Ci}\,t'_i][_S\,\text{Bill left}\,t_i]]]]]]]]$

In conformity with the ordering proposed here, Affect-alpha applied first. Then and only then could Free A′ indexing apply, coindexing the adjunct and its traces. Next, head indexing could apply, since it is freely ordered with respect to Affect-alpha and must also be allowed to follow Free A′-indexing (if it couldn't, the LF representation of *Why did John go?* would necessarily violate the ECP, because Comp could not be indexed). Thus, Comp and V were indexed. Now the most deeply embedded trace t is assigned $[+g]$, since it is antecedent-governed by the head C. Further, t'_i, occupying Comp, is also assigned $[+g]$, since it too is antecedent-governed, in this case by the head V. If the ECP is violated, the result we want, it must be that t'' occupying Spec of V″ is $[-g]$. But does this result follow? If it does, we must ask why the indexed head V (i.e., "said") does not antecedent-govern the trace in Spec of V″. These two categories are coindexed, and there is certainly no barrier dominating the trace in Spec of V″ that fails to dominate the verb "said." Why, then, does this verb fail to antecedent-govern the trace in Spec of V″? The answer is that c-command is required for antecedent government to obtain (i.e., for a category X to antecedent-govern Y, X must c-command Y, as is proposed in L&S). Given this, the head V does not antecedent-govern t'', despite the fact that it is coindexed with and m-commands t'', and is separated from t'' by no barriers. (For discussion of the relation m-command, see Aoun and Sportiche 1983 and Chomsky 1986b.) Under the c-command requirement, t'' is assigned $[-g]$ and the ECP is violated, a correct result.

Finally, in an LF representation similar to (142), only lacking the trace in Spec of V″ (and therefore also lacking an index on the V "said"), we have a further argument for the exact nature of the c-command condition. Consider

(143) $[_{S'}[_{C_i}\text{Why}_i][_S \text{do you wonder}[_{S'} \text{whether}[_S \text{John said}$
    $[_{S'}[_{C_i} t_i][_S \text{Bill left } t_i]]]]]]$

Clearly, it is the trace in Comp that violates the ECP. Notice, however, that the indexed Comp, a head, is coindexed with the trace in Comp and no barriers separate the two. Nonetheless, C_i does not c-command the trace in Comp, assuming that c-command entails nondomination (as proposed in Reinhart, 1979). Thus, correctly, the ECP is violated.

Motivation for the Head Requirement in the Barriers Framework

In the last section we argued that the "that"–*t* effect provided motivation for adopting the following principle:

(135) Only a head can properly govern

In this section I shall very briefly argue that (135) provides a possible solution to what may be a very general problem confronted within the Barriers framework of Chomsky (1986b). Our arguments will be illustrated by discussing a specific instantiation of this problem. How this solution can be generally applied to this framework is left open.

To begin, notice that extraction of adjuncts from adjuncts results in the kind of severe ungrammaticality indicative of an ECP violation.[22]:

(144) *Why did you get angry because Mary bought it

Although the structure of sentences like (144) is not altogether clear, one possibility suggested by Fukui (1987), to whom example (144) is due, is the following (see Fukui [1987] for further discussion)[23]:

(145) $[_{S'}$ Why$_i$ $[_S$ did you get angry $[_{P''}$ because $[_{S'}$ t'_i $[_S$ Mary bought it t_i]]]]]

Assuming that this is the correct structure, more specifically, the LF representation, the L&S system incorrectly predicts that the ECP is satisfied, as Fukui (1987) notes. The ECP is satisfied; in particular, t' is antecedent-governed under the L&S analysis, because a given S' is not a barrier to antecedent government of a category in its Comp. Thus, within the L&S system, t' is antecedent-governed by the indexed matrix Comp; incorrectly, the ECP is satisfied. Fukui (1987) argues that providing such a structure-independent inventory of barriers, as within the L&S system, results in such overgeneration, since such approaches are insensitive to whether a trace in Comp, such as t' in (145), is separated from its antecedent by a noncomplement such as P''. Fukui argues that such cases favor the analysis in Chomsky (1986b), an analysis that is sensitive to the role of complementhood, more precisely, L-marking, in determining whether or not a category *as it occurs in a given structure* is or is not a barrier to antecedent government.

Let us now return to the LF representation (145) and its treatment within the Barriers framework. Notice first that t' must be present to g-assign t. Given this, it is t' in Spec of C″ that violates the ECP. This principle is violated because the adjunct P″ is not L-marked in this representation. Since it dominates t' it is a BC and a Barrier for this category. Consequently, t' is not antecedent-governed (i.e., it is not governed by a coindexed antecedent), with the result that t', necessarily present to g-assign t, violates the ECP.

Thus, extraction of an adjunct out of an adjunct should always violate the ECP; adjunct phrases are, by definition, not L-marked; hence, they are BCs and, if not I″, they are barriers for the categories they dominate. That is, categories dominated by an adjunct cannot be governed, hence antecedent-governed, from outside. We can apparently conclude, then, that extraction of an adjunct from an adjunct always violates the Barriers formulation of the ECP. But there is a problem. It is clearly the case that articulating the class of barriers, whether it is a categorial inventory or a structure-dependent classification, is without effect, with respect to the theory of movement, in the absence of a companion theory articulating the class of positions to which categories can be moved. Thus, to take an extreme example, one can readily see how the theory of Chomsky (1986b) would be undermined if the following were maintained:

(146) Adjunction to any category is allowed

The point is simply this: Any substantive theory of barriers must incorporate a theory of landing sites. What, then, is the theory of landing sites proposed within the framework of Chomsky (1986b)? Here we are concerned only with the principles determining the class of adjunction sites; the fundamental one being the following:

(147) Adjunction is possible only to a maximal projection (hence X″) that is a nonargument[24]

But now here is the problem. As we have seen, extraction of an adjunct from an adjunct phrase is supposed to violate the ECP, since adjunct phrases are, by definition, not L-marked; hence, they are barriers for the categories they dominate. But since adjunct phrases are also, by definition, nonarguments, adjunction to them is possible in conformity with (147). Consequently, categories being extracted from adjunct phrases can adjoin to them. What we see, then, is that (147) vitiates the substantive barrierhood of adjunct phrases (i.e., these categories do not block extraction).

Thus, for example, sentence (144) can have the following LF representation in which a trace is adjoined to the adjunct P″, thereby allowing this category to be antecedent-governed from without:

(148) $[_{S'}$ why$_i[_S$ do you$[_{V''} t_i'''[_{V''}$ get angry
       $[_{P''} t''_i[_{P''}$ because$[_{S'} t_i'[_S$ Mary bought it $t_i]]]]]]]]]$

Each trace in (148) is antecedent-governed; specifically, t'' antecedent-governs t', which in turn antecedent-governs t. t'' can be antecedent-governed by "why" (if P″ is not dominated by the matrix V″) or by the trace adjoined to the matrix V″ (if P″ is dominated by the matrix V″). Incorrectly, the ECP is satisfied. Thus, we see that the substantive "barrierhood" of adjunct phrases is, in every case, voided by permitting adjunction to such phrases, which are, by definition, nonarguments. This problem appears to be a general one; a large subset of the class of barriers consists of nonarguments. Adjunction to these barriers is therefore allowed by (147), with the result that these categories are wrongly predicted to be permeable to government from outside. Chomsky (1986b, p. 66) addresses the specific problem concerning extraction from adjuncts and suggests two possible solutions. First, he suggests that t' in (148) would violate the ECP if "government" were defined in terms of domination instead of exclusion. That is, adoption of (149), as opposed to (150), yields the prediction that t' in (148) is $[-g]$ (i.e., the ECP is violated):

(149) A governs B iff A m-commands B and every barrier for B dominates A

(150) A governs B iff A m-commands B and there is no C, C a barrier for B such that C excludes A

However, as Chomsky (1986b, p. 66) notes, the adoption of (149), as opposed to (150), raises numerous problems, given the interacting theories of government and adjunction proposed there (see Chomsky, 1986b, for extensive theory-internal arguments against (149)).

A second solution to the problem of overgenerating LF representations like (148) is to assume the following, as Chomsky (1986b) suggests:

(151) Only an N″ can adjoin to a P″

However, in the absence of a way to derive (151), this filter (or constraint on movement) remains a stipulation. Further, it is a category-based stipulation, hence seemingly unrelated to (147), which is argued to be a theta theoretic principle. Moreover, there is evidence that, regardless of whether or not this stipulation is derivable, it is too weak. Although (151) would ensure the absence of $t″$ (a non-N″ adjoined to P″) in (148), thereby correctly reducing the resulting representation to an ECP violation, it nonetheless allows representations such as the following:

(152) $[_{S'}$ what reason$_i$ $[_S$ did you get angry
       $[_{P''}t_i'''$ $[_{P''}$ because $[_{S'}$ t_i'' $[_S$ Mary bought it $[_{P''}$ t_i' $[_{P''}$ for t_i]]]]]]]]]]

The sentence represented should be analyzed as, at least, a Subjacency violation. However, such an analysis is precluded. Since the moved category is an N″, it can adjoin to the nonargument P″ (in fact, to both nonargument P″s), in conformity with the stipulation (149). Note, "short" extraction, as in *What reason did you go for?* should be analyzed as a weak Subjacency violation. But this is also precluded; given that the N″ *"what reason" can* adjoin to P″, no barriers are crossed.

Thus, neither (147) nor (151) appears to provide a satisfactory solution to the problem of ruling out LF representations such as (148). What, then, could exclude such representations? Suppose, as discussed earlier, that

(135) Only a head can properly govern

Notice that (135) dictates that the trace adjoined to P″ in (148), not being a head, cannot antecedent-govern. As a result, the trace in Comp cannot be antecedent-governed. Hence, the ECP would be violated. This concludes our brief "case study" of the motivation for the head requirement within the Barriers framework.

In summary, the Barriers theory, in particular its employment of adjunction, seeks to provide a unified analysis of Subjacency and the ECP while also providing a natural analysis within which VP is a barrier (cf. L&S). However, this theory apparently confronts potentially widespread problems of overgeneration. We have looked at the specific case of adjunct extraction from out of adjunct phrases, the latter of which are, by definition, barriers for the categories they dominate. We have noted that such extraction should be analyzed as a violation of the ECP. The general point is clear; barriers should block extraction. However, we have seen that this result does not appear to be attainable in any unified way within the Barriers theory. We have argued that this is a result of the fact that a large subclass of the class of barriers consists of nonarguments. Consequently, adjunction to these categories is permitted by the central tenet of the Barriers theory of adjunction, namely, (147). As a result, under the Barriers definition of "government," defined in terms of "exlusion," "barrierhood" is voided in every case of a nonargument barrier. (We place the term "barrierhood" in quotes because the category is, in fact, still a barrier for its dominees. When we say " 'barrierhood' is voided," we mean only that the category in question fails to block extraction under the theory of movement proposed.)

As one possible solution to this general problem of overgeneration, we have adopted the proposal that the class of proper governors be restricted, such that only a head can properly govern. (Recall that this restriction was motivated within our analysis so as to prevent the generation of "that"–t configurations that would be otherwise allowed given that g-assignment and Affect-alpha are freely ordered in the Syntax.) As shown, the facts concerning extraction from adjuncts follows from this restriction on the class of proper governors. How to make this principle compatible with other aspects of the Barriers framework remains an open issue. However, it should be noted that, with respect to the ECP, this restriction renders superfluous both the theory of adjunction and the definition of "government" in terms of "exclusion" (with which it is intimately related). That is, since adjoined nonheads cannot properly govern, formulating "government" in terms of "exclusion" does not have the desired effect of allowing adjoined *phrases* to antecedent-govern (under government).[25]

On Adjunction and Pronominal Variable Binding

In the preceding section we have adopted the proposal that only a head can properly govern. If this restriction on the class of proper governors is correct, then the theory of adjunction, as formulated in May (1985) (and employed in Chomsky, 1986b), in fact, plays no direct role in the formulation of the ECP. That is, the ECP provides no independent support for this theory of adjunction. In this section we present evidence that certain pronominal variable binding phenomena also fail to provide support for the theory of adjunction proposed in May (1985). There are four subsections. The first presents the Scope Principle from May (1985), including the concept "relative scope." In addition, the Path Containment Condition, as adapted by May (1985) from Pesetsky (1982), is introduced. In the second subsection the concept "absolute scope" and its role in the analysis of pronominal variable binding proposed in May (1985) are discussed. Certain problems concerning this analysis of pronominal variable binding are revealed in the third subsection. The fourth subsection provides a very brief discussion of the issues raised.

The Scope Principle, Relative Scope, and the Path Containment Condition

One of the central phenomena with which May (1985) is concerned is the contrast in interpretation between sentences such as the following:

(153) (= May's (12), p. 38)
    What did everyone buy for Max

(154) (= May's (16), p. 39)
    Who bought everything for Max

Sentence (153) is ambiguous; it can be interpreted as a single question or as a "distributed" question. Under the former interpretation, an appropriate answer would be, for example, *Everyone bought Max a car.* Under the latter interpretation, an appropriate answer would be, for example, *John bought Max a pen, Bill bought Max a pencil, and Fred bought Max a paper clip.* By contrast, sentence (154) displays no such ambiguity; it is interpretable only as a single (undistributed) question.

How is this contrast between sentences (153) and (154) to be accounted for? Within the framework of May (1985), the LF representation of (153) is derived by adjoining the quantifier phrase "everyone" to S, yielding

(155)   (= May's (14), p. 38)

     $[_{S'}$ what$_2$ $[_S$ everyone$_3$ $[_S$ e_3 bought e_2 for Max]]]

Under the analysis presented in May (1985), this single LF representation represents both interpretations of sentence (153). This follows from the proposal that a "single multiple quantified LF representation can be seen to manifest a uniquely specifiable *class* of interpretations just in case the quantified phrases . . . govern . . . one another" (May, 1985, p. 33). Following, in essentials, Aoun and Sportiche (1983), "government" and "c-command" are defined as follows:

(156)   (= May's (80, p. 33) A governs B $=_{df}$ A c-commands B and B c-commands A, and there are no maximal projection boundaries between A and B.

(157)   (= May's (9), p. 34) A c-commands B $=_{df}$ every maximal projection dominating A dominates B, and A does not dominate B.

Under these definitions, "what" and "everyone" c-command each other.[26] Further, these two operators govern each other. Notice that to derive this latter result there must be no maximal projection boundary between "what" and "everyone." Since the outermost S bracket is indeed a projection boundary occurring between "what" and "everyone" (see May, 1985, p. 38) May (1985, p. 34) assumes that

(158)   S is not a Maximal Projection

Hence, there is no maximal projection boundary between "what" and "everyone," with the result that these two operators govern each other. The ambiguity is then accounted for by

(159) The Scope Principle: ". . . members of a SIGMA-sequence are free to take on any type of relative scope relation." (May, 1985, p. 34)

(160) SIGMA-sequence: "a class of occurrences of operators PHI [is] a SIGMA sequence if and only if for any O_i, O_j a member of PHI, O_i governs O_j, where 'operator' means 'phrases in A′-positions at LF,' . . ." (May, 1985, p. 34)

Given that the ambiguity of (153) is accounted for, how is the interpretation of (154) predicted? Notice first that to predict the nonambiguity of (154), the following LF representation must not be generated:

(161) ($=$ May's (21), p. 41)
   $[_{S'}$ who$_3$ $[_S$ everything$_2$ $[_S$ e_3 bought e_2 for Max]]]

If such a representation were generated, the Scope Principle would apply, thereby predicting (wrongly) that (154) is ambiguous. To rule out representation (161), May (1985, p. 118) adapts the Path Containment Condition (PCC) of Pesetsky (1982), defining this condition as

(162) PCC: Intersecting A′-categorial paths must embed, not overlap

May (1985, p. 118) explicates this condition as follows:

> A *path* is a set of occurrences of successively immediately dominating categorial nodes connecting a bindee to its binder. . . . Each contiguous pair of nodes within a path constitutes a *path segment*, and a path, more precisely, is just a set of such segments. I will refer to a set of such paths associated with an LF representation as its *path structure*. Paths *intersect* only if they have a common path segment. Consequently, paths sharing a single node do not intersect. If the paths do intersect, then the PCC requires that one of the paths must properly contain all the members of the other.

The LF representation (161) is ruled out by the PCC, since it exhibits the following path structure (see May, 1985, p. 120):

(163) path e_3 {S,S,S′}
   path e_2 {VP,S,S}

The paths of e_3 and e_2 intersect, that is, they have a common path segment, namely, (S,S). Thus, the PCC is applicable. This principle is violated because neither path is a proper subset of the other.

Given that (161) is ruled out, what is the LF representation of sentence (154)? May (1985, p. 42) proposes that in the LF representation of (154) "everything" is adjoined to VP, yielding

(164) $[_{S'}$ who$_3$ $[_S$ e_3 $[_{VP}$ everything$_2$ $[_{VP}$ bought e_2 for Max]]]]

This representation has the following path structure:

(165) path e_3 {S,S'}
       path e_2 {VP,VP}

Notice first that (165) satisfies the PCC, which is, in fact, inapplicable, since the paths do not intersect. In addition, given that (164) is the only LF representation of (154), it is correctly predicted that this sentence is unambiguous. This prediction is derived because the Scope Principle fails to apply to (164); "who" and "everything" do not govern each other, since the maximal projection boundary of VP (i.e., the outermost VP bracket) intervenes between these two operators. Thus, the Scope Principle is inapplicable with the result that "the grammar will make available only a dependent interpretation, relative scope order being fixed simply as a function of constituency, determined in a 'top-to-bottom' fashion, from structurally superior to structurally inferior phrases" (May, 1985, p. 35). Thus, the relevant interpretive property of sentence (154) is predicted; in the LF representation (164), "everything" has *relative scope* narrower than "who."

In the next subsection, we shall discuss another type of scope, distinct from relative scope, called "absolute scope."

Absolute Scope and Pronominal Variable Binding

As seen in the LF representation (164), a VP-adjoined operator has *relative scope* narrower than an operator in the next higher Comp. Despite having different relative scopes, May (1985) argues that such operators have the same absolute scope. This distinction between relative and absolute scope is best explained in May (1985, pp. 58–59):

> What is the scope of [an] NP$_i$, adjoined to VP?- we see that it is its c-command domain, which is S'. This maximal projection is the mini-

mal one dominating NP_i, which is dominated not by the VP-projection, but only by its higher member node. Thus, the "absolute" scope of NP_i extends outside the VP to the clausal level as does the scope of S-adjoined quantifers and *wh*-phrases in COMP, although, as we have seen, VP-adjoined phrases will have relative scope shorter than their counterparts in COMP or adjoined to S.

Given this distinction between relative and absolute scope, May argues that the interpretive properties of "crossing co-reference" sentences such as the following are predicted (see May, 1985, p. 59):

(166) Which pilot who shot at it hit every MIG that chased him?

According to May, (166) exhibits the following two interpretive properties:

(167) The quantifier phrase "every MIG that chased him" is interpreted as having narrower scope than the wh-phrase "which pilot who shot at it," and

(168) The pronoun "it" can be interpreted as a variable bound by the quantifier phrase, and the pronoun "him" can be interpreted as a variable bound by the wh-phrase.

Notice first that (166) is like (154) in that it contains a subject wh-phrase and an object quantifier phrase. Thus, the object quantifier phrase must be adjoined to VP in the LF representation of (166); were it adjoined to S the PCC would be violated (see again (161)). Hence, I assume the LF representation of (166) must be the following, in which the wh-phrase occupies Comp while the quantifier phrase is adjoined to VP:

(169) $[_{S'}[_{NP_2}$ which pilot who shot it it$_3][_S e_2$
$\quad [_{VP}[_{NP_3}$ every MIG that chased him$_2]$ $[_{VP}$ hit $e_3]]]]]$

In (169) the Scope Principle is inapplicable; the quantifier phrase has narrower scope than the wh-phrase (see again (164)). Thus, (167) is accounted for. But given the LF representation (169), how is (168) accounted for (i.e., how is the possibility of "crossed" pronominal variable binding predicted)? To answer this we must first identify the conditions under which pronominal variable binding is allowed. May (1985, p. 21) assumes the following condition on LF representation:

(170) A ronoun is a bound variable only if it is within the scope of a
coindexed quantifier phrase.

Given that the term "scope," as it occurs in (170), is to be interpreted as "absolute scope" (which, recall, May (1985, pp. 58–59)
defines as c-command domain), it follows that each pronoun in
(169) is indeed a bound variable. Each pronoun is a bound variable because each pronoun is within the absolute scope (c-
command domain) of the operator with which it is coindexed.
Under this analysis, then, each pronoun in (169) is a bound variable, since each operator has *absolute scope* over S′ and can
therefore variable-bind the pronoun with which it is coindexed.
Nonetheless, in (169) the Scope Principle is inapplicable; the
quantifier phrase is interpreted as having *relative scope* narrower
than the wh-phrase.

Problems Concerning Pronominal Variable Binding

May (1985, Chapter 5, Section 5) assumes that all locally A′-bound
categories, be they empty categories or overt pronominals, generate paths to their binders.[27] Given this, consider the following
two sentences, only the latter of which allows a bound-variable
reading of the pronoun "his":

(171) Who does his mother admire?

(172) Who admires his mother?

The unavailability of the bound-variable reading of the pronoun
in (171) follows from the fact that the LF representation of such
a reading violates the PCC:

(173) (= May's (66), p. 146)
$$[_{S'}[_C \text{who}_2][_S[_{NP}[_{DET} \text{his}_2][_{N'} \text{mother}]][_{VP} \text{admire } e_2]]]]$$

Since (173) contains two locally A′-bound categories, its path
structure consists of two paths (see May [1985, p. 146]):

(174) path $\text{his}_2\{\text{NP,S,S}'\}$
       path $e_2\{\text{VP,S,S}'\}$

Thus, the PCC is violated.

By contrast, the LF representation of the bound-variable reading of the pronoun in (172) satisfies the PCC:

(175) (= May's (67), p. 147)
$[_{S'}[_C$ who$_2][_S e_2[_{VP}$ admires$[_{NP}[_{DET}$ his$_2][_{N'}$ mother]]]]]

As May (1985, p. 147) notes, the structure contains only a single A'-path, namely, that of "e_2"; "his" generates no path at all. Since the path structure of (175) consists of only one path, the PCC is, of course, satisfied. Because condition (170) is also satisfied, "his" is a bound variable.[28]

Consider next the quantificational analogs of (171) and (172)[29]:

(176) His mother admires every man

(177) Every man admires his mother

Example (176), like (171), disallows a bound-variable reading of the pronoun, whereas in (177), like (172), a bound-variable reading of the pronoun is available. The LF representation of (176) is

(178) $[_{S'}[_S$ everyman$_2$ $[_S[_{NP}[_{DET}$ his$_2][_{N'}$ mother]] $[_{VP}$ admires $e_2]]]]$

The path structure of (178) is like that of (173), violating the PCC:

(179) path his$_2${NP,S,S}
       path e_2{VP,S,S}

By contrast, consider the LF representation of (177):

(180) $[_{S'}[_S$ everyman$_2$ $[_S e_2[_{VP}$ admires $[_{NP}[_{DET}$ his$_2][_{N'}$ mother]]]]]]$

Given that "e_2" is the only locally A'-bound category, (180) has a path structure consisting of only one path, hence the PCC is satisfied. Thus, it appears that the contrast in interpretation between (176) and (177) is accounted for.

However, notice that to derive this contrast yet another LF representation of (176) must be ruled out. Recall that distinguishing the interpretive properties of sentences (153) and (154) rested on the possibility of adjoining quantifiers to VP in the LF component. Given this possibility, consider the following LF representation of (176):

(181) $[_{S'}[_S[_{NP}$ his$_2$ mother][$_{VP}$ every man$_2$ [$_{VP}$ admires $e_2]]]]$

Recall from the discussion of (169) that the absolute scope of a VP-adjoined quantifier is S'. Thus, "his" is within the scope of "every man." Since these phrases are coindexed, "his" satisfies principle (170) and is thus a variable bound by the quantifier adjoined to VP. Furthermore, the path structure of (181) satisfies the PCC. Giving the PCC the best possible chance of ruling out (181), assume that both "his" and e generate paths to "every man." Under this assumption, the path structure of (181) is

(182) path his$_2$ {NP,S,VP}
       path e_2 {VP,VP}

Recalling from the preceding discussion of the PCC that "paths sharing a single node do not intersect" (May, 1985, p. 118), the paths in (182), having only the higher VP node in common, do not intersect. Consequently, the PCC is satisfied.[30] Thus, it appears that (181) with the path structure (182) is generable, with the result that it is incorrectly predicted that sentence (176) allows a bound-variable reading of the pronoun.

A similar problem confronts the analysis of sentences such as

(183) Every MIG that chased him hit some pilot

May (1985, p. 147) claims that, regardless of the scope relations of the two quantifiers, the pronoun cannot be interpreted as a bound variable. However, consider the following LF representation of (183):

(184) $[_{S'}[_{S}[_{NP2}$ Every MIG that chased him$_3][_{S} e_2$
       $[_{VP}$ some pilot$_3[_{VP}$ hit $e_3]]]]]$

In (184), "him" is within the absolute scope of "some pilot" (just as "it" is within the absolute scope of "every MIG that chased him" in (169)). Since these phrases are coindexed, (170) is satisfied and the pronoun is thus a bound variable. Further, the PCC is satisfied, given that (184) has the following path structure:

(185) path him$_3$ {. . .NP$_2$,S,S,VP}
       path e_2 {   S,S   }
       path e_3 {   VP,VP}

Thus, it is incorrectly predicted that (183) allows a bound-variable interpretation of the pronoun.

Discussion

In this section we have argued that May's (1985) analysis of pronominal variable binding, as couched within his theory of adjunction, is overly permissive. As shown, sentences such as (176) and (183) are incorrectly predicted to permit bound-variable interpretation of the pronoun. Thus, a fully adequate account of such pronominal variable-binding phenomena is not provided under this analysis. Here I do not attempt to provide a solution to the problems we have discussed (see Epstein, 1989, for a more detailed examination of these issues). Rather, our only purpose in this section has been to show that the facts concerning pronominal variable binding noted here constitute no evidence in favor of this particular theory of adjunction.

Notes

1. The structure of Comp is a controversial issue, raising, for instance, the following questions:

(i) What is the status of Comp with respect to X' theory?
(ii) What category types does Comp accommodate?
(iii) What principles constrain the distribution of categories in Comp?
(iv) Is Comp indexed, and if so, how?
(v) Is the structure of Comp parameterized, and if so, in what way?

For a recent analysis of this category, somewhat different from that of L&S, see Chomsky (1986b).

2. The exact D-structure position of wh-adjuncts is not clear. For example, Huang (1982) assumes they are adjoined to VP, whereas L&S tentatively assume they are immediately dominated by S. I leave this issue open.

3. For interesting discussion of the elimination of redundancy from models of UG, see Chomsky (1986a, p. 181).

4. It might be argued that this analysis entails stipulating that filter (3) does not apply at S-structure. We have argued that S-structure application of the filter has no necessary effects and also forces the stipulation (1) so as to prevent the assignment of $[-g]$ to traces in Comp. The elimination of the filter at S-structure comports with Chomsky's (1986a) conjecture that the only constraints on S-structure are those imposed by its being the output of D-structure and the input to both PF and LF.

5. One might argue that "double" g-assignment is conceptually odd in that a given category could bear two different values of the same feature. Notice, however, that in all such cases the representation is filtered since $[-g]$ ap-

pears. We will continue to assume double g-assignment, although nothing crucial hinges on this.

6. Davis proposes this principle as part of an account of the complementary distribution of the expletives "it" and "there." Davis proposes that "there" lacks all syntactic features, while "it" is lexically specified as third person, singular, and neuter. She adopts a rightward movement analysis of "there"-insertion (i.e., the D-structure subject is postposed, leaving a trace in subject position). Since it lacks all syntactic features, "there" can then be licitly inserted into the trace position. To account for the impossibility of "it"-insertion in this same context, Principle (50) is proposed. Under this principle, "it" cannot be inserted into a position occupied by a trace, since this would entail obliteration (i.e., deletion of syntactic features, namely, those of the trace). Hence, the ungrammaticality of (i) is accounted for

(i) *It is someone here

7. Notice that (51) disallows index-changing rules such as the Predication rule proposed in Chomsky (1982, n. 11). Such index changing is ruled out by (51), given two assumptions: first, that indices are features, hence members of feature matrices (as proposed by Davis, 1982); second, that change of index entails deletion of index.

For one alternative to the index-changing Predication rule see Aoun (1983). Aoun argues that the index-changing Predication rule is unnecessary if it is assumed that contraindexed categories may receive coreferent interpretation. This approach leaves open the question of why coreferent interpretation is precluded in, for example,

(i) [John$_i$ likes him$_j$]

Notice also that it is tempting to generalize (51) to

(ii) Only entire feature matrices are subject to deletion and insertion.

This seems problematic in that it does appear that there are a number of independently motivated feature-inserting operations. For example, LF A'-indexing (as proposed in Chomsky, 1982), Comp-indexing, g-assignment, and perhaps Case and Theta-role assignment.

8. To the extent that principles such as the Projection Principle, the ECP, and No Vacuous Quantification are constraints on representation, they do not entail that (63), a derivational principle, hold. For example, the following D-structure to S-structure mapping satisfies these principles:

(i)   DS: [$_{S'}$[$_S$ Who$_i$ left]]
(ii) Move: [$_{S'}$ Who$_i$[$_S$ left]]
(iii) Move: [$_{S'}$[$_S$ Who$_i$ left]]
(iv) SS: [$_{S'}$ Who$_i$[$_S$ t_i left]]

9. Since parasitic gaps cannot occur within islands, a number of more recent analyses assume that these categories are traces of movement (specifically, movement of an O-operator). See, among others, Contreras (1984), Aoun and Clark (1984), Browning (1987), and the references cited therein. Whether par-

asitic gaps are base-generated or are traces of movement is orthogonal to the issue we are concerned with here. The fact that these constructions, by definition, exhibit S-structure A'-binding (distinct from that of an O-operator, if present) is the only feature with which we are directly concerned, since it is this aspect of the construction that provides crucial evidence concerning what are and are not defining characteristics of movement.

10. See Brody (1984) and Epstein (1984) for critical discussion of this algorithm.

11. Notice that although English prohibits "resumptive pronouns" (i.e., it incorporates the negative setting of (69), the universal (70) still has empirical consequences with respect to parasitic gap licensing in this language. Consider the following contrast (discussed in Epstein, 1983) between Topicalization and Left Dislocation with respect to parasitic gap licensure:

(i) *[John [$_{S'}$[$_S$ I liked him] before meeting PG]]]

(ii) [John [$_{S'}$[$_S$ I liked t] before meeting PG]]]

Assuming that the N″ "John" occupies An A'-position in (i), (70) dictates that this category is not indexed at S-structure. Consequently, the parasitic gap is not determinable as a variable. Therefore, the structure is excluded, as desired. By contrast, assuming a movement analysis of Topicalization (as proposed in Chomsky [1977]) involving either movement of an empty operator to Comp or movement of the topic phrase to topic position, it follows that in these constructions there can be an indexed A'-binder of the parasitic gap at S-structure. Hence, the parasitic gap is determinable as a variable, correctly predicting that the structure is well formed.

12. Furthermore, this indexing explains why adjuncts fail to license parasitic gaps. This fact follows; since adjuncts are indexless at S-structure, a parasitic gap cannot be licitly determined as a variable (i.e., as locally A'-bound). The indexing theory is further examined later and from it, it *might* be possible to derive the more general fact that non-NPs fail to license parasitic gaps.

13. Under the analysis presented here, if traces of syntactic adjunct movement are created, they are necessarily free A' empty categories at S-structure. It may be the case that such categories are disallowed at S-structure. Empirical evidence bearing on this issue is discussed later.

14. An alternative to creating traces by down and back movement is to insert them, as suggested by L&S. Notice also that Free LF A'-indexing must not be permitted to freely index Comp, an A'-position. If Comp could be freely indexed, LF representations such as (56) would be overgenerated.

15. Under this analysis we must assume that "whether," unlike "that," is inserted, an instance of Affect-alpha constrained by the Strict Cycle. Recall that we assume "that" is spelled out, since it has no semantic content. By contrast, since it has semantic content, "whether" is lexical; its introduction into phrase markers is therefore an instsance of insertion. Hence, the derivation just discussed violates the Strict Cycle.

Notice, however, that given the existence of Spec of V″ (see later), the following alternative derivation does not violate the Strict Cycle:

(i) [$_{S'}$[$_S$ you wonder [$_{S'}$[$_S$ John bought what$_i$]]]]

(ii) $[_{S'}[_S$ you wonder $[_{S'}[_S$ John $[_{V''}$ what$_i$ $[_{V'}$ bought $t_i]]]]]]$

(iii) $[_{S'}[_S$ you wonder $[_{S'}$ whether $[_S$ John $[_{V''}$ what$_i$ $[_{V'}$ bought $t_i]]]]]]]$

(iv) $[_{S'}[_S$ you $[_{V''}$ what$_i$ $[_{V'}$ wonder $[_{S'}$ whether $[_S$ John $[_{V''}$ t_i $[_{V'}$ bought $t_i]]]]]]]]$

(v) $[_{S'}$ What$_i$ $[_S$ do you $[_{V''}$ t_i $[_{V'}$ wonder $[_{S'}$ whether $[_S$ John $[_{V''}$ t_i $[_{V'}$ bought $t_i]]]]]]]]$

This derivation also satisfies Subjacency, given that S' is not a bounding node in English. Thus, this derivation is wrongly allowed. However, Subjacency, as formulated in Chomsky (1986b), is violated in this derivation, since the second movement of "what" crosses the barrier S'. Hence, excluding the example at hand appears to motivate Chomsky's (1986b) formulation of Subjacency.

16. Besides Chomsky (1986b), two recent analyses seeking to eliminate lexical proper government are to be found in Stowell (1981) and in Aoun (1985). For discussion of the latter see Lasnik and Uriagereka (1988).

17. In the Barriers framework such adjunction to V" is, in the absence of verb-raising, forced. Notice, however, that nothing within the L&S framework precludes the option of adjunction to V".

18. Recall from the preceding that SS to LF mappings such as the following were presumed to be generated:

(i) Who do you wonder whether John said $[_{C_i}t_i]$ $[t_i$ left]
$$[+g]$$

(ii) Who do you wonder whether John said $[_{C_i}][t_i$ left]
$$[+g]$$

As desired, the ECP is satisfied. Further, filter (131) is inapplicable (since the Comp in question is headless).

19. A similar analysis is proposed independently in Tiedeman (1987).

20. As Esther Torrego points out, deriving an LF representation of the following S-structure, without appealing to lexical proper government, may be problematic, since there are two wh-phrases yet only one specifier of V" position.

(i) $[_{S'}$ who $[_S t_i [_{V''}$ gave what$_j$ to whom$_k]]]$

One possibility is this: On its way to Comp, one of the wh-phrases in situ moves to Specifier of V" and, via Specifier–head indexing, gives its index to the head V "gave," while the remaining wh-phrase in situ does the same. The result is that the head V "gave" bears both the index of "what" (j) as well as the index of "whom" (k). Thus, proceeding from (i), the type of derivation we have in mind can be illustrated as follows:

(ii) $[_{S'}$ who$_i$ $[_S t_i [_{V''}$ what$_j$ gave$_j$ t_j to whom$_k]]]$

(iii) $[_{S'}$ what$_j$ who$_i$ $[_S t_i [_{V''}$ gave$_j$ t_j to whom$_k]]]$

(iv) $[_{S'}$ what$_j$ who$_i$ $[_S t_i [_{V''}$ whom$_k$ gave$_{j,k}$ t_j to $t_k]]]$

(v) $[_{S'}$ whom$_k$ what$_j$ who$_i$ $[_S t_i [_{V''}$ gave$_{j,k}$ t_j to $t_k]]]$

Notice, however, if V" is a cyclic node and the Strict Cycle constrains LF-movement, then this principle is violated by the movement of "whom" to Specifier of V" subsequent to the movement of "what" to Comp. If there is such a violation, it can perhaps be avoided by assuming the following: Immediately after "what" moves to specifier of V″, "what" adjoins to V″, an operation that, by hypothesis, occurs on the V″-cycle. Following this, "whom" can move to specifier of V″ (a V″-cycle operation) in conformity with the Strict Cycle. A well-formed derivation is completed by subsequently moving each wh-phrase to Comp on the S′-cycle.

21. With this indexing in mind, consider a sentence such as

(i) Why do you know how John left

Clearly, this sentence has no interpretation in which "how" modifies the matrix sentence and "why" modifies the embedded sentence; that is, there is no LF representation in which "how" occupies the matrix Comp and "why" the embedded Comp. But consider the S-structure

(ii) $[_{S'}$ why $[_{S}$ do you $[_{V''}$ know $[_{S'}$ how $[_{S}$ John left$]]]]]$

Recall that adjuncts have no indices at S-structure (and adjunct traces are, in effect, absent at this level). Given that adjuncts have no indices at S-structure, they do not induce Comp-indexing. As a result, the (index-sensitive) LF filter (131) (which is intended to prevent, among other things, any derivation in which Comp has one wh-head at S-structure and another at LF) is rendered inapplicable. Consequently (as Elaine McNulty and Andy Barss point out), we wrongly allow an S-structure such as (ii) to be mapped into an LF in which "how" occupies the matrix Comp and "why" occupies the embedded Comp. Proceeding from (i), this LF representation can be generated as follows (which is in conformity with the Strict Cycle, assuming this principle constrains LF movement):

On the matrix V″-cycle:

(iii) "how" moves to Specifier of the matrix V″ (leaving no trace in Comp)
$[_{S'}$ why $[_{S}$ do you $[_{V''}$ how know $[_{S'}[_{S}$ John left$]]]]]$

On the matrix S′-cycle

  (iv) "why" lowers and adjoins to the embedded S and then moves back up to the matrix Comp, leaving a trace adjoined to the embedded S:
$[_{S'}$ why $[_{S}$ do you $[_{V''}$ how know $[_{S'}[_{S}[_{S}$ John left$]$ $t]]]]]$

  (v) "why" lowers to the embedded Comp:
$[_{S'}[_{S}$ do you $[_{V''}$ how know $[_{S'}$ why $[_{S}[_{S}$ John left$]$ $t]]]]]$

  (vi) "how" moves to the matrix Comp (leaving no trace):
$[_{S'}$ how $[_{S}$ do you $[_{V''}$ know $[_{S'}$ why $[_{S}[_{S}$ John left$]$ $t]]]]]$

 (vii) "how" lowers and adjoins to the matrix S and then moves back up to the matrix Comp, leaving a trace adjoined to the matrix S:
$[_{S'}$ how $[_{S}[_{S}$ do you $[_{V''}$ know $[_{S'}$ why $[_{S}[_{S}$ John left$]$ $t]]]]$ $t]]]$

(viii) Free LF A′ indexing then applies yielding
$[_{S'}$ how$_i$ $[_{S}[_{S}$ do you $[_{V''}$ know $[_{S'}$ why$_j$ $[_{S}[_{S}$ John left$]$ $t_j]]]]$ $t_i]]]$

One way to exclude such derivations is to assume that

(ix) LF movement cannot *originate* from Comp (see Huang, 1982b, and Chomsky, 1986b, for discussion).

Although this does indeed prevent the unwanted derivation, it would appear to be overly restrictive. Recall that there can be no well-formed adjunct traces at S-structure under our analysis. Hence, to create adjunct traces at LF (as required by the principle barring Vacuous Quantification) we have proposed that adjuncts occupying Comp at S-structure move down and back at LF so as to create trace-variables at this level. But this violates (ix). Nonetheless, suppose we maintain this constraint, and assume that, in conformity with it, adjunct traces can be created at LF without ever moving the adjunct from Comp. This result can be achieved if traces can be inserted (see L&S). Thus, (ix) excludes the unwanted derivation, and at the same time adjunct traces can be created at LF (in conformity with this constraint) via trace-insertion.

22. For detailed discussion of such extraction see Huang (1982a). The example (144) is due to Fukui (1987), who compares the analyses of such phenomena (and others) within the frameworks of L&S and Chomsky (1986b).

23. Another possibility, suggested by Howard Lasnik, is that "because" occupies Comp, immediately explaining the ill-formedness of "because that John left."

24. Chomsky (1986b) suggests that (147) may derive from theta theory.

25. Beyond the examples discussed in text, the Barriers theory of adjunction similarly overgenerates representations such as the following:

(i) $[_{C''}$ who$_i$ $[_{I'}$ do you $[_{V''} t_i$ $[_{V''}$ wonder $[_{C''}$ whether
$[_{I'} t_i$ $[_{I'}$ John $[_{V''} t$ $[_{V''}$ likes $t_i]]]]]]]]]$

(ii) $[_{C''}$ why$_i$ $[_{I'}$ did you $[_{V''} t_i$ $[_{V''}$ whisper $[_{C''} t_i$ $[_{C''} t_i$
$[_{I'}$ John $[_{V''} t_i$ $[_{V''}$ left $t_i]]]]]]]]]$

(iii) $[_{C''}$ why$_i$ $[_{I'}$ do you $[_{V''} t_i$ $[_{V''}$ like $[_{N''}$ the man $[_{C''} t_i$
$[_{C''}$ who$_j$ $[_{I'} t_i$ $[_{I'} t_j$ $[_{V''} t_i$ [left $t_i]]]]]]]]]]]$

Adjunction to nonarguments, as depicted in each case, is allowed. Consequently, no principles are violated (see Chomsky, 1986b, and Fukui, 1987, for further discussion).

26. Regardless of whether S is assumed to be maximal or not, "everyone" c-commands "what," since, under the theory of adjunction proposed in May (1985), "everyone" is not dominated by the S projection but rather is dominated by only one node of this projection.

27. Although I believe this is May's assumption, there seems to be some potential unclarity surrounding the question of which categories generate paths to their binders. Consider the following from May (1985):

(i) "paths are more generally associated with all A'-bound elements, regardless of whether they are lexical or not. More specifically, . . . locally A'-bound pronouns generate paths to their binders. . ." (p. 146).

(ii) With respect to the LF representation $[_{S'}$ who$_2$ $[_S e_2$ admires his$_2$ mother]]; "this structure contains only a single A'-path, that of the trace. The pronoun generates no path at all, since it is locally A-bound by the trace" (p. 147, para. 1).

(iii) "all A'-bound categories give rise to paths" (p. 147, para. 2).

(iv) With respect to the following LF representation in which "every pilot" is in an A'-position and both c-commands and is coindexed with "him":

$[_S[_{NP2}$ every pilot] $[_S e_2 [_{VP}[_{NP_3}$ some MIG that chased him$_2][_{VP}$ hit $e_3]]]]$

"Here the pronoun is no longer A'-bound; its local binder is the empty category in the subject position. That is, it is A-bound and therefore not associated with a path" (p. 148, para. 1).

(v) "all A'-bound categories, be they empty or lexical, generate paths. . ." (p. 154).

As further concerns this potential unclarity, I should add that I am unable to locate definitions of "binds," "locally binds," and "locally A'-binds" in May (1985).

28. Although I am unable to find any discussion of example (166) within the context of the PCC (see May, Chapter 5, Section 5), its LF representation, namely (169), should be discussed with respect to this principle. Recall that (169) must be well formed, since it is the LF representation of what is assumed to be an available interpretation of (166). I assume the path structure of (169) is as follows and therefore satisfies the PCC:

(i) path e_2 {S,S'}
    path e_3 {VP,VP}
    path it_3 {. . .NP$_2$,S',S,VP}

A number of comments regarding this path structure are in order. First, by analogy with (175), I assume that "him" in (169) is not associated with a path. Second, following May (1985, p. 148) I use ". . ." to refer to the nodes in the path of "it," each of which has the following two properties: (i) it dominates "it," and (ii) it is dominated by NP$_2$. Finally, I assume "it" is associated with a path (see the previous footnote). Notice the status of "it" in (169) is very much like that of "him" in the following LF (i.e., each pronoun is c-commanded by a coindexed phrase occurring to its right)

(ii) (= May's (68a), p. 148)
    $[_S[_{NP_3}$ Some MIG that chased him$_2][_S[_{NP_2}$ every pilot] $[_S e_2$ hit $e_3]]]$

Crucially, May assumes that "him" in (ii) is indeed associated with a path; the path structure of (ii) violates the PCC as desired (see May, p. 148) precisely because the paths of "him" and "e" overlap yet fail to embed

(iii) path e_2 {S,S}
    path him$_2$ {. . .NP,S,S}
    path e_3 {VP,S,S,S}

Thus, given that "him" in (ii) generates a path, I assume "it" in (169) does too.

29. The discussion of Weak Crossover and the PCC in May (1985, Chapter 5, Section 5) concerns only wh-phrases, not quantifier phrases.

30. To see why it must be the case that paths sharing a single node do not intersect, consider, for example, inversely linked sentences such as

(i) Somebody from every city despises it

May (1985, p. 151) claims that the pronoun can be interpreted as a bound variable. He assumes the following LF representation and path structure of this bound-variable interpretation of (i):

(ii) (= May's (74b), p. 151)

$[_S[_{NP_3}$ every city$_2$ $[_{NP_3}$ somebody from $e_2]]$ $[_S$ e_3 $[_{VP}$ despises it$_2]]]]$

(iii) path e_2 $\{\ldots NP_3, NP_3\}$
     path it$_2$ $\{VP, S, S, NP_3\}$
     path e_3 $\{S, S\}$

The assumption that such structures are well formed motivates the condition that paths sharing a single node do not intersect. If such paths did intersect, (ii) would be ruled out by the PCC; the paths of e_2 and "it$_2$" share a single node (the higher NP$_3$ node), yet neither path is a proper subset of the other (see May, 1985, p. 152).

Given that paths sharing a single node do not intersect, the PCC in fact fails to apply to (181)–(182).

3

Determining the Properties of A-Chains

In this chapter we attempt to determine the nature of the principles of UG governing the structure of A-chains. Throughout, it is our intention to eliminate, or at least simplify, chain-specific conditions, showing that, to a large extent, the properties of A-chains follow from independent principles of grammar. In the first section, the role of the ECP and Condition C in determining A-chain structure is discussed. Following this, the Local Binding Condition, a chain-specific condition, is motivated, and its proper formulation is investigated in detail. In the following section, this condition is substantially simplified, certain properties being reducible to independent principles.

The ECP and Condition C

Recall that in the preceding chapter we adopted the proposal that only heads are proper governors. In addition, we have assumed that application of head indexing can both precede and follow application of Affect-alpha in the syntax. (Recall that the assumption that this ordering obtains in LF allows for the elimination of lexical proper government of verb complements). As we have seen, this ordering in the syntax entails that "that"–*t* configurations can satisfy the ECP. We have therefore proposed other means by which such representations can be excluded. The proposed ordering of the head indexing rule has syntactic consequences beyond the "that"–t effect. Here we are concerned with NP-movement. To begin with, let us consider how well formed cases of NP-movement are to be treated. Consider, for example:

(1) $[_{S'}[_S \text{John}_i \text{INFL}_i [_{V''} \text{was arrested } t_i]]]$

(2) $[_{S'}[_S \text{John}_i \text{INFL}_i [_{V''} \text{is likely } [_S t_i \text{to go}]]]]$

(3) $[_{N''} \text{Rome's}_i [_{N'} \text{destruction}_i t_i]]$

In deriving each case, Affect-alpha applies, followed by the application of Spec-Head indexing. In the representations derived, the NP-trace satisfies the ECP (i.e., it is properly governed by a coindexed head, namely, INFL in (1) and (2), and N in (3)).

Now let us consider some cases of NP-movement that must be excluded. To begin, consider "super-raising," as in the following example (adapted from Chomsky, 1986b):[1]

(4) DS:
$[_{S'}[_S e \text{ seems}[_{S'}[_S e \text{ is considered}[_S \text{he}_i \text{ intelligent}]]]]]$

(5) SS:
$[_{S'}[_S \text{he}_i \text{ seems}[_{S'}[_S \text{it is considered}[_S t_i \text{ intelligent}]]]]]$

Since t is not properly governed, this S-structure representation is mapped into an LF representation violating the ECP. However, other possible derivations must also be examined. Suppose the N'' "he" first moved to SPEC of the V'' headed by "consider," and, while occupying this position, it triggers Spec–head indexing. Following this, suppose "he" then moves to matrix subject position. This derivation results in the following S-structure representation:

(6) $[_{S'}[_S \text{he}_i \text{ seems}[_{S'}[_S \text{it is}[_{V''} (t'_i)[_{V'} \text{considered}_i$
     $[_S t_i \text{intelligent}]]]]]]]$

Notice first that, under the proposed ordering of the head indexing rule, the head "considered" can bear an index at S-structure, regardless of whether or not a trace occupies Spec of V'' at this level. Further, since Subjacency constrains only movement, it follows that no principle either requires or prohibits the presence of a trace in Spec of V'' at S-structure (i.e., the presence of this category is optional). We may assume that the application of

Spec–head indexing is also optional. Given that such indexing can be generated as in (6), the ECP is satisfied; t is assigned $[+g]$, since it is properly governed by the head V "considered," whereas t' can be absent at S-structure or delete in LF. The problem, then, is how to rule out such representations. One possible approach to this problem is to adopt Chomsky's (1986b) treatment of very similar representations by appealing to Condition C of the Binding theory, as formulated in Chomsky (1986a):

(7) Condition C: An R-expression must be A-free in the domain of the head of its chain[2]

Of course, if Condition C is to rule out a representation such as (6), this representation must first be analyzed as containing an R-expression, otherwise Condition C will be inapplicable. There are, in fact, two independently motivated algorithms by which (6) is analyzed as containing an R-expression. Under each, t is determined to be just such a category. The first algorithm we will call the Intrinsic Features Hypothesis (IFH). With respect to empty categories created by movement originating from an A-position, the IFH contains the following principles, which we state as conditionals, given that creation of traces is optional (as discussed earlier).

(8) Intrinsic Feature Hypothesis (IFH)

    a. If movement to an A'-position leaves a trace, it is an R-expression

    b. If movement to an A-position leaves a trace, it is an anaphor

Recall that in the derivation resulting in (6), t was created by movement of the N" "he" to Spec of V", an A'-position. Under the IFH, then, t is by definition, an R-expression. Given this characterization of t, the representation can be ruled out as follows. First, we assume chains are freely formed (see later). Consequently, the N" "he" can be a singleton chain, but the resulting representation is independently excluded by the Theta Criterion, since this argument would not be in a chain containing a theta position. To satisfy the Theta Criterion, the N" "he" must form a chain with t, a category that occupies a theta position. However, if this chain formation occurs, as is necessary, the representation is ruled out, in fact, for two independent reasons. First, it is excluded by the Theta Criterion, since the chain ["he," t] contains

tains two arguments. Recall, under the IFH, t is, by definition, an R-expression. Given that all R-expressions are arguments, t is an argument. Hence, the Theta Criterion is violated. In addition, (6) is also excluded by Condition C, since t, an R-expression, is not A-free in the domain of the head of its chain. Notice that the chain of t minimally consists of the N"s "he" and t. The head of this chain is "he," which occupies an A-position. Given that the domain of "he" includes "he," it follows that t is A-bound in the domain of the head of its chain (i.e., Condition C is violated).

Thus, under the IFH, (6) is ruled out, since t is an R-expression. Nonetheless, we will now show that the Condition C–IFH approach fails to provide an adequate analysis of super-raising, because alternative derivations are possible under which the empty category occupying subject position of "intelligent" is not determined as an R-expression by the IFH. This renders both Condition C and the Theta Criterion incapable of excluding the resulting representations. Beginning with the D-structure (4), suppose the N" "he" first moves to an A-position. Under the IFH, the empty category created by such movement is not an R-expression; rather, it is, by definition, an anaphor. Assuming now that application of Affect-alpha is constrained only by Subjacency and the Strict Cycle, consider, for example, the following derivation (one of a number of possible derivations originating from the following D-structure, given the minimal constraints on Affect-alpha assumed here):

(9) a. DS:
$[_{S'}[_S e$ seems$[_{S'}[_S e$ is $[_{V''}[_{V'}$considered
$[_S$ he$_i$ to be intelligent]]]]]]]]

b. Move 1: A-to-A
$[_{S'}[_S e$ seems$[_{S'}[_S$ he$_i$ is $[_{V''}[_{V'}$ considered
$[_S t_i$ to be intelligent]]]]]]]]

c. Move 2: A-to-A′
$[_{S'}[_S e$ seems$[_{S'}[_S e$ is $[_{V''}$ he$_i[_{V'}$ considered$_i$
$[_S t_i$ to be intelligent]]]]]]]]

(Note this move leaves no trace and also triggers Spec–head indexing)

d. "it"-INSERT:
$[_{S'}[_S e$ seems$[_{S'}[_S$ it is $[_{V''}$ he$_i[_{V'}$ considered$_i$
$[_S t_i$ to be intelligent]]]]]]]]

    e. Move 3: A′-to-A
      $[_{s'}[_s\,\text{he}_i\,\text{seems}[_{s'}\,[_s\,\text{it is }[_{v''}\,(t'_i)\,[_{v'}\text{considered}_i$
      $[_s\,t_i\,\text{to be intelligent}]]]]]]]$

The crucial aspect of this derivation is that Move 1 was to an A-position. Consequently, if a trace is left by such movement, as in (9b), it is determined to be an anaphor under the IFH. (Notice a number of other possible derivations beginning with the D-structure (9a) and resulting in the S-structure (9e) have this property, though I will not go through them here.) As a result of characterizing t as an anaphor, Condition C is now rendered inapplicable; t is an anaphor, and, as we have seen, t', occupying Spec of V″, need not be present. Thus, the representation need not contain any R-expressions whatsoever. Furthermore, the Theta Criterion can be satisfied by freely forming a chain consisting of the argument "he," occupying a thetaless position, and the nonargument anaphor empty category, occupying a theta-marked position. Finally, as was discussed earlier, the ECP can be satisfied, since t can be properly governed by the head V "considered." Thus, under the IFH–Condition C analysis, such derivations are overgenerated.[3]

But before abandoning this approach, we should take a closer look at derivations such as (9). Recall that if t, the most deeply embedded empty category, is determined as an R-expression, the resulting representation is ruled out by Condition C and the Theta Criterion. However, derivations such as (9) show that, under the IFH, coupled with minimal constraints on the application of Affect-alpha, the most deeply embedded empty category is not necessarily determined as an R-expression. Rather, if the first movement of the N″ "he" is to an A-position and this movement leaves a trace, the trace is determined as an anaphor by the IFH. Thus, under the IFH, the derivations that are overgenerated (proceeding from the D-structure (9)) have the following property, exhibited by (9):

(10) "He" is first moved to an A-position

Notice that, continuing with a derivation such as (9), other generalizations concerning the unwanted derivations can also be made. To satisfy the ECP, Spec–head indexing must occur, so as to index the head V "considered." For such indexing to occur, the following must occur:

(11) ((10) applies, then), "He" must move to Spec of V″, an A′-position

Finally, the following may also be inferred, given Case-theoretic considerations:

(12) ((11) applies, then), "he" must ultimately move to a Case-marked position, an A-position

To summarize, the overgenerated derivations seem to exhibit the following defining characteristic (using (9) as an example): "he" must first move to an A-position (so that the empty category created by the movement is determined as an anaphor under the IFH). Next, "he" must move to Spec of V″, an A′-position (so as to trigger head indexing of V, required by the ECP). Finally, "he" must move to matrix subject position, so as to satisfy Case requirements. Thus, the derivations incorrectly permitted by the IFH/Condition C approach to super-raising appear to have the following property:

(13) Movement is from an A-position to an A′-position to an A-position

Within the Revised Extended Standard theory, it has been argued that the ill-formedness of representations derived by such movement is predictable. In particular, May (1979, 1981) has argued that the ill-formedness of such representations is theorematic within the framework proposed in Chomsky (1980). May suggests that the configurations derived by this type of movement necessarily contain a category displaying a kind of indexing, the interpretation of which is anomalous. (See May [1979, 1981], but also see Chomsky [1981, p. 288] for arguments against this analysis.) However, we have seen that within the framework assumed here, despite the fact that the overgenerated derivations exhibit movement as in (13), Condition C is inapplicable, since the IFH fails to determine any empty category in the S-structure representation as an R-expression. This failure is the result of two factors: First, since the most deeply embedded empty category can be created by movement to an A-position, it is, by definition an anaphor, under the IFH. Second, every other movement need not leave a trace, since we adopt the optimal assumption that creation of traces is optional under movement. Thus, because the representation contains no R-expression, Condition C is inapplicable.

We have just seen that the Condition C/IFH approach overgenerates derivations like (9), even though they display movement as in (13). One might now suppose that if we could somehow independently exclude movement like (13), the Condition C–IFH approach could be retained, since it would properly treat the remaining cases of super-raising (i.e., those not involving movement of the type in (13)). We will now show that this is not the case. That is, even if we could somehow derive the ill-formedness of derivations exhibiting movement as in (13), the Condition C–IFH approach would not provide a satisfactory solution to the problem of super-raising. To see this, notice that derivations of the following kind are still generable under this hypothetical analysis (i.e., movement of the form (13) does not occur, nor is Condition C violated in derivations of the following kind):

(14) a. DS:

$[_{S'}[_{S_1} e \text{ seems}[_{S'}[_{S_2} e \text{ is }[_{V''}[_{V'} \text{considered }[_S \text{who}_i \text{intelligent}]]]]]]]$

    b. "it"-INSERT:

$[_{S'}[_{S_1} e \text{ seems}[_{S'}[_{S_2} \text{it is }_{V''}[_{V'} \text{considered }[_S \text{who}_i \text{intelligent}]]]]]]$

    c. Move 1: A-to-A

$[_{S'}[_{S_1} \text{who}_i \text{seems}[_{S'}[_{S_2} \text{it is }[_{V''}[_{V'} \text{considered }[_S t_i \text{intelligent}]]]]]]]$

    d. Move 2: A-to-A$'$

$[_{S'} \text{who}_i[_{S_1} t_i \text{seems}[_{S'}[_{S_2} \text{it is }[_{V''}[_{V'} \text{considered }[_S t_i \text{intelligent}]]]]]]]$

    e. Move 3: A$'$-to-A$'$

$[_{S'}[_{S_1} t_i \text{seems}[_{S'} [_{S_2} \text{it is }[_{V''} \text{who}_i[_{V'} \text{considered}_i [_S t_i \text{intelligent}]]]]]]]$

    f. Move 4: A$'$-to-A$'$

$[_{S'} \text{who}_i[_{S_1} t_i \text{seems}[_{S'}[_{S_2} \text{it is}[_{V''} (t_i')[_{V'} \text{considered}_i [_S t_i \text{intelligent}]]]]]]]$
          [+g]　　　　　　　　　　　　　　　[+g]

As concerns this derivation, notice first that "it" is absent at D-structure, a consequence of our assumption that this level is a pure representation of GF-Theta, lacking expletives such as "it" (which therefore must be inserted in the syntax). One might now ask why "it"-insertion has applied first? To begin, recall that the IFH will determine the most deeply embedded empty category as an anaphor (thereby voiding application of Condition C) only if the first movement of "who" is to an A-position. There are two possibilities, then, movement to the matrix subject position or movement to the embedded subject position. If the first movement of "who" is to matrix subject position, then subsequent insertion of "it" would violate the Strict Cycle.[4] If the first movement is to the embedded subject position, then "who" must vacate this position to allow subsequent insertion of "it." When "who" vacates embedded subject position, it cannot move out of S_2; if it did, subsequent insertion of "it" would violate the Strict Cycle. Consequently, "who" must move to some position internal to S_2. The only possible landing site is therefore Spec of V''. But this is an A'-position and, recall, Case-theoretic requirements force subsequent movement of "who" to matrix subject position, an A-position (i.e., this would represent movement as in (13), precisely the type of movement we wish to avoid). We therefore conclude that "it" is inserted before "who" is moved. After "it"-insertion applies, "who" moves directly to matrix subject position (an A-position). The empty category created by this movement is determined to be an anaphor under the IFH. Following this, "who" moves to the matrix Comp, an A'-position. The third movement of "who" is movement to Spec of V'', also an A'-position (this allows Spec/Head indexing so as to satisfy the ECP). Finally, "who" is moved back to the matrix Comp, an A'-position. The crucial property of this derivation is that movement of the type (13) does not occur, and, in addition, the ECP is satisfied, as are the Theta Criterion and Condition C. Thus, the IFH–Condition C approach is still inadequate, even if movement as in (13) is somehow independently excluded. This inadequacy is further demonstrated by the possibility of derivations such as the following:

(15) a. DS:

     $[_{S'}[_S$ who$_i$ said $[_{S'}[_S e$ seems$[_{S'}[_S e$ is $[_{V''}[_{V'}$ considered
     $[_S$ he$_i$ intelligent$]]]]]]]]]$

  b. "it"-INSERT:

$[_{S'}[_S \text{who}_i \text{ said}[_{S'}[_S e \text{ seems}[_{S'}[_S \text{it is}[_{V''}[_{V'} \text{considered } [_S \text{he}_i \text{intelligent}]]]]]]]]]$

  c. Move 1: "he" A-to-A

$[_{S'}[_S \text{who}_i \text{ said}[_{S'}[_S \text{he}_i \text{seems}[_{S'}[_S \text{it is} [_{V''}[_{V'} \text{considered } [_S t_i \text{intelligent}]]]]]]]]]$

  d. Move 2: "who" A-to-A'

$[_{S'} \text{who}_i[_S t_i \text{ said}[_{S'}[_S \text{he}_i \text{ seems}[_{S'}[_S \text{it is} [_{V''}[_{V'}\text{considered } [_S t_i \text{intelligent}]]]]]]]]]$

  e. Move 3: "who" A'-to-A'

$[_{S'}[_S t_i \text{ said}[_{S'}[_S \text{he}_i \text{ seems}[_{S'}[_S \text{it is} [_{V''} \text{who}_i[_{V'}\text{considered}_i [_S t_i \text{intelligent}]]]]]]]]]$

  f. Move 4: "who" A'-to-A'

$[_{S'} \text{who}_i[_S t_i \text{ said}[_{S'}[_S \text{he}_i \text{ seems}[_{S'}[_S \text{it is} [_{V''} (t_i')[\text{considered}_i[_S t_i \text{intelligent}]]]]]]]]]$

$$[+g]$$

Derivations of this type demonstrate that a given category C need not be the category triggering indexing of the head that properly governs the trace of C (i.e., a category distinct from C can trigger indexing of the head properly governing the trace of C). In this particular derivation, "who" and "he" are coindexed at D-structure.[5] In the syntax, "it" is inserted, and then "he" moves to an A-position, leaving what is an anaphor under the IFH, with which "he" can form an A-chain. Following this, "who," which is coindexed with "he," moves to the matrix Comp, then to Spec of V'', then back to the matrix Comp. While occupying Spec of V'', "who" triggers indexing of the verb. Thus, the N'' "who" triggers head indexing, resulting in proper government of the trace of "he." Movement as in (13) fails to occur. Further, under the IFH, Condition C is satisfied. So are the ECP and the Theta Criterion. We conclude that the IFH–Condition C approach is inadequate even if supplemented with some principle prohibiting movement as in (13). We therefore abandon this approach.

We have now seen that Chomsky's (1986b) Condition C approach to super-raising requires an algorithm determining empty categories in such a way that the trace of super-raising is necessarily an R-expression; the IFH fails to do this. Suppose, then, that we try to maintain a Condition C approach by incorporating

a different algorithm for determining empty categories. Consider
the Functional Determination algorithm proposed in Chomsky
(1982):

(16) Functional Determination of Empty Categories (FD): An empty cat-
      egory is a variable if it is in an A-position and is locally A′-bound.
      An empty category in an A-position that is not a variable is an
      anaphor . . . a pronoun is either free or locally A-bound by an an-
      tecedent with an independent theta role.

The most fundamental difference between (16) and the IFH is that
the latter represents a derivational classification of empty categories created by movement (i.e., the classification of such a category depends entirely on the type of movement that created it).
By contrast, FD provides a representational classification of
empty categories. This algorithm is insensitive to the manner in
which an empty category is created; rather, the classification of
an empty category depends entirely on the properties of the representation in which it occurs. Under a Condition C approach to
super-raising, the representations derived by this type of movement will be uniformly excluded only if some empty category is
necessarily determined as an R-expression and is also A-bound
in the domain of the head of its chain. FD dictates that an empty
category is a variable (equivalently, an R-expression) if it is in an
A-position and is locally A′-bound.[6] We will now show that the
FD–Condition C approach (like the IFH–Condition C approach)
also provides an inadequate analysis of super-raising. Since FD
is representational, all we have to do to reveal the inadequacy of
this analysis is reconsider S-structure representations such as (9e)
or (14f). Consider the former. As noted, no principle requires the presence of t' occupying Spec of V″, an A′ position, at
S-structure. In particular, the ECP does not require the presence
of this category. This principle requires only that t be properly
governed. This dictates that the head "considered" must be coindexed with t. But this indexing can be produced in the absence
of t' at S-structure, since Spec–head indexing can both precede
and follow Affect-alpha (an assumption we originally made so as
to eliminate lexical proper government of verb complements).
Thus, representations such as the following satisfy the ECP:

(17) $[_{S'}[_S$ he$_i$ seems$[_{S'}[_S$ it is $[_{V''}[_{V'}$considered$_i$ $[_S$ t_i intelligent$]]]]]]]$

Furthermore, such representations can be derived in conformity with Subjacency as a constraint on movement. Now, since t' is absent, t is not locally A′-bound. Therefore, t is not a variable, equivalently, not an R-expression under FD. Rather, t is an anaphor. Condition C is now inapplicable. Further, the Theta Criterion can be satisfied by freely forming a chain consisting of the argument "he," occupying a nonargument position, and the nonargument anaphor t, occupying an argument position. Thus, we see that the FD/Condition C approach fails to provide an adequate analysis of the ill-formedness of super-raising representations.

We therefore conclude that within the broader framework of principles assumed here, the FD–Condition C analysis of super-raising cannot be maintained. More generally, we cannot maintain the Condition C analysis in any form, since no algorithm for determining empty categories is restrictive enough to ensure the presence of an R-expression in representations derived by super-raising. In fact, we have shown only the inadequacy of the IFH and FD algorithms in this regard. But notice that the free assignment algorithm proposed in Brody (1984) is also inadequate, since this maximally permissive algorithm allows every classification allowed by the IFH as well as every classification allowed by FD. Therefore, it encounters all the problems confronted under the conjunction of the IFH and FD. We therefore abandon the Condition C approach altogether. Later we shall propose an analysis of super-raising compatible with the framework assumed here. But before doing this, we shall briefly review the Condition C approach to super-raising as it was originally proposed within the framework of Chomsky (1986b), an approach we could not successfully incorporate into our framework. The question we are concerned with is this: Is the Condition C approach to super-raising adequate as proposed within the framework of Chomsky (1986b)?

Consider the following derivation:

(18) a. DS:

$\quad\quad[_{S'}[_S e$ seems$[_{S'}[_S e$ is $[_{V''}$considered $[_S$ John$_i$ intelligent$]]]]]]]$

b. Move 1: A-to-A′

$[_{S'}[_S \, e \text{ seems}[_{S'}[_S \, e \text{ is } [_{V''} \text{John}_i \, [_{V''} \text{considered}_i \, [_S \, t_i \text{intelligent}]]]]]]]$

c. "it"-INSERT:

$[_{S'}[_S \, e \text{ seems}[_{S'}[_S \text{ it is } [_{V''} \text{John}_i[_{V''} \text{considered}_i \, [_S \, t_i \text{intelligent}]]]]]]]$

d. Move 2: A′-to-A

$[_{S'}[_S \text{John}_i \text{ seems } [_{S'}[_S \text{ it is } [_{V''} (t_i') [_{V''} \text{considered}_i \, [_S \, t_i \text{intelligent}]]]]]]]$

Chomsky (1986b, p. 22) suggests that a derivation like (18) is excluded, since the "process of V″-adjunction is barred . . . under standard assumptions blocking 'improper movement'[20]" Footnote 20 of Chomsky (1986b, p.22) then reads: "Thus t [in our (18d) (S.D.E.)] would be an A′-bound R-expression that is A-bound in the domain of the head of its chain, violating Condition C of the Binding Theory. . . ."

Thus, it is argued that Condition C is violated, since t is an R-expression disallowed by this principle. But how is t determined as an R-expression? As we have seen, the IFH fails to determine t as an R-expression in other possible derivations (permitted, at least within our framework) in which t could be created by direct movement to an A-position. Suppose, then, that t is an R-expression because t is locally A′-bound in (18d). As we have argued, this approach will not work within our framework, since no principle requires the presence of t' at S-structure. But does some principle require the presence of this category within the framework of Chomsky (1986b)? First, we might ask whether the ECP requires the S-structure presence of t', occupying V″-adjoined position. This is not clear. Although the elimination of lexical proper government of verb complements appears to rest on the assumption that g-assignment and Affect-alpha are freely ordered in the LF component, it is not at all clear whether Chomsky assumes that the same ordering characterizes the syntax. If it does (and we see no principled way of preventing this), then g-assignment can occur in (18b); that is, while the N″ "John" occupies V″-adjoined position, this category can assign $[+g]$ to its trace. Following this, the N″ "John" can move from V″-adjoined position and the ECP would not require a trace to be left in this position. Suppose, then, that it is Subjacency that requires the presence of t' (a category adjoined to V″) at S-structure. If this inference is right, it has potentially interesting consequences. First, if it is Subjacency that requires the S-structure presence of t' adjoined to V″ (thereby rendering Condition C applicable), this entails that Subjacency is a constraint on representation (and not a condition on movement). Although the status of this principle is left open in Chomsky (1986b, n. 25), this analysis apparently decides the issue. That is, if Condition C is to rule out (18c), this representation must contain an R-expression. This requires that t be locally A′-bound at S-structure (hence, an R-expression). Therefore, t', adjoined to V″, must be present at this level, so as to locally A′-bind t. This requirement can be enforced if Subjacency is a constraint on representation, thereby ensuring the presence of t' at S-structure.

Thus, one might tentatively conclude that Subjacency constrains representation within the Barriers framework, since this appears to be prerequisite to a successful analysis of super-raising as a violation of Condition C. However, we will now suggest that this Condition C analysis, resting on the assumption that Subjacency constrains representation, is unmaintainable. If we are correct, this has at least two notable consequences. First, the apparent evidence that Subjacency constrains representation, provided by this analysis, disappears (i.e., since the analysis is unsound, it provides no evidence concerning the status of Subjacency). Second, if the analysis in question cannot be maintained, then, if our inferencing is correct, this shows that the Condition C analysis is untenable within the Barriers framework, as it is within ours. This, then, leaves open the correct analysis of super-raising.

To begin, suppose we assume that the following analysis (which we inferred earlier) is the analysis dictated within Barriers:

(19) a. Subjacency is a constraint on representation,

    b. therefore, Subjacency forces the presence of t', adjoined to V″,

    c. therefore, t is determined as an R-expression,

    d. therefore, Condition C is violated

There is a potentially questionable feature of any such analysis that should be noted. Under analysis (19), a "weak" principle (Subjacency) requires a representation to exhibit a certain property (the presence of t'). Since the representation exhibits this property, this results in the violation of a "strong" principle (Condition C). Adapting a term from standard phonological theory, we may say that, within such an analysis, a weak principle "feeds" a strong principle. The predictive content of such an analysis is intended to be as follows; the ungrammaticality of the sentence represented is necessarily of a strong type (i.e., it is not the type of ungrammaticality exhibited by sentences the representations of which violate only the weak principle). Thus, (19) is intended to characterize the string represented as necessarily strongly ungrammatical, since its representation necessarily violates Condition C, a "strong" principle. But is this result in fact derivable within the analysis proposed? We shall now argue that it is not. Consider again (19a) and (19b). To the extent that it is clear, this inference seems wrong (i.e., given that Subjacency is a constraint on representation, we assume that the creation of a trace in Spec V'' is entirely optional with respect to Subjacency). Indeed, it would be odd to assume Subjacency constrains representation while also claiming that this principle requires certain traces to be created by movement. Rather, if a trace is created, Subjacency is satisfied; if no trace is created, this principle is violated. We conclude that Subjacency does not require a trace to be created in V''-adjoined position. Now, as concerns the ECP, recall that if g-assignment and Affect-alpha are freely ordered in the syntax, satisfaction of this principle does not require the S-structure presence of a trace adjoined to V''. We may conclude, then, that trace-leaving is optional, the optimal assumption. Suppose, then, that a trace is not present in V''-adjoined position, an available option. Although the ECP can be satisfied, Subjacency, a weak principle, is violated. But notice that, as a result of violating Subjacency, Condition C, a strong principle, is now satisfied. Consequently, there is a derivation of the sentence violating only Subjacency, and this is an incorrect result. If the discussion here is right, no analysis in which a weak (representational) principle feeds a strong one can be maintained (if the intent is to provide a uniform analysis as a strong violation).

In summary, it may be the case that this analysis is like ours in that a Condition C account of super-raising cannot be maintained within either. In the following section an alternative analysis is proposed.

The Local Binding Condition

Let us begin by re-creating the problem we confront. Recall, to eliminate lexical proper government of verb complements, head indexing can both precede and follow Affect-alpha in the LF component. We assume an identical ordering in the syntax, since we have no principled means by which to exclude it. Consequently, S-structure representations such as the following are generated:

(20) $[_{S'}[_S$ John$_i$ seems $[_{S'}[_S$ it is $[_{V''}$ considered$_i[_S$ t_i intelligent]]]]]]
$$[+g]$$

As a result of this ordering, the ECP is satisfied. Since we assume Subjacency constrains only movement, this principle too is satisfied in (20). As concerns Condition C, neither the IFH, FD, nor Free Assignment ensures the presence of an R-expression; hence, this principle is, in fact, inapplicable. (Given that the three algorithms are identical in this respect, we provisionally adopt the optimal one, Free Assignment.) Finally, the Theta Criterion is also satisfied. Since we assume that chains are freely formed, a chain consisting of the N'' "John" (an argument in a nonargument position) and t (a nonargument in an argument position) may be formed, thereby satisfying this principle. Given the derivational freedom displayed by this system (including free ordering of head indexing and Affect-alpha, free assignment of features to empty categories, and free formation of chains), one would suspect that a principle of representation must be violated. Accordingly, we propose that representations such as (20) are indeed ruled out by a principle of representation, namely, the following, originally proposed in Chomsky (1981)[7]:

(21) The Local Binding Condition on Chains:
      $C = (a_1, \ldots, a_n)$ is a chain only if a_i locally binds a_{i+1}
      (preliminary version)

Under (21), every link of a chain must exhibit local binding. Before providing a more precise definition of this condition and examining its application to representations derived by super-raising, we shall briefly review some independent motivation for this condition.

Lasnik (1985) notes that Chomsky (1981) provides no explicit motivation for incorporating a local binding condition on chains. Lasnik argues, however, that precisely such a condition appears to be required to exclude the S-structure representations he presents, such as

(22) *$[_{S'}[_S$ John$_i$ is believed $[_{S'}$ that $[_S$ he$_i$ likes t_i]]]]

As Lasnik notes, (22) satisfies Condition A of the Binding theory, that is, the trace is bound in its governing category. However, under the Theta Criterion, ["John"-"t"] must form an A-chain in this representation, yet this required chain structure is precluded by the Local Binding Condition. Correctly, then, the structure is excluded.

Rizzi (1982b) provides the first motivation for a local binding condition on A-chains. In Italian, constructions containing an anaphoric clitic bound by a derived subject, are ungrammatical:

(23) *Gianni si   è stato affidato
      Gianni to-himself was entrusted
      "Gianni was entrusted to himself"

Rizzi observes that the Theta Criterion requires that the representation of such sentences contains two chains, ["Gianni," t] and ["si," t']:

(24) *$[_{S'}[_S$ Gianni$_i$ $[_{V''}$ si$_i$ è stato affidato t_i t'_i]]

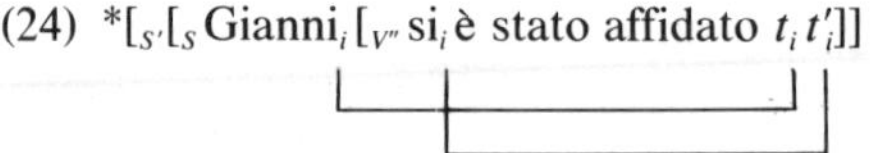

The ill-formedness of such representations is claimed to be the result of violating the Local Binding Condition on A-chains (for further discussion, see the works cited, as well as Chomsky [1986a] and Epstein [1986a].)

Baker, Johnson, and Roberts (1987), extending an analysis proposed in Jaeggli (1986), provide yet another argument for a local binding condition on chains. As they note, the understood subject of an Agentless passive cannot be interpreted as coreferential with the S-structure subject. Thus, for example, (25) cannot be interpreted as (26):

(25) They were admired

(26) They were admired by themselves

Baker, Johnson, and Roberts provide an account for this fact. They assume that in the analysis of (25), the passive affix "en" is an indexed argument that receives the external (subject) theta role assigned by the V''. It is also assumed that there is a V''-internal empty category (which they call "IMP") that shares the underlying subject theta role with "en" and is also coindexed with "en." Under these assumptions, the only representation of (25) that could be interpreted as (26) is

(27) $*[_{S'}[_S \text{They}_i \text{ were kill } + \text{en}_i\, t_i\, \text{IMP}_i]]$

Baker, Johnson, and Roberts argue that representations of this kind are excluded by the Local Binding Condition, thereby accounting for the unavailability of the interpretation.

Having now reviewed some of the independent motivation for a Local Binding Condition, let us now return to super-raising representations:

(28) $[_{S'}[_S \text{John}_i \text{ seems } [_{S'}[_S \text{ it is considered}_i[_S t_i \text{ intelligent}]]]]]$

The Theta Criterion is satisfied provided the N'' John and the N'' t form an A-chain, an available option if chains are freely formed. Further, the ECP is satisfied, since "considered" properly governs the trace. In particular, "considered" antecedent-governs the trace, since it is a head that binds the trace (under c-command) and no barrier to antecedent government separates these two categories. But notice that this antecedent government of the trace by "considered" necessarily results in a violation of the Local Binding Condition; the N'' "John," the head of the A-chain, does not locally bind t, since "considered" is an "intervening" binder. With this approach in mind, we may now begin to determine the exact definition of "local binding" as this term occurs in the definition of the Local Binding Condition. One possible definition of "local binding" (discussed in Epstein, 1986a) is the following:

(29) A locally binds B iff A X-binds B and there is no C such that A X-binds C and C X-binds B, where "X" is uniformly replaced by either "A" or "A'" throughout

Under this definition, for a category C to prevent A from locally binding B, C must occupy a position-type (A or A′) identical to that of category A. With respect to A-chains, (29) predicts that; only categories in A-positions can prevent the head of a (potential) A-chain from locally binding the tail. The purpose of proposing this definition is twofold. First, following Lasnik and Rizzi, we wanted to provide a definition of "local binding" accounting for the ill-formedness of S-structures such as (22) and (24). Under (29), each case is correctly ruled out as a violation of the Local Binding Condition. In (22) the N″ "he" occupying an A-position prevents the N″ "John," which also occupies an A-position, from locally binding t. Therefore, there can be no chain consisting of "John" and t, with the result that the Theta Criterion is violated. In (24), $t′$, occupying an A-position, prevents "Gianni," occupying an A-position, from locally binding t. Consequently, ["Gianni," t] cannot be an A-chain and the Theta Criterion is violated. Thus, (29) correctly accounts for both cases. But where is the motivation for the restriction in (29) that A and C must occupy the same position-type? Lasnik's and Rizzi's cases ((22) and (24)) provide no such motivation, since each would be ruled out even in the absence of the restriction that A and C must occupy the same type of position. The motivation for this restriction can be seen by first considering the grammaticality of sentences of the following kind:

(30) John was entrusted to himself

The S-structure representation is as follows:

(31) $[_{S′}[_S \text{John}_i \text{ was entrusted } t_i [_{P″} \text{to himself}_i]]$

Clearly, to allow this representation, any definition of "local binding" is sufficient, since the N″ "John" is the only binder of t and is hence the local binder of this category. But assuming Chomsky's (1986a) analysis, under which overt anaphors are "cliticized" at LF (see also Lebeaux, 1983) the S-structure (31) is mapped into the following LF representation in which the N″ "himself" is "cliticized" onto INFL:

(32) $[_{S′}[_S \text{John}_i \text{himself}_i[_{V″} \text{ was entrusted } t_i [_{P″} \text{to } t′_i]]]]$

Now, given that "himself" binds t, the well-formedness of such representations provides motivation for the requirement expressed in (29) that A and C occupy the same type of position. Without this restriction, the LF representation (32) would be incorrectly deemed ill formed; "John" and *t* could not constitute the requisite A-chain, since "John" binds "himself" and "himself" binds *t* (i.e., "John" would not locally bind *t*). However, given the restriction in (29) that A and C must occupy the same type of position, the LF representation is correctly allowed; in particular, "himself," *which occupies an A'-position, does not* prevent "John," *occupying an A-position, from locally binding t.* Thus, (29) was motivated to the extent that it allowed the LF representation (32) while it simultaneously excluded Lasnik's and Rizzi's S-structures (22) and (24). Nonetheless, (29) must now be abandoned, since it fails to rule out super-raising representations such as (28). Recall that we assume (28) is to be ruled out as a violation of the Local Binding Condition as follows: the N" "John" fails to locally bind *t* because of the presence of the verb "considered," which is both bound by "John" and binds *t*. But given that "John" occupies an A-position, whereas the verb "considered" patently does not, (29) predicts that "John," the only A-binder of *t,* does indeed locally bind *t.* Hence, these two categories can be an A-chain and the Theta Criterion can therefore be satisfied, an incorrect result. Therefore, we abandon (29), because the definition of "local binding" needed to rule out examples such as (28) must predict that an X^0, such as the verb "considered," can prevent an N" in an A-position, such as "John" in (28), from locally binding its trace.

For the purpose of ruling out (28) as a violation of the Local Binding Condition, suppose we modify definition (29) of "local binding" by simply eliminating the requirement that A and C occupy the same type of position. This results in the following definition of "local binding" (from Chomsky, 1986a, p. 181):

(33) A locally binds B iff A binds B and there is no C such that A binds C and C binds B

This definition predicts that in (28), "John" does not locally bind *t,* since "John" binds "considered" and "considered" binds *t*. Therefore, "John" and *t* cannot be an A-chain and the Theta Criterion is violated. Thus, under (33), (28) is correctly excluded. Furthermore, under (33), the S-structures (22) and (24) are also correctly predicted to be ill formed. Despite this, we cannot maintain (33), since it has two incorrect consequences. First, it incorrectly excludes the LF representation (32). Under (33), "John" does not locally bind t, since "John" binds "himself" and "himself" binds t (i.e., the Theta Criterion is violated and the sentence represented is wrongly predicted to be ungrammatical). The second unwanted consequence is similar. Consider again well-formed cases derived by N''-movement:

(1) $[_{S'}[_S \text{John}_i \text{INFL}_i \text{ was arrested } t_i]]]]$

(2) $[_{S'}[_S \text{John}_i \text{INFL}_i \text{ is likely}[_S t_i \text{ to go}]]]]]$

(3) $[_{N''} \text{Rome's}_i[_{N'} \text{ destruction}_i t_i]]$

In (1) and (2) the head INFL properly governs the trace. In (3) the head N is a proper governor. But given this, under (33) the requisite A-chain in each representation is now precluded. In (1) and (2), "John" binds INFL and INFL binds t; hence, "John" does not locally bind t. In (3), "Rome's" binds "destruction" and "destruction" binds t; hence, "Rome's" does not locally bind t. Therefore, (1) through (3) each violate the Theta Criterion. Under (33), then, each sentence represented is wrongly predicted to be ungrammatical.

Thus far we have seen that both definition (29) and definition (33) of "local binding" are inadequate. Consider again the illicit case of super-raising:

(28) $[_{S'}[_S \text{John}_i \text{ seems } [_{S'}[_S \text{it is considered}_i[_S t_i \text{ intelligent}]]]]]]$

Recall that if we are to rule out such representations as violations of the Local Binding Condition, then X^0 categories must be able to prevent local binding between A-positions. But if this is so, the question we now face is this: How is it that the X^0 categories INFL and N do not prevent local binding in the well-formed cases (1) through (3), but the X^0 "considered" does prevent local binding in (28)? We can begin to see the answer by making the following observation: In the well-formed cases, the X^0 categories INFL and N are "very close" to the head of the chain, whereas, in the case of super-raising, the X^0 "considered" is "very far" from the head of the chain. For the purpose of formally instantiating this distinction, we propose that "local binding" be defined as follows (adapted from Chomsky, 1981, p. 185):

(34) A locally binds B iff A binds B and if C binds B, then either C binds
A or C = A

Under this definition, the case of super-raising violates the Local
Binding Condition, the desired result. "John" does not locally
bind *t,* because "considered" binds *t* yet fails to bind "John."
Consequently, ["John," *t*] cannot be an A-chain, with the result
that the Theta Criterion is necessarily violated.

Notice that the same correct result is obtained with respect to
both Lasnik's and Rizzi's examples, (22) and (24). In each the
Local Binding Condition, incorporating (34), prohibits the chain-
structure required by the Theta Criterion; hence, these structures
are also ruled out.

Now let us examine the predictive content of (34) with respect
to the cases that should be allowed. Consider the following in
more detail:

(1) $[_{S'}[_S \text{John}_i[_{I'}\text{INFL}_i[_{V''} \text{ was arrested } t_i]]]]$

Under definition (34), does "John" locally bind *t*? Given that
INFL binds *t,* (34) predicts that "John" locally binds *t* only if
INFL also binds "John." Does INFL bind "John"? This, of
course, depends on the definition of "binding." Consider the following definitions:

(35) A binds B iff A c-commands and is coindexed with B

(36) A binds B iff A m-commands and is coindexed with B

(37) C-command: A c-commands B if neither A nor B dominates the
other and the first branching node dominating A dominates B (Reinhart, 1976)

(38) M-command: A m-commands B if neither A nor B dominates the
other and the minimal maximal projection dominating A dominates
B (adapted from Aoun and Sportiche, 1983)

Under definition (35), INFL does not bind "John." But under
definition (36), INFL does bind "John." Therefore, we assume
that definition (36) is the definition of the final occurrence of
"binds" in definition (34). Thus, in (1), "John," by definition (34),
locally binds *t.* Therefore, these categories can constitute an A-
chain and the Theta Criterion is satisfied. The same correct result
obtains with respect to the other representations derived by licit

N"-movement, such as (2) and (3). Furthermore, the LF representation (32) is also correctly allowed under (34). Thus, in every case discussed, definition (34) of "local binding" provides the correct result.

To summarize thus far, we have proposed that super-raising representations such as (28) are ruled out by (21):

(21) The Local Binding Condition:
   $C = (a_1, \ldots, a_n)$ is a chain only if a_i locally binds a_{i+1}

(34) Locally Binds: A locally binds B iff A binds B and if C binds B, then either C {binds} A or C = A

(36) {binds}: A binds B iff A m-commands and is coindexed with B

(38) M-command: A m-commands B if neither A nor B dominates the other and the minimal maximal projection dominating A dominates B

We may now proceed to determine further properties of the Local Binding Condition.

Consider once again the illicit representation derived by super-raising:

(28) $[_{S'} [_S \text{John}_i \text{ INFL}_i \text{ seems } [_{S'} [_S \text{it is considered}_i [_S t_i \text{intelligent}]]]]]$

We have seen that the Local Binding Condition excludes a representation in which "John" and t constitute a chain. But suppose a chain is freely formed consisting of the three categories "John," "considered," and t. Since the verb "considered" is part of the chain, the Local Binding Condition is satisfied. That is, each link of the chain, namely, "John"–"considered" and "considered"–t, satisfies the Local Binding Condition; "John" locally binds "considered," which in turn locally binds t. Thus, if "considered" can be part of the chain, the Local Binding Condition can be satisfied (i.e., the representation would be wrongly allowed). We must therefore preclude the inclusion of "considered" in the chain. This can be achieved by modifying the Local Binding Condition (21) as follows (from Chomsky, 1981, p. 333):

(39) The Local Binding Condition:
   $C = (a_1, \ldots, a_n)$ is a chain iff

 (i) a_i is an N"

(ii) a_i locally A-binds a_{i+1} where "locally A-binds" is defined as

(40) X locally A-binds Y iff X locally binds Y and X A-binds Y, where X A-binds Y only if X binds Y and occupies an A-position (adapted from Chomsky, 1981, p. 185)

Under these definitions, each link in a chain must exhibit local A-binding, that is, a_i must be in an A-position and must locally bind a_{i+1}. Consequently, there can be no chain consisting of the three categories ["John," "considered," t]. Specifically, the link "considered"–t is barred, since "considered," which fails to occupy an A-position, does not locally A-bind t. Given that this link is precluded, satisfaction of the Theta Criterion now requires a direct link between "John" and t. But as shown, this too is precluded by the Local A-binding Condition, since "John" fails to locally bind t.

Thus, under the Local A-binding Condition, no X^0 can be a chain internal binder because, by virtue of being an X^0, it cannot be an A-binder. This is precisely the result we want; the Local Binding Condition is formulated in such a way that an X^0 can "break" a chain and, in addition, cannot be included in a chain. (Later we attempt to derive this from other principles.)

We can now proceed to determine, in even more detail, the exact definition of "local binding." Consider the following representation:

(41) $[_{S'}[_S \text{John}_i \text{ INFL}_i \text{ seems } [_S t_i \text{ INFL}_i \text{ to be intelligent}]]]$

Notice first that, under the requirement that only a head can properly govern, infinitivals (such as the embedded S in (41)) must contain INFL. If INFL were absent in infinitivals, the ECP would be violated in representations such as the following (thereby wrongly predicting the sentence represented to be ungrammatical):

(42) $*[_{S'}[_S \text{I}_i \text{ INFL}_i \text{ want } [_S \text{John}_j \text{ to seem } [_S t_j \text{ to be intelligent}]]]]]$

The ECP is violated because there is no head properly governing the trace. To avoid this result, there must be an INFL element in infinitivals, such as (42), as well as (41). Notice that the same holds true for small clauses such as "I consider John likely to win." With this in mind, notice that in (41) the ECP is satisfied because the trace is properly governed by the *matrix* (tensed)

INFL. In this representation, "John" and t must be an A-chain. Notice that under the Local A-binding Condition, the matrix INFL cannot be part of the chain, since this category does not locally A-bind t. Therefore, "John"–t is not only a chain, but also a link. The exclusion of the matrix INFL from the chain does not prevent "John" from locally binding t, precisely because the matrix INFL binds "John" (assuming, as we have, definition (36)). But now consider the embedded INFL. Given that "binding" is defined in terms of "m-command," this INFL also binds t. In addition, the embedded INFL fails to bind "John." Consequently, "John" does not locally bind t (i.e., the Local Binding Condition is violated and the sentence represented is therefore incorrectly predicted to be ungrammatical). There are two possible approaches to this problem. First, since the embedded INFL is "breaking" the requisite chain between "John" and t, we might suppose that this INFL can be put into the chain. Recall that the Local A-Binding Condition precludes the possibility of an X^0 being a chain internal binder, precisely because it does not occupy an A-position. However, it does not preclude an X^0 from being a chain internal nonbinder (i.e., a tail). Thus, to prevent the problem of the embedded INFL "breaking" the chain consisting of ["John," t], we could incorporate the embedded INFL into this chain (i.e., suppose the following chain is freely formed ["John," t, "embedded INFL"]). This, in fact, provides no solution at all. If the chain consists of ["John," t, "embedded INFL"], then, since INFL is not an A-binder, it cannot be a linkhead. Therefore, the two links of this three-membered chain must be "John"–t and t–"embedded INFL." But as we have seen, the former link does not satisfy the Local Binding Condition (i.e., "John" does not locally bind t, because the embedded INFL binds t and fails to bind "John." The fact that the embedded INFL is in a chain with "John" and t is irrelevant; the definition of "local binding" is not theta-sensitive. Thus, putting the embedded INFL in the chain is without effect; the Local Binding Condition is still violated, since "John" does not locally bind t. Thus, we are still faced with the following problem: How can we generate (41); in particular, how can we allow a chain = ["John," t], given that the embedded INFL binds t and not "John," in violation of the Local Binding Condition? We assume that the Local

Binding Condition is satisfied in (41) as a result of the fact that the embedded INFL does not c-command "John" (i.e., the embedded INFL fails to bind t under definition (35) of "binds"). Consequently, the Local Binding Condition is satisfied (i.e., the embedded INFL does not bind the trace in the relevant sense of binding; hence, the embedded INFL does not break the chain).

Notice that this analysis now entails that the Local Binding Condition incorporates two distinct definitions of "binds," one including the term "c-command" and another including "m-command." To see this clearly, consider again the chain ["John," t] in (41). It is allowed by the Local Binding Condition, that is, "John" is predicted to locally bind t as follows. First, even though the matrix INFL binds t, since the matrix INFL m-commands and is coindexed with "John," the matrix INFL does not prevent "John" from locally binding t. As concerns the embedded INFL, if it were to bind t, then, since it does not bind "John," the Local Binding Condition would be violated. Therefore, we assume that the embedded INFL does not bind t in the relevant respect (i.e., the embedded INFL does not c-command t). Thus, to allow the chain ["John," t] in (41) (a chain excluding both INFLs, as dictated by the Local A-Binding Condition), "local binding" must be defined as follows:

(43) Local Binding:
A locally binds B iff A binds B and if C [binds] B, then either C <binds> A or C = A,

(35) [Binds]: A [binds] B iff A c-commands and is coindexed with B

(36) <Binds>: A <binds> B iff A m-commands B and is coindexed with B

Under (43), (41) is allowed; that is, ["John," t] is an A-chain, since "John" locally binds t.

Thus, the Local Binding Condition, incorporating definition (43), correctly allows licit N'' movement, whereas any super-raising representation satisfying the ECP is excluded. Notice that the analysis proposed here extends directly to "classic improper movement representations" such as

(44) $*[_{S'}[_S \text{John}_i \text{INFL}_i \text{seems}[_{S'} [_{Ci} (t_i)][_S t_i \text{left}]]]]$

(45) $*[_{S'}[_S \text{John}_i \text{INFL}_i \text{is illegal}[_{S'} [_{Ci} (t_i)][_S t_i \text{to go}]]]]$

In each representation, satisfaction of the ECP requires that Comp be indexed. This indexing, however, entails that the chain structure required by the Theta Criterion violate the Local Binding Condition. Hence, any "improper movement representations," like any super-raising representations, will necessarily violate either the ECP or the Theta Criterion.

Summary

Modifying proposals of Chomsky (1986b), we argued in Chapter 2 that freely ordering Affect-alpha and head indexing in the LF component allows for the elimination of lexical proper government of verb complements. Having no principled way to exclude such ordering in the syntactic component, we assume this ordering obtains in the syntax as well. We have also shown that the assumed syntactic ordering allows representations derived by super-raising and "improper Movement" to satisfy the ECP. Following Chomsky (1986b), we attempted to provide an analysis of the ill-formedness of such representations in terms of Condition C of the Binding theory. However, given the broader framework of assumptions we adopt, a Condition C analysis was shown to be inadequate, since no algorithm for determining empty categories (neither the IFH, FD, nor Free Assignment) ensures the presence of an R-expression in such representations. Hence, Condition C is not necessarily applicable, that is, the Condition C approach is inadequate within our framework. (We then tentatively suggested that the Condition C approach to super-raising, as proposed by Chomsky 1986b, might be inadequate within that framework as well, since the analysis proposed there may consist of a "weak" principle "feeding" a "strong" one, a type of ordering we have argued to be problematic.) Consequently, we abandoned the Condition C approach, and instead have proposed an analysis under which any representation derived by super-raising or improper movement violates either the ECP or the Local Binding Condition on A-chains. In constructing this analysis, the following definition of the Local Binding Condition (adapted from Chomsky, 1981) was motivated:

(46) The Local Binding Condition:

$C = (a_1, \ldots, a_n)$ is a chain only if

a. a_1 is an N", and

b. a_i locally A-binds a_{i+1}

Locally A-Binds:

X locally A-binds Y iff X locally binds Y and X A-binds Y

Locally Binds:

A locally binds B iff A binds B and if C [binds] B, then either C <binds> A or C = A

[Binds]:

A [binds] B iff A c-commands and is coindexed with B

<Binds>:

A <binds> B iff A m-commands and is coindexed with B

C-command:

A c-commands B if neither A nor B dominates the other and the first branching node dominating A dominates B

M-command:

A m-commands B iff neither A nor B dominates the other and the minimal maximal projection dominating A dominates B

A-Binds:

X A-binds Y iff X binds Y and X occupies an A-position

Simplification of the Local Binding Condition: Deriving Conditions on A-Chains

In the preceding section, we proposed an analysis incorporating the following condition on chain links:

(46) The Local Binding Condition:

$C = (a_1, \ldots, a_n)$ is a chain only if

a. a_1 is an N", and

b. a_i locally A-binds a_{i+1}

As is clear from the definitions provided at the end of the previous section, the condition (46b) in fact imposes three distinct requirements on a chain link:

(47) a_i must occupy an A-position

(48) a_i must bind a_{i+1}

(49) If some category C binds a_{i+1}, then C must bind a_i (as discussed in detail earlier)

The purpose of this section is to show that requirement (48) is theorematic (i.e., it need not be stipulated that links of an A-chain must exhibit binding, since this follows from independent principles). We shall argue that the binding requirement on chain links is derivable from two principles in particular, the ECP and (49). Given that the binding requirement on chain links is derivable, the statement of the Local Binding Condition can be accordingly simplified (i.e., (48) is eliminable).

Because we want to show that it follows, without stipulation, that a chain link exhibits binding, the formal objects we need to consider are argument chains consisting of at least one link (i.e., consisting of more than one member). How does a chain consisting of more than one member, call it C2, arise; that is, what properties must it exhibit? Under the Projection Principle, we know that this chain must contain one and only one argument. But how is the argument "introduced into" C2? That is, how does it become a member of C2? To answer this we must first determine how arguments are introduced into syntactic derivations, hence representations, in general. Given that D-structure is a pure representation of Theta Structure, an argument can appear at this level only if it occupies a theta position, and if a theta position appears, it must be occupied by an argument. Thus, the only way for an argument to be introduced into a syntactic derivation is for it to appear in a theta position at D-structure. We now know the site of origin of the argument member of a chain. Notice that from the assumed definition of D-structure, it follows that at this level, all chains are single membered. Thus, by definition, our chain C2, consisting of more than one member, arises at a level of representation that is not equivalent to D-structure. However, under the Projection Principle, we may assume that the level of representation containing C2 is like D-structure in that it conforms to the Theta Criterion. That is, the argument (originating in a theta position) is the only argument in C2 and, in addition, C2 consists of only one theta position. If the argument remains in the theta position in which it occurs at D-structure, the chain is, by definition, a singleton chain. Therefore, we know that C2 has the following property: The argument member of C2 does not occupy the theta position it occupied at D-structure. What (kind of) position does the argument occupy? By the Recoverability Condition, the argument must occupy a thetaless position. Recall that (47) dictates further that a_i occupies an A-position. Thus, we have now derived that the argument of C2 occupies a thetaless A-position, of which there are two kinds: Specifier of I″ and Specifier of N″. For the sake of simplicity, we shall restrict our attention to the case in which C2 is a two-membered chain. We assume that the following arguments extend naturally to chains of greater length. Given that C2 is two-membered, we have now determined one half of its properties (i.e., one member of the chain is an argument occupying the thetaless Specifier position of I″ or N″). From the Theta Criterion, we can now infer that the other member of the chain consists of a nonargument category that occupies a theta position. What are the properties of this category? The nonargument occupies a theta position. Recall that at D-structure, all theta positions are occupied by arguments. Therefore, the nonargument was not base generated in the theta position it occupies as a member of C2. Further, under Recoverability, we assume that the nonargument could not have been moved into the theta position it occupies. Thus, the nonargument was absent at D-structure; equivalently, we may infer that

(50) The nonargument is a trace

Given that wh-trace is, by definition, an argument, it follows that the nonargument member of C2 is an NP-trace. Thus, the categorial status of such chain members need not be stipulated (see Brody, 1984; Sportiche, 1983). The properties of C2 that we have now derived can be schematically represented as follows:

(51) C2 = [+ ARG] .... [− ARG]
       thetaless   NP-trace
       A-position   theta position
       (= Spec I″
       or Spec N″)

Given that the nonargument is a trace and given that such categories must be bound, one might suppose that we can now derive what we intended to derive, namely, the fact that chain links must exhibit binding. However, this is not so. Although the trace must indeed be bound, we have not shown that the argument, with which the trace forms a link (and a chain), must be a binder of the trace. Rather, it could be that some link-external (or even chain-external) category binds the trace, thereby providing the trace with the binder it requires, while the category with which the trace forms a link does not bind the trace (see later). Given this, we have yet to show that it is derivable that chain links exhibit binding.

To determine further properties of C2, we now turn our attention to the ECP, a principle that applies to the trace by definition. Under the ECP, this category must be properly governed. Tentatively assuming the elimination of lexical proper government, as proposed in Chomsky (1986b) and modified earlier, proper government of the trace requires that there be a head (i.e., an X^0) that binds the trace. Thus, conformity with the ECP demands a representation schematically depicted as follows:

(52) C2 = [+ARG] .... Head$_i$ .... [−ARG]$_i$
        thetaless   trace
        A-position   theta position
        (Spec I″ or
        Spec N″)
    where the Head binds [−ARG]

As concerns the binding requirement on proper government (i.e., the requirement that the head bind the trace, we have seen at a number of junctures, that the binding in question entails c-command, as opposed to m-command. Thus, the binding requirement dictates that the head c-command (and be coindexed with) the trace in (52). With this in mind, consider the (core) X' schema

(53) $[_{X''} \text{Spec}[_{X'} X]]$

Since the ECP demands that the trace in (52) be c-commanded by the head (for purposes of binding), we can now licitly infer that the trace falls within the X' projection of the head (i.e., within the c-command domain of the head).

(54) $[_{X''} \text{Spec}[_{X'} \text{Head}_i \ldots \text{trace}_i]]$

Under the ECP, it is necessary, but not sufficient, that the head bind the trace. In addition to the head-binding requirement, the ECP imposes a locality requirement, demanding that there be no category C, C = N″ or S′, such that C dominates the trace yet fails to dominate the head. That is, satisfaction of the ECP requires the following:

(55) $[_{X''}$ Spec$[_{X'}$ Head$_i[_Z$ . . . trace$_i$. . .]]], where Z (if present) is neither an N″ nor an S′

We have now determined the relation between the head and the trace, where, recall, the trace is the [−ARG] member of C2, a two-membered chain consisting of a single link, which in turn consists of the trace and some argument. We now turn our attention to the argument member of C2. We have just seen that the trace must be bound by a head. Since a head, by definition, is not in an A-position, the head cannot be a member of the A-chain C2; equivalently, it cannot be a member of the single link of C2. Since the head both binds the trace and cannot be a link member, the following condition on chain links (discussed earlier) becomes relevant:

(49) If some category C binds a_{i+1}, then C must bind a_i

Given that the trace is equivalent to a_{i+1}, (49) is applicable to (55) (i.e., some category C—namely, the head—*does* bind the trace). Condition (49) thus requires that the head bind, under m-command (see earlier), the argument (i.e., the category with which the trace forms a link). By definition, a head can m-command only those categories that are dominated by the minimal maximal projection dominating the head. Thus, it follows from (49) that (i) the argument member of the chain C2 must occur within the minimal maximal projection dominating the head and (ii) the argument and the head are coindexed.

In summary, we have determined that, under the ECP, there must be a head that binds (under c-command) the trace, whereas under (49), this head must bind (under m-command) the argument with which the trace forms a link. By modifying (55) so that it is consistent with these inferences, we derive the following:

(56) $[_{X''} [_{X'} \text{Head}_i [_Z \text{trace}_i]]]$

   where

   (i) Z (if present) is not an NP or an S′ (as required by the ECP), and

   (ii) There is an argument with which the trace forms a chain, and, as required by (49), this argument is bound (under m-command) by the head; equivalently, the argument occurs within X″ and bears the index i

In somewhat simplified terms, the following configuration is forced by the ECP and condition (49):

(57)

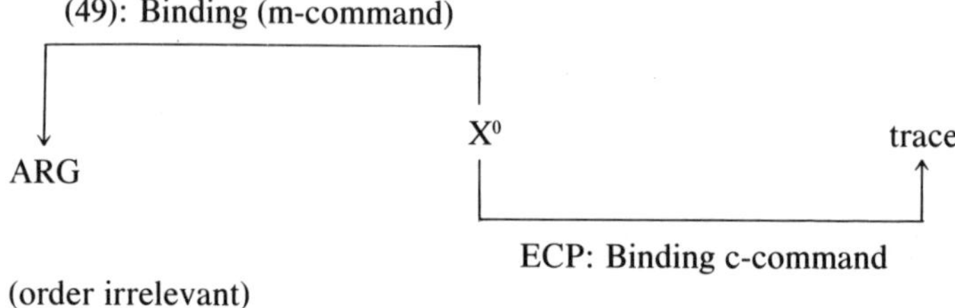

(order irrelevant)

From the requirements that (i) the head must bind the trace and (ii) the head must bind the argument, we can now in part derive the binding requirement on links. Consider the following sentence, for example:

(58) *After the thief seemed that the police left,
       it seemed to rob the bank.
       (cf. After it seemed that the police left,
       the thief seemed to rob the bank)

The D-structure to S-structure derivation of (58) is as follows:

(59) a. $[_{S'_1}[_{S'_2}$ After e seemed that the police left]
        $[_{S'_3} e$ seemed $[_S$ the thief to rob the bank]]]

(59) b. $*[_{S'_1}[_{S'_2}$ After the thief$_i$ seemed that the
        police left] $[_{S'_3}$ it seemed$[_S t_i$ to rob the bank]]]

To satisfy the ECP, either the verb "seemed" of S'_3 or INFL of S'_3 must bind the trace. This can be achieved by syntactic movement of the N″ "the thief" through Specifier of V″ or Specifier of I″, thereby triggering Spec–head coindexing (a rule that we have seen can apply at intermediate levels). To satisfy the Theta Criterion, the N″ "the thief" must form a chain (and a chain link) with the trace in (59b). One way to rule out a representation in which these two categories form a link would be to appeal to (48) (i.e., the requirement that members of a chain link must exhibit binding). Since "the thief" and the trace are not in a relation of binding, this requirement is violated. Therefore, these categories cannot form a link (or a chain) and the Theta Criterion is consequently violated. But notice that it is unnecessary to appeal to a binding requirement on links. As we have seen, the ECP demands that either INFL or V of S'_3 binds the trace. But since one of these heads must bind the trace (which is the tail of a chain link) Condition (49) requires that whichever head binds the trace must also bind "the thief." Since neither INFL nor V of S'_3 binds "the thief," (49) is violated. Thus, such structures are ruled out without appeal to a stipulated binding requirement on links. Hence, the binding requirement on links is, at least in part, derivable.

We have just examined a case in which an X^0 binds the trace (in conformity with the ECP), yet this X^0 fails to bind the argument, thereby violating (49). We will now consider examples in which both the ECP and (49) are satisfied, that is, examples in which the schema (57) is displayed. As concerns this schema, we might ask, "What are the possible binding relations between the argument and the trace within such a structure?" The following four logical possibilities exist (we repeat (57) here for convenience):

(57)

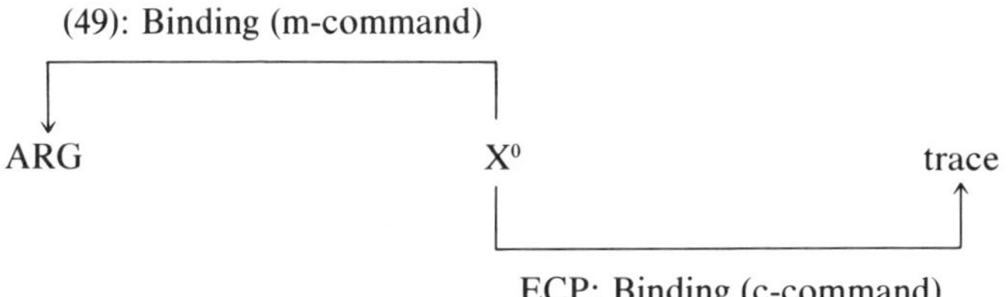

(order irrelevant)

a. The trace and the argument are not in a binding relation (i.e., neither binds the other).

b. The trace and the argument bind each other

    c. The trace binds the argument but not conversely

    d. The argument binds the trace but not conversely

Notice, if we can somehow independently exclude examples like (57a), we will then have derived the binding requirement on chain links. This follows because in cases (57b)–(57d) there is a binding relation between the argument and the trace (i.e., the link members). The binding relation between these categories is not necessarily well formed (see, for example, (57c)), but there is a binding relation nonetheless, and it is merely this relation that we seek to derive at this point.

We will now attempt to show, by examining what we hope is a representative case, that examples of (57a) can be excluded without appealing to a binding requirement on chain links (i.e., the binding requirement is shown to follow from independent principles). To begin, consider a licit site for an NP-trace, as in, for example, the following (partially represented) S-structure (where, for the moment, we ignore matrix subject position and the location of the argument):

(60) $[_{s'}[_{I''}\underline{\quad\quad}$ INFL $[_{V''}[_{V'}$ seems$[_{I''}$ trace$_i$ . . .]]]]]]

Now, in case (57a), which we are now attempting to construct, the trace and the argument are coindexed, yet they are not in a binding relation. It therefore follows that the trace does not c-command the argument. As concerns (60), we can therefore infer that

(61) The argument does not occur within the embedded I″

By the ECP there must be a head binding the trace. Suppose, via movement of the argument to or through Spec of V″, Spec–head indexing applies and the V "seems" is indexed and thereby properly governs the trace. But now, under (49), since "seems" binds the trace, it must bind (under m-command) the argument (i.e., the argument must occur within V″). But recall from (61) we also know that the argument is not within the embedded I″. The only possible NP position within V″ but not within the embedded I″ is Spec V″. For whatever reason, arguments do not occur in this position. Therefore, we can conclude that

(62) "seems" is not indexed

What other head could properly govern the trace? Consider INFL. By moving the argument to or through Spec of I″, INFL could be indexed i and thereby properly govern the trace. But now, since INFL binds the trace, (49) dictates that INFL must bind (under m-command) the argument. The m-command domain of INFL is the matrix I″. Therefore, if the structure is to be well formed,

(63) The argument occurs within the matrix I″

Recall from (61) that we know the argument does not occur within the embedded I″. Further, we have seen that the argument does not occur in Spec of V″. Where, then, could the argument occur? One possibility is that the argument is in subject position of the matrix I″, as in

(64) $[_{S'}[_S \text{ARG}_i \text{INFL}_i \text{seems}[_S t_i \text{to be here}]]]$

Of course, (64) is not equivalent to (57a) (the case we seek), since the argument and trace in (64) *are* in a binding relation; in fact, this represents a well-formed chain.

There is, however, another possibility. The argument member of the chain could still be bound (under m-command) by INFL, thereby satisfying (49) if this argument were moved to a thetaless position *inside* some complex NP occupying matrix subject position. The following (partially) illustrates the case we have in mind

(65) $[_{S'}[_{N''} \text{The man who}_j \, t_j \text{thinks ARG}_i \text{seems that Bill left}] \text{INFL}_i \text{seems}$
      $[_S t_i \text{to be here}]]$

This is an example of (57a), the structure we seek; both the ECP and (49) are satisfied, while the ARG and the trace are not in a binding relation. But the structure is ill formed. First, since the subject position is thetaless, the complex N″ occupying this position must have moved into this position. We naturally assume (without proof here) that the chain structure associated with this N″ is ill formed. Further, recall that INFL must be indexed i to satisfy the ECP. But notice that subject agreement dictates that the complex N″ occupying subject position is also indexed i. With this in mind, recall that since INFL binds the trace, (49) dictates that INFL bind the ARG. But this means ARG is also indexed i.

Thus, ARG, INFL, and the matrix subject are coindexed. This, however, results in a violation of the i-within-i principle. The structure is therefore excluded by this principle as well.

To the extent that our investigation of this particular case of raising is representative of the general case, (57a) cannot exist. That is, it follows without stipulation that chain links exhibit binding.

Although we have now derived that links exhibit binding, we have not examined the nature of this binding relation. There are three cases to examine, namely, (57b)–(57d). Consider first (57b), "the trace and the argument bind each other." Of course, to construct such an example, we need two A-positions in a relation of symmetric c-command or m-command. The only possible example of this is

(66) $[_{N''} \text{Romes}_i [_{N'} \text{destruction } t_i]]$

This is a case of (57b) to the extent that the argument binds (under c-command) the trace, while the trace binds (under m-command) the argument. Of course, this case is well formed. The only other *possible* case of such symmetric binding between an argument and trace is the following:

(67) $[_{N''} t_i [_{N'} \text{destruction}_i \text{ the barbarians}_i]]$

This, however, is not a case of (57b). The head does not bind the trace (i.e., the ECP is violated). Further, the Theta Criterion is violated, since the N" "the barbarians" was moved into a theta-position. We conclude that, to the extent that (57b) exists, structures like (66) are the only instantiations of it. That is, it follows from independent principles that (57b), if extant, is well formed.

Consider next (57c), "The trace binds the argument, but not conversely." An example of this is the following, in which an argument is "lowered" from its D-structure position[8];

(68) $[_{S'} [_S \text{I want}[_S \text{it to be told}_i t_i [_{S'} [_S \text{PRO}_i \text{ to seem } [_{S'} \text{that Bill left}]]]]]]]$

By first moving the argument PRO into Specifier of V", Spec–head indexing produces an index on the verb "told." The verb properly governs the trace in conformity with the ECP. Further, (49) is satisfied (i.e., since the verb binds t, it must bind PRO), and it does. Notice, the Theta Criterion is satisfied to the extent that the chain = [*t*, "PRO"] consists of one and only one argument as well as one and only one theta position. Further, Recoverability is satisfied in that movement was strictly to a thetaless position. In addition, movement was a "last resort" (i.e., without movement, a governed PRO would appear). One might argue that the example is excluded by the Visibility Principle of Chomsky (1981), since the chain is headed by neither PRO nor a Case-marked category. Although this principle would indeed exclude the example, we present extensive evidence against it in the following chapter, including evidence that there are well-formed A-chains headed by neither PRO nor a Case-marked category. Next, we might assume that the structure is excluded because the trace must be bound and isn't (it is an independent question as to what principle [or principles] enforce the requirement that trace be bound). However, in the following modification of the example, the trace is bound, yet grammaticality is not improved:

(69) $[_{S'} [_S \text{I}_i \text{ want}[_S \text{it to be told}_i t_i [_{S'} [_S \text{PRO}_i \text{ to seem } [_{S'} \text{that Bill left}]]]]]]$

If an even stronger binding requirement were imposed on the trace, namely, Condition A of the Binding theory, this structure would then be excluded; the trace is not bound in its governing category. The example is interesting in this regard in that it demonstrates that satisfaction of both the ECP and (49) does not entail satisfaction of Condition A. This is worth examining further. As is clear from (56), the ECP demands that a trace be bound by a head and that there exists no NP or S' dominating the trace that fails to dominate the binding head. Further, under (49), if an NP-trace is bound by a head, as it must be under the ECP, the head must bind the category with which the trace forms a link. Thus, the ECP and Condition (49) appear to come very close to enforcing satisfaction of Condition A for NP-trace. The fact that satisfaction of Condition A is not enforced by our particular formulation of the ECP (and (49)) can be seen as the direct result of the existence of intermediate-level application of Spec–head indexing (a rule ordering we proposed in the interest of eliminating lexical proper government). Under intermediate level Spec–head indexing, the category triggering indexing of the head need not occur in Spec at the derived level of representation. This is seen clearly in the example at hand, in which PRO moves to Specifier of V", triggering Spec–head indexing (i.e., indexing of "told"), but then is lowered. Consequently, the ECP can be satisfied, as can (49), yet Condition A is violated. This state of affairs thus seems to be one cost of eliminating lexical proper government by allowing intermediate-level application of Spec–head indexing. At any rate, appeal to Condition A would apparently exclude (69). But, in fact, a Condition A account is problematic. If expletives function only as "weak" Specified Subjects (see, e.g., Chomsky, 1986a), then, given also the distribution of Tense in (69), this example would be analyzed only as a "weak" violation of Condition A, akin to

(70) $[_{S'}[_S$ The men$_i$ want$[_S$ it to surprise each other$_i$
        $[_{S'}$ that it's a holiday]]]]

Thus, a Condition A account is suspect to the extent that the sentence represented in (69) seems substantially worse than the one represented in (70).

Next, notice that an account in terms of Subjacency is untenable, since movement occurred in conformity with this principle.

As yet another attempt to exclude this structure, we could assume the following condition on chain links (from Aoun, 1985):

(71) C is a chain iff . . . S' does not intervene between a_i and a_{i+1}

Under this principle, the trace and PRO in (69) could not form a chain link, since S' intervenes. Consequenetly, the Theta Criterion is violated. Notice that the following permutation of (69), in which S' does not intervene between the trace and the "lowered" argument, satisfies (71):

(72) *$[_{S'}[_S$ John$_i$ said $[_{S'}[_S$ it seems $[_S t_i$ to want
        $[_S$ ARG$_i$ to seem $[_{S'}$ that Bill left]]]]]]]]

We will now suggest that such a structure is independently excluded, since no argument can licitly occupy the position marked by ARG in this example. An R-expression, whether overt or empty, in the position of ARG would violate Condition C of the Binding theory. PRO would violate Condition B, as would a pure pronominal. The only argument type remaining is an overt anaphor, such as "each other." What precludes a category of this kind from occurring in the position of ARG in (72)? Notice that

the argument "each other" would be bound in conformity with
Condition A. Further, we know nothing precludes binding "each
other" with an NP-trace. This occurs in well-formed examples
such as the following:

(73) $[_{S'} [_S$ the men$_i$ seem $[_S t_i$ to like each other$_i$]]]

What, then, excludes (72) in the event that an overt anaphoric
argument (e.g., "each other") occurs in the position of ARG?
One possibility, which I will not pursue in detail here, is that such
structures are excluded, since they exhibit a kind of illicit "circularity." This is the result of the fact that the argument is the
"antececdent" of the trace (as is usually the case), whereas the
trace is, in turn, the "antecedent" of the argument (since it binds
the argument). I leave this approach open. Another possibility is
that if "each other" occupies the position of ARG in (72), the
Theta Criterion is violated. This result can be obtained from the
following proposal:

(74) The Theta Criterion–Projection Principle applies cyclically

Under (74), in deriving each syntactic level of representation
(D-structure, S-structure, and Logical Form) the Theta Criterion
is applied first to the most deeply embedded cyclic node (where
the class of cyclic nodes includes at least S and S'). If the most
deeply embedded cyclic node satisfies the Theta Criterion, the
next highest cyclic node is examined. If it satisfies the Theta Criterion, the procedure is iterated until finally the matrix S' (i.e.,
the entire structure) is checked for conformity with the Theta Criterion. If, at any point, the Theta Criterion is violated, the structure is excluded. Notice that cyclic application excludes any
structure excluded by noncyclic application. Under the latter ordering, the Theta Criterion is applied to the entire structure. This
also occurs (on the last cycle) under the former ordering. Thus,
cyclic application is at least as restrictive as noncyclic application. Consider now the structure in question:

(75) $[_{S'} [_{S_1}$ They$_i$ said$[_{S'} [_{S_2}$ it seems$_i [_{S_3} t_i$ to want
        $[_{S_4}$ each other$_i$ to seem $[_{S'}$ that Bill left]]]]]]]]

Cyclic application of the Theta Criterion excludes this example,
as desired. On the S_4 cycle, the Theta Criterion is violated; the
argument "each other" cannot be a singleton chain, since it does

not occupy a theta position, nor can it form a well-formed chain with any other category within S_4, since no nonargument occurs in this domain. Crucially, notice now that cyclic application of the Theta Criterion presumably excludes all instances of (57c) (= the NP-trace binds the argument). Consequently, we no longer need to appeal to (71) (= S' breaks a chain) to exclude examples of (57c) such as (69). This is a welcome result, since (71) is an independent, chain-specific condition, precisely the type of for- mal object we seek to eliminate here.

We have now suggested that cyclic application of the Theta Cri- terion excluded the examples at issue. We have also noted that cyclic application is at least as restrictive as noncyclic applica- tion. But is it overly restrictive? As concerns nonmovement cases, cyclic and noncyclic application are equivalent. So con- sider cases of A' and A movement:

(76) $[_{s'}\text{who}_i[_s e_i \text{left}]]$

(77) $[_{s'} [_s \text{John}_i \text{seems} [e_i \text{to go}]]]$

Before examining these structures, let us be a little more explicit about the organization of grammar we assume. We propose the following:

(78) a. D-structure

    b. Apply Theta Criterion cyclically

    c. Affect-alpha

    d. Freely assign the features $[\pm a, \pm p]$ to empty categories (Brody, 1984)

    e. Apply Theta Criterion cyclically

    f. S-structure

    g. Affect-alpha

    h. Freely assign the features $[\pm a, \pm p]$ to any empty categories not present at S-structure

    i. Apply Theta Criterion cyclically

    j. LF

As concerns (78h), notice that *reassignment* of features at LF to a category that was assigned features at S-structure, entails dele- tion of features, an operation that we have proposed is proscribed under principle (50) of Chapter 2. (Recall that this was assumed so as to prevent gamma-changing in LF.) We assume that (78d) and (78e) may be freely ordered with respect to each other and that the same is true for (78h) and (78i).

With this organization in mind, consider now syntactic application of the Theta Criterion on the S-cycle of (76).

(79) [$_s$ *e* left]

Given that (78d) and (78e) are freely ordered, the Theta Criterion might apply to this S before assignment of features to *e*. If so, since *e* is devoid of features, the Theta Criterion is violated (i.e., a category devoid of features cannot be an argument). If *e* is assigned [$+a$, $-p$], again, the Theta Criterion is violated. If *e* is assigned [$+a$, $+p$], the Theta Criterion is satisfied, since PRO is an argument. However, the structure is ultimately excluded on later cycles by at least Binding theory. Finally, if *e* is assigned [$-a$, $-p$], the Theta Criterion and, ultimately, all other principles are satisfied. Thus, (76) is allowed only if *e* is a variable.

Consider now (77). Applying in the syntax, the Theta Criterion encounters the following on the S cycle:

(80) [$_s$ *e* to go]

If no features are present, the Theta Criterion is violated. If *e* is assigned [$+a$, $+p$]. the Theta Criterion is satisfied on this cycle, but the Binding theory and the Theta Criterion are ultimately violated on later cycles. If *e* is [$-a$, $-p$], the Theta Criterion is satisfied, but Condition C and the Theta Criterion are violated on subsequent cycles. Consider finally the assignment of [$+a$, $-p$] to *e*. If a [$+a$, $-p$] empty category is, by definition, a nonargument, then the Theta Criterion will exclude (80) yet again, since under this feature assignment, it contains a nonargument singleton-chain occupying a theta-position. Thus, we are apparently left with no way to generate (77), since no feature assignment results in satisfaction of the Theta Criterion applying (cyclically) to (80). As just noted, if a [$+a$, $-p$] empty category is, by definition, a nonargument, then *e* cannot bear these features in (80); the Theta Criterion, applying cyclically, excludes this. As a solution to this problem, suppose we abandon the assumption that a [$+a$, $-p$] empty category is a nonargument. Assume instead that such a category is freely taken to be either an argument or a nonargument. In fact, following McNulty (1984), let us adopt the optimal assumption that *any empty category* is freely taken to be an argument or a nonargument. Given this, consider the following substructure of (77) and the cyclic application of the Theta Criterion to it:

(81) $[_s e$ to go]
    $[+a, -p]$

Given that a $[+a, -p]$ empty category can be an argument, the Theta Criterion can now be satisfied on this cycle. But consider now the subsequent application of the Theta Criterion on the matrix cycle:

(82) $[_{s'} [_s \text{John}_i \text{ seems}[_s e_i \text{ to go}]]]]$
            $[+a, -p]$

How is this permitted by the Theta Criterion? We assume that this structure satisfies the Theta Criterion because ["John," *e*] is a well-formed chain. This, of course, entails that *e,* on this matrix cycle, is now taken to be a nonargument, whereas, on the lower S-cycle, it was taken to be an argument. But given that an empty category is freely taken to be an argument or a nonargument, the optimal assumption, this is allowed. Hence, the derivation is permitted, precisely the result we desire. (Notice that the status of *e* 'changed' from nonargument to argument. Since we have proposed that features cannot change (i.e., cannot be deleted) we conclude that there is no *feature* [± argument] (see McNulty [1984] for further discussion of the notion "argument"). Thus, under cyclic application of the Theta Criterion, well-formed cases of NP-movement are permitted, but the unwanted cases, like (57c), are excluded. This concludes our attempt to show that case (57c) is independently excluded. In summary, we have seen that Condition A may play some part in excluding such structures, but the kind of violation occurring in (69), for example, does not appear to be strong enough to provide an adequate account. We have also speculated that some form of a ban on "circularity" may exclude such structures, but we have left the details of this approach open. Finally, we have proposed that cyclic application of the Theta Criterion interacting with a maximally free theory of empty categories may provide a general account of the ill-formedness of case (57c).

We have now discussed (57a)–(57c). We have shown that (57a) (the case in which an argument and a trace form a link of an A-chain but neither binds the other) cannot exist. Hence, it is derivable that chain links are in some relation of binding (i.e., a binding requirement on links need not be stipulated). We then suggested that, to the extent that case (57b) exists, independent principles allow only well-formed instantiations of it. With regard to (57c), in which the trace asymmetrically binds the argument, we have just argued that this case is also independently excluded. This leaves only (57d), the case in which the argument asymmetrically binds the trace. Of course, this is characteristic of a well-formed A-chain. Thus, without appealing to any stipulation that there must be a binding relation between members of a chain link, it appears that independent principles ensure not only that there is such a binding relation but that the argument binds the trace. Since the binding relation between members of a link follows, we can now eliminate the stipulated binding requirement on links from the statement of the Local Binding Condition (i.e., (48) is now eliminable). Thus, the Local Binding Condition can be simplified as follows:

(83) The Chain Link Condition:
$C = (a_1, \ldots a_n)$ is a chain only if
a. a_i is an NP, and
b. a_i occupies an A-position, and
c. If some category C binds a_{i+1}, then C binds a_i

We have renamed the Local Binding Condition, since in its original form it states that "a_1 must locally A-bind a_{i+1}," which, of course, entails the stipulation that "a_i must bind a_{i+1}." As argued earlier, this latter requirement on links need not be stated.

Before concluding this section we should like to simplify this condition further. Consider the requirement (83b), dictating that each member of an A-chain must occupy an A-position. Recall that this condition was needed to exclude super-raising structures such as the following:

(84) $[_{S'}[_S \text{John}_i \text{ seems } [_{S'} \text{that}[_S \text{it is considered}_i[_S t_i \text{ intelligent}]]]]]$

If a chain consisting of ["John$_i$", "considered$_i$", t_i] were allowed, no violation of the Local Binding Condition (i.e., (83c)) would occur and the structure would be wrongly allowed. Under the stipulation (83b), "considered" cannot be part of an A-chain, since it does not occupy an A-position. Hence, (83c) is necessarily violated. But suppose now that we eliminate the stipulation (83b). What would prevent including "considered" in the chain? Following Chomsky (1986a), let us assume that an A-chain is the abstract representation of an argument. Given this conception, suppose, under the elimination of (83b), that the verb "considered" is freely incorporated into the A-chain (i.e., suppose the structure (84) contains the A-chain ["John$_i$", "considered$_i$", t_i]. This chain satisfies (83c). But if a *chain is the abstract representation of an argument* (in this case "John"), it now follows that *"considered" is "part of" the representation* (albeit abstract) *of an argument*. Given that an argument has no status apart from its representation, we can conclude that *"considered" is "part of" the argument*. It now seems natural to assume that if X is "part of" an argument, X cannot, for example, assign Case or assign a theta-role. Thus, if "considered" is part of the A-chain, then, by definition, it cannot assign a theta-role to its S complement. That is, the structure is excluded by the Theta Criterion. If this line of argument is correct, we can now eliminate condition (83b) from (83). Hence, the latter can be further simplified as follows:

(85) The Chain Link Condition:
      $C = (a_1, \ldots a_n)$ is a chain only if

    a. a_i is an NP, and

    b. If some category C binds a_{i+1}, then C binds a_i

In the following chapter we shall argue that the stipulation (85a) is eliminable (see also Sportiche, 1983, Chapter 2, n. 1). Given this, the condition with which we began is reduced to the following single requirement:

(86) The Chain Link Condition:
      $C = (a_1, \ldots, a_n)$ is a chain only if

    a. If some category C binds a_{i+1}, then C binds a_i

The reduction of this condition awaits further research.

In the following chapter, we examine Case requirements on NP-trace and wh-trace. To the extent that such categories are members of chains, this investigation can be seen as an extension of the current chapter.

Notes

1. The categorial status of "small clauses," such as $[t_i$ intelligent] in (5), is controversial. We assume that the clause is sentential, whereas Chomsky (1986b) proposes that it is an AP. The categorial status of such clauses is of no direct concern to the present, or ensuing, discussion.

2. For discussion of Condition C see, for example, Freidin and Lasnik (1981). For different attempts to eliminate this principle see Higginbotham (1980, 1981), Koopman and Sportiche (1982), and Chomsky (1982).

3. Notice that if t is an anaphor, Principle A of the Binding theory is violated. However, this analysis alone is inadequate. The violation of Principle A is only a weak one, since expletives such as "it" function only as weak *subjects*. Thus, under a Principle A analysis, (9e) would be analyzed as only a weak violation. For further discussion of this aspect of Binding and the relation between ECP and Principle A, see Chomsky (1986a, 1986b) and later.

4. We assume that "it" is inserted, an instance of Affect-alpha subject to the Strict Cycle. Another possibility is that expletive "it" (like "that") is the spell-out of certain syntactic features, an operation not constrained by the Strict Cycle. We leave this option open. Notice, however, that if "it" is a spell-out, then the derivation under discussion would still be allowed, and it is the generation of such wh-movement that we wish to examine here.

5. If indices cannot be deleted, as was argued earlier, and variable-bound interpretation of pronominals requires coindexation with an operator, then, within the framework proposed here, variable-bound interpretation of pronouns must always arise from Operator–pronoun coindexation at D-structure. This is to be contrasted with the indexing assumed in the analysis of pronominal variable binding provided in Higginbotham (1980) incorporating a reindexing rule, entailing the deletion of indices, which is prohibited on our assumptions. For the possibility of a filter-based analysis of such phenomena, rendering the reindexing rule unnecessary, see Epstein (1983).

6. Under Functional Determination, the subject trace in the following example is, by definition, a variable, since it is locally A′-bound:

(i) $[_{S'}$ who$_i$ $[_S$ does he$_i$ think $[_{S'}$ t_i $[_S$ t_i left]]]]

Consequently, under the functional account of strong crossover (eliminating Condition C, as applied to empty categories), this type of structure is over-generated. (See Koopman and Sportiche, 1982, for possible solutions to this problem. See also Epstein, 1984, for other problems facing the functional account of Strong Crossover.)

7. See also Barss (1986, Chap. 4) for discussion of super-raising and the Local Binding Condition.

8. We are using PRO here for the purpose of avoiding Case-marking requirements on chains imposed in other examples.

4

Case Requirements on Traces

The Case Requirement on Wh-Trace

There is a Case requirement on wh-trace that is apparently independent of all other principles. Consider the following S-structures:

(1) *[$_{S'}$ Who$_i$ [$_S$ did John try [$_{S'}$ t'_i [$_S$ t_i to go]]]]

(2) *[$_{S'}$ Who$_i$ [$_S$ did it seem [$_S$ t_i to go]]]

The central observation concerning such ill-formed examples has been that wh-movement originates from a position that is not Case-marked. Given this, structures such as (1) and (2) could be readily excluded by somehow formally expressing the following observation:[1]

(3) Wh-trace must be Case-marked

Within recent analyses there have been two general approaches to capturing (3): the Case-filter approach and the Visibility Condition. We shall now briefly review these two accounts, arguing that each is problematic. Following this, we offer a new approach to the problem of formally expressing the generalization (3).

The Case Filter Approach

Freidin and Lasnik (1981) propose the following filter:

(4) *NP Filter:
    *NP, where NP is lexical or the trace of wh and has no Case

The filter excludes (1) and (2). In each, both the wh-phrase and the wh-trace have no Case. Given that each example violates both disjuncts of filter (4), it might be supposed that the requirement that wh-trace have Case (enforced by (4)) could be eliminated. One could claim that (3) is simply false and it might be assumed instead that examples such as (1) and (2) are ill formed only because the lexical *wh-phrase* "who" fails to bear Case. Under this line of argument, filter (4) could be simplified as follows:

(5) *NP Filter: *NP where NP is lexical and has no Case

(1) and (2) would then be ruled out by (5), because the lexical NP "who" fails to bear Case. The status of the wh-trace would then be irrelevant. This approach is, in fact, inadequate. As Lasnik and Freidin (1981) note, examples such as the following are ungrammatical, just like (1) and (2), yet neither contains a Caseless lexical NP.

(6) *I like the man $[_{S'} [_S$ John tried $[_{S'} t_i [_S t_i$ to go]]]
(7) *I like the man $[_{S'} [_S$ it seems $[_S t_i$ to go]]]

The ungrammaticality of examples like (6) and (7), each of which contains no overt (i.e., lexical) Operator, thus indicates that filter (5) is insufficient; the requirement that wh-trace have Case is not derivable from the requirement that lexical NPs have Case. Clearly, the converse also holds (i.e., the requirement that lexical NPs have Case is not derivable from the requirement that wh-trace have Case). Hence, Lasnik and Freidin propose filter (4). The filter is, however, problematic. Although each of the two disjuncts of the filter appears empirically motivated, the filter (4) is, on conceptual grounds, odd in that it imposes a disjunctive requirement on an arguably unnatural class of categories, namely, lexical N"s and wh-traces. Further, since the Case filter requires that wh-trace be Case marked, it cannot be interpreted as imposing a purely morphological requirement. It is this unnaturalness that constitutes the primary motivation for Chomsky's (1981) attempt to eliminate the Case filter.

The Visibility Principle

Chomsky (1981) proposes the following principle governing the assignment of theta roles to chains:

(8) The Visibility Principle: Suppose that the position P is marked with the theta role R and C = $(a_1, \ldots, a_n)$ is a chain. Then C is assigned R by P if and only if for some i, a_i is in position P and C has Case or is headed by PRO

where "C has Case" is defined as

(9) The chain C = $(a_1, \ldots, a_n)$ has the Case K if and only if for some i, a_i occupies a position assigned K by b

The Theta Criterion is formulated as follows:

(10) The Theta Criterion: Given the structure S, there is a set K of chains, K = $\{C_i\}$, where $C_i = (a^i_1, \ldots, a^i_n)$ such that:
   (i) if a is an argument of S, then there is a C_i that is a member of K such that $a = a^i_j$ and a theta role is assigned to C_i by exactly one position P.
   (ii) if P is a position of S marked with the theta role R, then there is a C_i that is a member of K to which P assigns R, and exactly one a^i_j in C_i is an argument.

Under (8), a well-formed chain must either be headed by PRO or contain a Case-marked position. Chomsky (1981) suggests that the Case filter is eliminable under these principles. Although he was assuming a chain-based formulation of the Case filter, slightly different from (4), we can nonetheless employ his arguments in eliminating the formulation of the Case filter provided in (4). Consider first the second disjunct, "*NP, where NP is the trace of wh and has no Case." As Chomsky notes, this aspect of the filter is eliminable under (8) and (10). As an illustration of how these principles enforce the requirement that wh-trace bear Case, consider again examples (1) and (2). These structures are ruled out as follows. The wh-trace is an argument. The Theta Criterion thus requires that it be the single member of a chain that is assigned a theta role, by the theta position the wh-trace occupies. Under the Visibility Principle, the chain of which the wh-trace is the sole member, is assigned a theta role only if the chain is headed by PRO or has Case. Since the chain is not headed by PRO, it now follows that the chain is assigned a theta role only if some member of the chain has Case. Given that the wh-trace is the only member of the chain, the chain is assigned a theta role only if the wh-trace has Case. Since the wh-trace is Caseless, the chain is not assigned a theta role. Consequently, the Theta Criterion is violated, the wh-trace is not a member of a theta-assigned chain. Thus, under the Visibility approach, the Case filter, as applied to wh-trace, appears to be eliminable (i.e., the fact that wh-traces require Case is now expressed by the Visibility Principle applying in conjunction with the Theta Criterion). Chomsky suggests that the remainder of the Case filter, that is, the requirement that lexical NP have Case, is also derivable from the Visibility Principle. With regard to lexical argument NPs, this can be illustrated by considering, for example:

(11) *$[_{s'} [_s$ I tried $[_{s'} [_s$ John to go]]]]

The N″ "John" (like the wh-trace in (2)) is an argument that must be a single member of a chain. This chain must be assigned a theta role by the theta position "John" occupies. Since it is not headed by PRO, a theta role is assigned to the chain only if the chain has Case. Given that "John" is Caseless, the chain has no Case. Consequently, the chain is assigned no theta role and the Theta Criterion is violated. Consider next nonargument lexical NPs such as "there" and "it." How does the Visibility Principle, a principle governing theta assignment to argument chains, require that these nonarguments bear Case? Consider, for example:

(12) I want there to be a man outside

(13) *I tried there to be a man outside

At first glance it would appear that the Visibility Principle is incapable of enforcing the requirement that expletives bear Case. Since expletives, by definition, are not theta marked, the Visibility Principle (i.e., the requirement that Case is prerequisite to theta marking) seems inapplicable to such nonarguments. Thus, it would appear that examples such as (13) are incorrectly allowed by the Visibility Principle. In fact, the Visibility Principle has been argued to exclude examples such as (13) containing a Caseless expletive (see Chomsky, 1986a, p. 93; and Chomsky, 1981, p. 336, for discussion). The argument is as follows. Consider first example (12). With respect to such structures it is assumed that the argument N″ "a man" occupies a Caseless position. Now if this argument were a singleton chain (like the wh-trace in (1) or the N″ "John" in (11)), (12) would be excluded by the Theta Criterion. The chain containing only the N″ "a man" has no Case (nor is it headed by PRO), thereby precluding theta assignment to the chain. Thus, to allow (12) under the Visibility Principle, "a man" cannot be a singleton chain. Rather, this N″ must form a chain with some other category displaying two properties. First, this other category must have Case so that the chain containing "a man" will be visible for theta assignment. Second, this other category must be a nonargument, since the Theta Criterion allows but one argument per chain. The expletive "there" meets both requirements. In (12), then, ["there," "a man"] is assumed to constitute a chain. This chain is visible for theta assignment precisely because the expletive "there" occupies a Case-marked position. Consider now the ungrammatical (13). In this example, the expletive "there" is Caseless. Consequently, the chain ["there," "a man"] has no Case. Therefore, under the Visibility Principle, it is not assigned a theta role and the Theta Criterion is violated. Thus, (12) is allowed by Visibility only because "there" has Case, rendering the chain ["there," "a man"] visible for theta assignment. By contrast, (13) is excluded precisely because the expletive lacks Case, making the chain invisible for theta assignment. In this way, the Visibility Principle appears to enforce the requirement that the expletive "there" must bear Case.

A similar requirement is imposed on expletives such as "it." Consider, for example:

(14) I want it to be likely [that John will leave]

(15) *I tried it to be likely [that John will leave]

In (14) the clausal complement to "likely" is an argument in a Caseless position; the adjective "likely" is not a Case assigner. Therefore, under Visibility, the clause cannot be a singleton chain. However, the Visibility Principle can be satisfied, provided the clausal complement and the Case-marked expletive "it" form a chain; the chain then has Case and is therefore visible for theta-role assignment. By contrast, in (15), the expletive is Caseless, with the result that a chain consisting of this category and the clausal complement is invisible for theta assignment. The Theta Criterion is consequently violated. Thus, the Visibility Principle appears to require that nonargument "it" have Case, much in the same way that it enforces the requirement that nonargument "there" have Case.

Summarizing to this point, we have seen that the Case filter (4) displays an unnatural disjunct, requiring that both lexical NP and wh-trace have Case. This filter is arguably eliminable under the Visibility Principle (see Chomsky, 1981, 1986a). However, in the next section a number of problems confronting the Visibility Principle will be reviewed.

Some Problems with Visibility

D-STRUCTURE APPLICATION

As has been noted, one potential conceptual problem confronting the Visibility Principle concerns D-structure application. Clearly, there are well-formed D-structures containing Caseless arguments, more precisely, containing chains of length 1, which do not have Case. The D-structure underlying "passive" and "raising" are examples. Application of the Visibility Principle at this level would therefore incorrectly filter such D-structures. Thus, the Visibility Principle, a principle governing theta assignment, must not apply at D-structure, a level of representation characterized as a pure representation of theta structure. This is an arguably odd, yet necessary, aspect of the Visibility analysis.

FORMAL STATEMENT OF THE VISIBILITY PRINCIPLE

Earlier, we provided a sketch of how the Case filter is argued to be eliminable under the Visibility Principle. In the next subsection, empirical problems encountered by the Visibility Principle will be discussed. But before examining the predictive adequacy of the Visibility Principle, we should note two general properties of the previously discussed reduction of the Case filter to the Visibility Principle. First, as Chomsky (1981, p. 337) notes, the Case filter has not been reduced to independently motivated principles of grammar. Rather, the Case filter is eliminated by incorporating Visibility, a similarly Case-theoretic principle. Second, recall that the elimination of the Case filter is a desirable result in that it appears, in certain respects, to be an unnatural principle of grammar, incorporating an unappealing disjunctive requirement. However, the elimination of the Case filter is not cost-free; the price is the Visibility Principle, and it is important to notice that this principle also displays a rather unnatural disjunct, namely, the requirement that a chain "has Case or is headed by PRO."

Beyond the conceptual problems noted earlier, the Visibility Principle encounters a number of empirical problems. Consider again the requirement that expletives such as "there" must be Case-marked. As noted earlier, this requirement is argued to be derivable from the Visibility Principle by assuming that the postcopular NP in, for example, (12) is in a Caseless position and is thereby "forced" into a chain with "there," a category that must have Case for theta assignment to occur in conformity with Visibility. With this analysis in mind, consider the following data due to Lasnik (1989):

(16) I want there to be a man outside

(17) *I want there to be usually a man outside

As Lasnik notes, under the Visibility analysis, there is no explanation for the ungrammaticality of (17). The N″ "a man" is an argument in a Caseless position, but since "there" occupies a Case-marked position, the chain ["there," "a man"] is visible for theta assignment in (17) (just as a chain consisting of the same two categories is visible in (16)). Thus, the Visibility Principle incorrectly fails to distinguish the ill formed (17) from the well formed (16). How can they be distinguished? Following Lasnik (1989), assume, contrary to the Visibility analysis, that "be" assigns Case to "a man" in (16). Under this analysis, the ungrammaticality of (17) is readily explained. English observes a strict adjacency condition on Case assignment, under which a Case-assigner and the category to which it assigns Case must be adjacent (see Stowell, 1981). In (17), "be" is not adjacent to "a man." The Case filter (4), unlike the Visibility Principle, excludes this structure because the lexical N″ "a man" is Caseless. Thus, given that "be" is a Case assigner, the distinction between (16) and (17) can be accounted for by the Case filter.[2] As we have seen, no such distinction is expressible within the Visibility approach. Now, given that "be" assigns Case to an adjacent N″, consider again the following:

(13) *I tried there to be a man outside

In (13), "a man" is assigned Case by "be." If "a man" is a singleton chain, an available option, Visibility is satisfied (i.e., the chain has Case and is therefore theta assigned in conformity with the Theta Criterion). The status of the nonargument "there" is irrelevant to Visibility. Incorrectly, (13) is allowed. By contrast, the Case filter (4) correctly excludes (13), since the lexical N″ "there" is Caseless. As Lasnik shows, this inadequacy of the Visibility Principle is similarly demonstrated by examples of the following type:

(18) I consider there to be a solution

(19) *I consider there a solution

Again, under the Visibility approach, this contrast is inexplicable. In particular, the chain ["there," "a solution"] is, in both examples, visible for theta assignment, since, in each, "there" occupies a Case-marked position. The contrast is, however, explained by appeal to the Case filter. In (18) each lexical NP is Case marked, whereas in (19), the lexical N″ "a solution" is not Case assigned and thereby violates this filter. Lasnik provides further evidence. Consider

(20) There arrived a man

(21) *There arrived quickly a man

Once again, Visibility fails to provide an account of the distinction. A chain consisting of ["there," "a man"] is equally visible in the two examples. However, if it is assumed that like the copula in Existentials, the impersonal predicate "arrived" is a Case assigner, as Belletti (1986) argues, then the Case filter predicts just such a contrast.

Pollock (1981) presents evidence of a different kind, indicating that in French, corresponding impersonal constructions also involve direct Case assignment to the postverbal N″ by the verb. Pollock (1981) notes the following contrast in grammaticality between stylistic inversion sentences such as (22) and impersonal sentences such as (23) (see also Davis [1984] for discussion):

(22) De quoi t_i ont été contents [tes amis]$_i$
      "Of what have been happy your friends"

(23) *De quoi est-il, contents [trois de tes amis],
    "Of what is (il) happy three of your friends"

In (22), the case of stylistic inversion, the lexical N″ "tes amis" can "inherit" Case from its trace. By contrast, in the ungrammatical impersonal construction, the postadjectival N″ apparently cannot inherit Case from the expletive and thereby violates the Case filter. Given that such inheritance is precluded, the well-formedness of the following example indicates that the impersonal verb assigns Case directly to the postverbal N″ (for further discussion and analysis, see Pollock, 1981, and Davis, 1984).

(24) A la vision de quel spectacle s'est-il
    "At the sight of what show was ("il")
    enthousiasmé [trois de tes amis]
    enthused   three of your friends"

For present purposes, what is important is that, once again, the Visibility approach appears inadequate. It would presumably allow (23) by virtue of the fact that the chain ["il," "trois de tes amis"] contains a Case-marked member, namely "il," and is therefore visible for theta assignment. By contrast, the Case filter correctly excludes (23), since the postadjectival N″ "trois de tes amis" is not Case marked.

Davis (1986, n. 5) raises additional problems the Visibility approach encounters in attempting to enforce the Case requirement on lexical nonarguments. Consider

(25) *$[_{N''}$ my desire$[_{S'}$ $[_S$ it to be raining]]]
(26) Es wurde getanzt
    "There was danced"

In (25), there is no argument present (i.e., there is no argument "associated with" weather "it"). Consequently, there is no theta assignment, with the result that Visibility is inapplicable. Hence, Case marking of "it" is wrongly predicted to be unnecessary. As Davis notes, the problem might be avoided by appealing to the "quasi-argument" status of weather "it" as advocated by Chomsky (1981, p. 325). However, as Davis observes, examples like (26) remain problematic for the Visibility approach, since there is absolutely no theta assignment in such structures. Of course, such examples are readily handled by the Case filter.

The Visibility approach encounters other problems as well. Consider again examples like the following:

(14) I want it to be likely that John will leave

(15) *I tried it to be likely that John will leave

Recall that, under Visibility, the expletive "it" must have Case, so that the chain consisting of "it" and the Caseless argument S′ is visible for theta assignment. But as Chomsky (1981) notes, examples of the following kind pose a problem for this analysis.

(27) We are proud [$_{S'}$ that Bill is intelligent]

(28) My belief [$_{S'}$ that Bill is intelligent]

These examples are well formed, yet the argument S′ in each occupies a Caseless position and, in addition, cannot form a chain with a Case-marked expletive, since no such category is present. Visibility thus predicts that the examples are ill formed, because the argument S′, a singleton chain, is not visible for theta assignment. One solution to this problem, suggested by Chomsky (1981, p. 338) is to stipulate that a chain head is, by definition, an N″. Under this stipulation, the S′s in (27) and (28) are not chains; hence, Visibility is inapplicable. However, as Chomsky notes, this approach is stipulative. But in addition to being ad hoc, it is important to note that this stipulation that a chain-head must be an N″ is empirically adequate precisely because it mimics the Case filter in this respect (i.e., under this stipulation, Visibility, in effect, requires only that N″s not S′s, be Case marked). The need for this particular stipulation thus provides yet another argument in favor of the Case filter.

In the absence of stipulating that a chain head must be an N″, examples such as (27) and (28) can be made compatible with Visibility if it is assumed, following Chomsky (1986a), that adjectives and nouns assign Case. As Davis (1986) notes, under this assumption, the argument S′s in these examples can be singleton chains, since they are Case marked (by the adjective in (27) and the noun in (28)). Hence, each is visible for theta marking. The assumption that adjectives are Case assigners is also necessary to permit the following type of example (see Davis, 1986):

(29) $[_{S'} [_S \text{John}_i \text{ is likely } [_S t_i \text{ to leave}]]]$

If the adjective "likely" were not a Case assigner, the complement S, an argument, would not be visible for theta assignment, since it occupies a Caseless position. As in (27), (29) contains no Case-marked nonargument with which the postadjectival argument could form a visible chain. Thus, the assumption that adjectives are Case assigners appears to provide a way of rendering the postadjectival arguments visible for theta assignment. However, Davis (1986) notes a number of problems facing this proposal, which we will now briefly review. First, consider the following:

(30) We are $[_{A''} \text{happy } [_{S'} \text{that you won the race}]]$

(31) *We are $[_{A''} \text{happy (of) } [_{N''} \text{your success}]]$

If the adjective "happy" assigns Case to the S′ argument in (30), then it should assign Case to the N″ argument in (31). To rule out (31), then, it appears that "happy" must be analyzed as a category that is not subcategorized by an N″ complement. But, as Davis notes, this requires that subcategorization is a primitive (i.e., an irreducible property of lexical entries that is not derivable from Case and theta theory (see Stowell, 1981).

Davis notes a second problem with the assumption that adjectives assign Case. If, in (29), "likely" assigns Case to the S complement, then examples of the following form should be allowed:

(32) *It is likely Fred to be here

The adjective "likely" must be an S′ deleter if antecedent government of the trace is to obtain in (29). But if "likely" deletes S′ and is also a Case assigner, then, in these respects, "likely" is indistinguishable from "believe" (i.e., it is an Exceptional Case Marking predicate) and, as a result, (32) is wrongly predicted to be well formed.

As Davis notes, under Visibility, not only must adjectives and nouns be assumed to be Case assigners, but raising verbs such as "seem" must also be assumed to assign Case. This is necessary to allow, for example:

(33) $[_{S'} \text{They}_i \text{ seem } [_S t_i \text{ to be intelligent}]]$

But again this assumption similarly results in the incorrect analysis of "seem" as an Exceptional Case Marking predicate, permitting an infinitival complement containing a lexical subject.

A separate problem noted by Davis concerns passive participles. Consider

(34) [$_{S'}$ They$_i$ are believed [$_S$ t_i to be intelligent]]

Since there is no Case-marked nonargument with which the complement S can form a chain, it must be assumed that this category is Case marked by "believed." But affixation of the "-en" morpheme is supposed to result in the loss of the Case-assigning feature of the base verb. Under the assumption that "believed" is a Case assigner, the ungrammaticality of the following remains to be explained (see Davis [1986] for further discussion):

(35) *It was believed [$_{N''}$ that rumor]

Finally, Davis argues that if raising predicates can assign Case to their complements, then there is no longer any Case requirement on the expletive category occurring in these constructions. That is, structures of the following form are incorrectly predicted to be grammatical:

(36) *It seems it to be likely [$_{S'}$ that John will leave]

Once again, the Case filter derives the correct prediction and the Visibility Principle does not.

In this section we have reviewed a number of conceptual and empirical problems confronting the Visibility Principle. As we have seen, each empirical problem encountered by Visibility is readily handled by the Case filter (4). However, as noted earlier, adoption of the Case filter (4) is problematic to the extent that this filter expresses the requirement that lexical N''s and wh-traces, an unnatural class of categories, must have Case. Recall, it was this property of the Case filter that warranted its elimination and thereby led to the postulation of the Visibility Principle. But if this unnaturalness could somehow be eliminated from the Case filter, we would then have a principled account of the phenomona discussed in the previous section, phenomona that the Visibility Principle cannot explain.

Simplification of the Case Filter

Both disjuncts of the Case filter (4) appeared to be motivated by data such as

(37) *I tried John to go

(38) *Who did you try to go

(39) *The man you tried to go

As noted earlier, the requirement that wh-trace have Case is not reducible to the requirement that lexical N″ have Case; this is demonstrated by examples like (39) (from Freidin and Lasnik, 1981). Thus, it appears that the Case filter must require that lexical N″ have Case while also requiring that wh-trace have Case. However, there is evidence that the requirement imposed on wh-trace by the Case filter is overly restrictive. Equivalently, there is evidence that the descriptive generalization (3) (= wh-trace must be Case marked) is false. Recall that in English, Case assignment obeys a strict adjacency condition. Thus, for example, consider the following contrast:

(40) John believes Bill to be the best man

(41) *John believes sincerely Bill to be the best man

The S-structure representations are as follows:

(42) $[_{S'}[_S$John believes$[_S$ Bill to be the best man]]]

(43) *$[_{S'}[_S$ John believes sincerely $[_S$ Bill to be the best man]]]

In (42), the lexical N″ "Bill" is Case marked by the adjacent verb "believe." However, in (43), "believes" does not Case-mark "Bill," since these categories are not adjacent to one another. Consequently, the Case filter is violated. Now if it is true that wh-trace must be Case marked, just as a lexical N″ must be Case marked, then the following (from Chomsky and Lasnik, 1977) should be ungrammatical, just like (43) is

(44) Who does John believe sincerely to be the best man?

However, (44) is grammatical. Thus, as Chomsky and Lasnik (1977, p. 478) point out, lexical N″ and wh-trace behave differently in the following context (see also Chomsky, 1981, p. 281):

(45) VERB + ADUNCT [$_S$ wh-trace/*lexical N″ to VP]

The S-structure of (42) is

(46) [$_{S'}$ Who$_i$[$_S$ does John believe sincerely[$_S$ t_i to be the best man]]]

The structure is well formed yet the wh-trace is not Case-marked, a result of the fact that it is not adjacent to the Case marker "believe." Such structures provide direct evidence that the descriptive generalization (3) is wrong; that is, (46) indicates that

(47) Wh-trace need not be Case marked

Notice (47), as evidenced by (46), represents another problem for Visibility. Since this principle makes Case assignment a prerequisite to theta assignment, structures like (46) are wrongly excluded. Such structures similarly represent a problem for the Case filter (4), which requires that wh-trace by Case marked. So as to allow (46), suppose we abandon the Case filter (4) and replace it with the following formulation:

(5) *NP, where NP is lexical and has no Case

This formulation of the Case filter correctly allows (46) because it imposes no Case requirement on wh-trace. Crucially, notice that (5) not only correctly allows (46) (whereas (4) does not), but also eliminates the disjunct in the Case filter (4). Further, the Case filter (5) handles all the problems encountered by the Visibility Principle, as discussed earlier.

Although (5) is desirable in each of these respects, adopting this formulation of the Case filter leaves us with no explanation of the ill-formedness of the following structures:

(48) *[$_{S'}$ Who$_i$[$_S$ did John try [$_{S'}$ t_i[$_S$ t_i to go]]]]
(49) *[$_{S'}$ Who$_i$[$_S$ did it seem [$_S$ t_i to go]]]
(50) *[$_{S'}$[$_S$I like [$_{N''}$ the man[$_{S'}$[$_S$ John tried [$_{S'}$ t_i[$_S$ t_i to go]]]]]]]
(51) *[$_{S'}$[$_S$ I like [$_{N''}$ the man [$_{S'}$[$_S$ it seems [$_S$ t_i to go]]]]]]

Although (48) and (49) might be ruled out by (5) (since the lexical N″ "who" lacks Case), the Case filter (5) fails to exclude (50) and (51); in these structures each lexical N″ has Case.[3] We therefore propose the following principle, which uniformly excludes these structures while allowing (46):

(52) A variable must be governed by a Case assigner

Notice that (52) is only slightly weaker than the requirement that wh-trace be Case marked. But the distinction is crucial. Under this principle, well-formed examples like (46) are correctly allowed; no principle requires wh-trace to be Case marked, and (52), dictating only that wh-trace be governed by a Case assigner, is satisfied. More generally, (52) and the simplified Case filter (5) account for all the data discussed in this section.

In summary, examples such as (46) (noted in Chomsky and Lasnik, 1977), indicate that wh-trace need not be Case marked. The descriptive generalization that wh-trace requires Case is simply false. It was this generalization that motivated the disjunctive and therefore unnatural formulation of the Case filter (4) requiring both lexical N″ and wh-trace to be Case marked. To eliminate this unnaturalness, while still imposing similar requirements, Chomsky (1981) attempted to eliminate the Case filter by reducing it to the Visibility Principle. We have seen that this Principle encounters a number of conceptual and empirical problems that do not arise under the Case filter. The primary problem confronting the Case filter is thus the unnatural class to which it applies. But we have seen that this unnaturalness is ill motivated; wh-trace need not be Case marked. Achieving empirical adequacy therefore demands that we drop the requirement that wh-trace be Case marked. The Case filter can therefore be simplified so as to apply only to lexical N″. The unmotivated unnaturalness is thereby eliminated. Those structures thought to be violations resulting from the presence of Caseless wh-trace can then be excluded by imposing a weaker requirement on wh-trace, namely, that such categories be governed by a Case assigner. The resulting analysis displays no unnaturalness and it confronts none of the problems encountered by Visibility. In the following subsections some further consequences of the proposed analysis are examined.

Consequences

PREDICATE N″S

Before investigating some consequences of the requirement that a variable be governed by a Case assigner, one consequence of the Case filter (5) will be examined. Chomsky (1986a, p. 95) notes that any formulation of the Case filter that requires that lexical N″ be Case marked differs from the Visibility Principle in the following way: The Case filter requires that a predicate N″ be Case marked (if lexical), whereas Visibility imposes no such requirement on any predicate N″, since such categories are not theta marked. Consider the predicate N″ in, for example:

(53) John is [$_{N''}$ a fine mathematician]

Chomsky (1986a) suggests that the grammaticality of such examples argues in favor of Visibility and against the Case filter. The assumption is that the predicate N″, a lexical N″, is not in a Case-marked position. Hence, the Case filter wrongly predicts ungrammaticality, whereas the Visibility Principle yields the correct prediction here. But is the predicate N″ in a Caseless position? Consider the following examples:

(54) I want John to be [$_{N''}$ a good performer]

(55) *I want John to be often [$_{N''}$ a good performer]

Why is (55) ungrammatical? Assume, following Lasnik (1989), that the copula "be" is a Case assigner in such structures. In (54), then, "be" Case-marks the N″ "a good performer." By contrast, in (55) "be" does not Case-mark this N″; it cannot, because it is not adjacent to this category. Given that the predicate N″ in (55) is Caseless, Visibility wrongly allows the example; the predicate N″ need not have Case, since it is not theta marked. However, the Case filter yields the correct result. The predicate N″ is lexical and Caseless; therefore, the structure is excluded.

Thus, what was thought to be an argument for Visibility and against the Case filter may in fact be exactly the opposite. In the following section we discuss a number of consequences of the proposal that wh-trace need not be Case marked, but rather, must be governed by a Case assigner.

"WANNA" CONTRACTION

The phenomenon of "wanna" contraction has been studied extensively, and there is now a vast literature on this topic, which I will not review here. Rather, I would like to examine and attempt to resolve an apparent incompatibility between the requirement on wh-trace proposed here and one analysis of "wanna" contraction, namely, the analysis advocated in Pesetsky (1982). The following core data are now familiar:

(56) I wanna sleep

(57) Who do you wanna see

(58) *I wanna John sleep

(59) *Who do you wanna sleep

To account for such data, Jaeggli (1980) proposes an analysis under which contraction of "want" and "to" is blocked when a Case-marked category intervenes between these two categories. In the S-structure analyses of (56) and (57), prior to contraction, PRO appears between "want" and "to." Since PRO is Caseless, contraction is allowed. In both (58) and (59), a Case-marked category appears between "want" and "to," namely, "John" in (58) and wh-trace in (59). Consequently, contraction is blocked in these examples (see Jaeggli [1980] for further discussion). This analysis seems to be descriptively correct (i.e., Case-marked categories seem to block contraction whereas Caseless ones do not). However, Pesetsky (1982) argues that this is derivable without stipulation. Following Stowell (1981), Pesetsky assumes that the order of constituents follows in large part from principles governing Case assignment. Thus, in an infinitival S complement to "want," a lexical subject must be S-initial to receive Case from "want" (since Case assignment obeys an adjacency requirement [as discussed earlier]).

(60) $[_{S'}[_S$ I want$[_S$ John to sleep]]]

By contrast, in an infinitival S′ complement to "want," a PRO subject need not occur S-initially, since PRO need not be Case marked. Hence S-structures of the following type are generable:

(61) $[_{S'}[_S$ I want $[_{S'}[_S[_{V''}$ to sleep] PRO]]]]

As Pesetsky notes, given his analysis, it no longer has to be stipulated that Case-marked categories block contraction whereas Caseless categories do not. Rather, the contraction rule can be simplified so that it applies whenever "want" and "to" are adjacent.[4] Contraction is then correctly allowed in (61) (yielding (56)) and is prohibited in (60), correctly predicting the ungrammaticality of (58). We have now examined cases of PRO subjects and lexical subjects. Consider next, wh-trace. Pesetsky assumes that wh-trace must be Case marked. Therefore, S-structures of the following form are excluded:

(62) $[_{S'}\text{Who}_i [_S \text{do you want} [_S [_{V''} \text{to sleep}] t_i]]]$

This representation is excluded because t is not adjacent to "want" and is therefore Caseless, violating the assumed requirement that wh-trace bear Case. The exclusion of (62) is, of course, a correct result. Were it not excluded, contraction could apply ("want" and "to" are adjacent), thereby yielding the ungrammatical (59). But the exclusion of (62) clearly rests on the assumption that wh-trace must be Case marked, and we have rejected this assumption, arguing that wh-trace need not bear Case, but rather, must satisfy only the weaker requirement that it be governed by a Case assigner. We therefore confront a problem: The S-structure (62) meets this weaker requirement on wh-trace; hence, it is generable. Consequently, we wrongly predict that contraction is possible, since "want" and "to" are adjacent.

(63) S-structure/PF
$[_{S'} \text{Who}_i [_S \text{do you want} + \text{to} \rightarrow \text{wanna} [_S [_{V''} \text{sleep}] t_i]]]$

To exclude such structures, we propose that they violate the requirement that wh-trace be governed by a Case assigner. This requirement is violated under the assumption that cliticization of "to" to "want" results in the loss of the Case assigning feature of "want." That is,

(64) Verb + "to" (e.g., "wanna") is not a Case assigner

Notice that if this approach is correct, the adjacency requirement could be eliminated from the statement of the contraction rule (i.e., *I wanna John go* exhibits licit application of contraction, but the derived structure violates the Case filter, since the lexical N″ "John" is Caseless).

TRACES OF ADJUNCTS AND LOWERED QUANTIFIERS

Although we have proposed that wh-trace must be governed by a Case assigner, we have not been absolutely explicit as to the level(s) at which this constraint applies. Consider again examples of the types of sentences we have argued are excluded by this requirement:

(65) *The man you tried to sleep

(66) *Who do you wanna sleep

Clearly, application of the constraint at S-structure would be sufficient to account for (65). Whether S-structure application is sufficient to exclude (66) depends on the level of application of contraction and the precise formulation of the rule. If contraction applies only at PF and "want" is a Case assigner prior to Contraction (see earlier), then the constraint must also apply at PF. Let us then assume the following formulation:

(67) A variable must be governed by a Case assigner at S-structure and at PF

As Howard Lasnik points out, this may provide another way (distinct from the proposal in Chapter 2) of deriving the following:

(68) Only an argument receives a *g*-feature at S-structure

Recall that in Chapter 2 we derived (68) from independently motivated properties of the indexing algorithm from which it follows that adjuncts and their traces have no indices until LF. As a result, antecedent government of adjunct traces (the only form of proper government available for such traces) is precluded at S-structure; antecedent government requires indexation, yet adjuncts bear no indices at S-structure. Principle (67) may provide yet another way of deriving (68). An adjunct trace is, by definition, a category that is not lexically governed (i.e., not governed by an X^0 category). Since every Case assigner is lexical (i.e., an X^0), it follows that an adjunct trace is not governed by a Case assigner. Under (67), then, an adjunct trace cannot exist at S-structure, since it cannot satisfy the S-structure requirement that it be governed by a Case assigner. This explains, without appeal to (68), why it is that adjunct traces are not *g*-assigned at S-structure; such categories are necessarily absent and hence unavailable for *g*-assignment at this level.

As concerns LF representation, the principle barring vacuous quantification requires that a wh-adjunct bind a variable (i.e., an adjunct trace) at this level of representation. In the LF component, then, an adjunct trace can be created by movement. In the LF representation, the wh-adjunct binds the adjunct trace, thereby satisfying the prohibition against vacuous quantification. But notice now that the existence of adjunct traces at LF dictates that (67), the requirement that a variable be governed by a Case assigner, does not apply at this level. An adjunct trace that is a variable cannot be governed by a Case assigner at LF any more than it can be at S-structure.

On the contrary, one might propose that, at LF, an adjunct trace could always be governed by a Case assigner, by virtue of the LF application of INFL adjunction to S (see L&S, forthcoming, for discussion of this rule in the context of the ECP). But this proposal is inadequate. Consider wh-adjunct extraction from an infinitival complement, yielding LF representations of the following kind:

(69) $[_{S'}[_S$ I wonder$[_{S'}$ why$_i[_S$ INFL $[_S$ you$_j$ tried
$[_{S'}$ $t'_i[_S$ INFL $[_S$ PRO$_j$ to go] $t_i]]]]]]]$

Despite LF INFL adjunction, t is not governed by a Case assigner; the embedded INFL is not a Case assigner and the matrix INFL does not govern t. The grammaticality of the sentence represented therefore indicates that (67) does not apply at LF.

Thus, to allow LF representations like (69), we assume that (67) does not constrain LF.

In summary, we have presented evidence against a requirement that variables must be Case marked. Instead, we have proposed the weaker requirement that a variable must be governed by a Case assigner. We have argued that this principle constrains S-structure and PF but does not constrain LF representation. Under this organization, we have suggested that the asymmetry in g-assignment expressed by (68) is derivable.[5]

Our proposal that (67) fails to apply at LF is independently motivated by the existence of LF representations derived by the application of Quantifier Lowering (see May [1977, 1985] for discussion of this rule). Consider Lowering as in the following SS to LF mapping:

(70) SS
$[_{S'}[_S$ Some senator$_i$ seems $[_S t_i$ to be intelligent]]]

(71) LF

$[_{S'}[_S \, e$ seems $[_S$ some senator$_i[_S \, t_i$ to be intelligent]]]]

As Chomsky (1981, p. 91) notes, such structures violate the requirement that variables must have Case (i.e., in the LF representation (71), t is a variable, yet this category is Caseless). Notice, however, that the principles proposed here are satisfied. In (71) t is a Caseless variable and, in addition, this category is not even governed by a Case assigner. It is inconsequential that t is Caseless, since no principle requires that variables have Case. Further, the fact that t is not even governed by a Case assigner causes no problem, since (as discussed earlier), the requirement that a variable be governed by a Case assigner does not apply at LF. Thus, the existence of LF representations derived by quantifier lowering, containing a (Caseless) variable that is not governed by a Case assigner, are not problematic.

FRENCH WH-MOVEMENT

Kayne (1981) discusses the following contrast:

(72) *Je crois Jean être le plus intelligent de tous
"I believe John to be the most intelligent of all"

(73) Quel garçon crois-tu être le plus intelligent de tous
"Which boy do you believe to be the most intelligent of all"

Kayne argues that the ungrammaticality of (72) is attributable to a violation of the Case filter.

The SS of (72) is as follows:

(74) *$[_{S'}[_S \, $Je crois$[_{S'}[_S \, $Jean être le plus intelligent de tous]]]]

The N″ "Jean" is not governed by the V "crois," with the result that this N″ is Caseless, thereby violating the Case filter. But now how is the grammaticality of (73) to be explained? Kayne argues that in the derivation of (73), successive cyclic wh-movement of the N″ "quel garçon" can void a violation of the Case filter. The following type of derivation is assumed:

(75) a. DS

$[_{S'} \, [_S \, $tu crois$[_{S''} \, [_{COMP}] \, [_S \, $quel garçon être le plus intelligent. . .]]]]$

    b. Move 1

       $[_{S''}[_S$tu crois$[_{S''}[_{COMP}$ quel garçon$_i]$ $[_S t_i$ être le plus intelligent. . .]]]]

    c. SS

       $[_{S'}$quel garçon$[_S$ crois-tu$[_{S'}[_{COMP} t_i]$ $[_S t_i$ être le plus intelligent. . .]]]]

The N″ "quel garçon" cannot receive Case in the DS (75a) (even if there is Case assignment at this level) for the same reason that the N″ "Jean," occupying an identical position, cannot receive Case in (72). "Crois" does not govern subject position; hence, Case assignment is blocked. However, in (75b) after movement to Comp, the verb "crois" does govern "quel garçon" and can therefore assign this category Case. Kayne then assumes that the Case feature is carried along, as well as copied, under movement. Therefore, at SS, "quel garçon," as well as the trace in Comp, bears objective Case.[6] Hence, the Case filter is satisfied. Thus, the contrast in grammaticality between (72) and (73) is accounted for. Government (hence Case assignment), across S and S′ does not obtain, whereas government of Comp, across S′, does obtain. As Rizzi (1982, p. 90) notes, under the assumption that Comp is the head of S′, these phenomena indicate that maximal projections block government with one exception (see Belletti and Rizzi, 1981) "the head of a maximal projection (and only the head) is accessible to an external governor. . ."[7].

Kayne's analysis of French wh-movement raises a potential problem with the constraint on wh-trace we have proposed. Consider the SS representation of (73) in more detail:

(76) $[_{S'}$quel garçon$[_S$ crois-tu $[_{S'}[_{Comp} t']][_S t$ être le plus intelligent. . .]]]
       + Case   + Case − Case

First, given that t is a Caseless variable, notice that the well-formedness of such structures provides further evidence that variables need not be Case marked. However, remember that we have also proposed that at S-structure, a variable must be governed by a Case assigner. This seems to be violated in (76), wrongly predicting ungrammaticality in this case. Recall that the purpose of incorporating such a principle was to rule out structures that are very similar to (76) in that they contain a variable in subject position of an infinitival S'. Of course, the structures in question do differ, (76) displays Case marking into Comp, while the ill-formed structures do not. We will now exploit this distinction and argue that, in fact, (76) does satisfy the requirement that a variable be governed by a Case assigner at S-structure. Following Rizzi, we assume that in (76), Comp, and only Comp, can be governed across S' by the verb. Given that Case assignment requires government, it follows that the verb can assign Case to Comp, and only to Comp. Thus, the N" "quel garçon," upon occupying Comp, is not directly assigned Case by the verb, since this N" is not the head of S'. Rather, it must be that the verb assigns Case to Comp, whereas the wh-phrase occupying Comp somehow acquires the Case feature from Comp (see Davis, 1984, p. 199; 1987, for discussion). But in this "extended" sense, Comp is a Case assigner (i.e., it has a Case feature assigned to it by the verb that it in turn assigns to the N" "quel garçon" when this category occupies Comp). With this in mind, consider again the S-structure (76). We have now proposed that in this representation, Comp is a Case assigner. Notice that Comp governs the variable t. Consequently, the requirement that t, a variable, be governed by a Case assigner is in fact satisfied. Thus, S-structures such as (76) are not problematic for the analysis proposed here.

Case assignment by Comp, to a category Comp dominates, is not Case assignment under government, given that government requires c-command which, in turn, requires nondomination. Thus, in at least this respect, Case assignment by Comp is some kind of marked option. We have seen that French and Italian exploit this option. Esther Torrego points out that Spanish does not; the analog of (73) is ungrammatical in this language. As concerns English, Kayne (1980) argues that a verb like "assure" is the equivalent of French "croire" in that both assign Case to Comp. Thus, the same contrast between a lexical subject and a wh-trace subject exhibited by an infinitival complement to "croire" is displayed in the following examples:

(77) *I assure you John to be the best man

(78) John, who I assure you to be the best man. . .

The S-structure representations are assumed to be as follows

(79) *[$_{S'}$[$_S$I assure you [$_{S'}$[$_S$John to be the best man]]]]

(80) John[$_{S'}$ who$_i$[$_S$I assure you[$_{S'}$$t'_i$[$_S$$t_i$ to be the best man]]]]
           [+obj]   [+obj]

Example (79) violates the Case filter, whereas it is argued that
(80) does not; "assure" is argued to Case-mark "who" when this
category occupies Comp. Thus, it appears that "assure" is like
"croire" in that Case assignment to Comp is possible while Case
assignment of the subject is precluded. There are, however, some
potential problems confronting this analysis. First, as Stowell
(1981, p. 417) notes, it is not clear how Case assignment to Comp
occurs in (80), since "assure" and t' are not adjacent (but see
Kayne, 1983, concerning the elimination of the Case Adjacency
Principle). A second potential problem with this unified treatment
of "croire" and "assure" is that these verbs do differ in at least
one crucial respect. Consider the following contrast:

(81) *I assure you to have made a mistake
(82) Je crois avoir fait une erreur
     "I believe to have made a mistake"

How is this contrast to be explained? The grammaticality of (82)
is readily accounted for. As Kayne argues, the verb "croire"
takes an S' complement with the result that a subject PRO is allowed. But the ungrammaticality of (81) indicates that when a
PRO subject occurs in the infinitival complement of "assure,"
some principle is violated. One straightforward way of accounting for the ungrammaticality of (81) is to assume that the subject
position of the infinitival complement is governed, thereby precluding PRO. Thus, let us assume that when "assure" takes an
infinitival complement, the complement is a bare S (not an S' as
in (79) and (80)):

(83) [$_{S'}$[$_S$ N″ assure N″ [$_S$ N″ to V″]]]

Thus, "assure" differs from "croire" in taking a bare S complement. This explains the ungrammaticality of (81), the S-structure
of which is

(84) *[$_{S'}$[$_S$I assure you[$_S$ PRO to have made a mistake]]]

This representation, under any indexation, is excluded by Binding theory, since PRO is governed. Consider next the occurrence of lexical N″ and of wh-trace in subject position of an infinitival complement to "assure":

(85) *[$_{S'}$[$_S$I assure you [$_S$ John to be the best man]]]

(86) John [$_{S'}$who$_i$[$_S$I assure you [$_S$ t_i to be the best man]]]

Example (85) is ruled out by the Case filter, "assure" is unable to Case-assign "John," since these two categories are not adjacent. By contrast, (86) is well formed. The variable t is Caseless, but this is allowed under our analysis. Further, the requirement that a variable be governed by a Case assigner is met, since "assure" governs t.

If this analysis is correct, "assure" does not Case-mark into Comp, but rather, takes a bare S infinitival complement, as is schematically depicted in (83). Notice that the existence of a verb like "assure," a verb taking a direct object N″ followed by a bare S infinitival complement, fills an assumed gap in the verbal paradigm. Such verbs are assumed not to exist, since it is assumed that no NP type could licitly occupy the subject position of the complement. But given that wh-trace need not be Case marked, there is no reason such verbs should be excluded (i.e., since subject position is governed by a Case assigner, wh-trace can licitly occupy this position).

MODERN HEBREW WH-MOVEMENT

On the basis of examples like the following, we have concluded that variables need not be Case marked:

(87) Who do you believe sincerely to be intelligent

Borer (1981) reaches the same conclusion on the basis of evidence from modern Hebrew. She argues that this language exhibits Caseless variables within well-formed structures. Modern Hebrew free relatives such as the following are considered:

(88) ma se hexlatnu ^{c}al-av
     "what that decided we on it"
     "whatever we decided on"

The S-structure of such well-formed strings is argued to be as
follows (see Borer, 1981, n. 7 for further discussion of this structure):

(89) (= Borer's (44))
     $X[_{NP}[e][_{S'}[_{COMP} ma_i]se [_S hexlatnu [_{PP} {}^{c}al\text{-}av\ t_i]]]]$

Case assignment where X
has Case assignment features

Following the analysis of free relatives proposed in Groos and van
Riemsdijk (1979), it is assumed that, in (89), the wh-word "ma"
occupies Comp of the headless relative and is assigned Case directly by the external Case assigner X. Consequently, the Case
filter is satisfied, since "ma" is assigned Case.
   Borer, however, argues that the variable t is Caseless. The PP
in the S-structure (89) appears at D-structure as

(90) (= Borer's (43a))
     $[_{P\ max}[_{P+clitic\ i} {}^{c}al\text{-}av_i] [_{N_i\ max} ma_i]]$
                 'on-it$_i$ what$_i$

The wh-phrase "ma" occupies a Caseless position, a result of the
fact that the clitic "av" has "absorbed" the Case assigned by the
preposition (see Borer, 1981). The crucial property of such constructions is this: At S-structure the wh-phrase occupies a
Case-marked position, whereas the wh-trace occupies a Caseless
position. Since these constructions are grammatical, Borer concludes that variables need not be Case marked. We have reached
the same conclusion earlier; hence, under the analysis proposed,
the Caselessness of the variable in (89) is nonproblematic. But
recall we have also proposed that a variable must be governed by
a Case assigner. This requirement too appears to be met in S-
structures such as (89), the PP of which occurs as

(91) $[_{P\text{-}MAX} [_{P+CLITIC_i} {}^{c}al\text{-}av_i] [_{N\text{-}MAX_i} t_i]]$

Notice first that the preposition "^{c}al" is a Case assigner. Thus (91), in which the clitic "av" intervenes between "^{c}al" and t, is very much like the following, in which an adverb intervenes between the Case-assigning verb and the trace:

(92) $[_{s'}$Who$_i[_s$. . . . . .believe sincerely $[_s t_i$ to. . .]]]

In both (91) and (92), Case assignment of the trace is blocked under the Case Adjacency Condition. But given that the preposition "^{c}al" governs t in (91), the requirement that a variable be governed by a Case assigner is presumably met in this representation as it is in (92). Hence, (88) is correctly generable.

The requirement that a variable be governed by a Case assigner straightforwardly excludes Free relatives of the following kind, in which the wh-trace is extracted from the subject position of an infinitival S':

(93) *mi$_i$ se amarti le Dan t_i le taken 'et ha-qu^{c}ara
     "Whoever that told-I to Dan   to fix   acc the sink"
     "*Whoever I told Dan to fix the sink"

Although no exact structure is provided for example (93), it is claimed that it is, in essentials, structurally identical to its English counterpart, given as

(94) *Whoever$_i$ I told John $[t_i [t_i$ to fix the sink]]

Under our analysis, (93) and (94) are correctly excluded, since the subject trace in each is not governed by a Case assigner. In the spirit of Kayne (1980), Borer (1981) excludes such examples by the ECP.[8] Borer formulates the ECP as

(95) ECP: A properly governs B if and only if A governs B
     and

   (i) A is $[\pm N]$, $[\pm V]$; or

   (ii) A has Case features and is coindexed with B

The subject traces in both (93) and (94) violate the ECP, since they are not lexically properly governed. Nor are they antecedent-governed, a result of the fact that the t in Comp is Caseless. As Borer notes, her ECP analysis extends directly to examples such as the following in which *t* violates the ECP, since *t'* is not Case marked.

(96) *The man*i*[that[you tried[t'*i*[t*i* to go]]]]

Summary

We began this section by reviewing two distinct approaches to expressing the requirement that *wh-trace must be Case-marked,* namely, the Case filter and the Visibility Principle. Each approach was argued to be problematic. The central problem confronting the Case filter is that it is formulated so as to impose a requirement on an unnatural class of categories, namely, wh-trace and lexical NPs. The primary appeal of the Visibility Principle is that its formulation avoids this particular unnaturalness. In particular, the requirement that wh-trace be Case-marked is expressed without stipulation. However, the Visibility Principle encounters a number of conceptual and empirical problems, which we reviewed. As was noted throughout, these problems are readily handled by the Case filter.

After reviewing the problems confronting each approach, we presented evidence that *wh-trace need not be Case marked.* This is important because the primary problem confronting the Case filter is that it must stipulate that wh-trace bear Case, whereas the central virtue of Visibility is that it expresses this requirement without stipulation. But, given that wh-trace need not be Case marked, the Visibility Principle's nonstipulative requirement that wh-trace must bear Case is, in fact, not a virtue but is, rather, yet another inadequacy of this approach. By contrast, if wh-trace need not be Case marked, the unnaturalness of the Case filter is eliminable (i.e., this filter can be applied to a natural class). Thus, the following formulation of this filter was adopted: **NP, where NP is lexical and has no Case.* It was then shown that this principle alone fails to account for the distribution of wh-trace. To account for this distribution, we proposed that *a variable must be governed by a Case assigner.* The consequences of this analysis were then examined with respect to the following: (i) the distribution of predicate NPs, (ii) "wanna"-contraction, (iii) the distribution of adjunct traces and quantifier traces, and (iv) certain wh-movement constructions in French and modern Hebrew. This concludes our discussion of the Case requirement on wh-trace.

The Case Requirement on NP-Trace

Many recent analyses express, in one way or another, the following constraint on the distribution of NP-trace[9]:

(97) NP-trace must not be Case marked

This requirement is violated in, for example, structures of the following form[10]:

(98) *$[_{S'} [_S$ John$_i$ strikes $t_i [_{S'}$ that he won]]]

(99) *$[_{S'} [_S$ I$_i$ bother $t_i [_{S'}$ that he won]]]

Notice that structures of this type are excluded as violations of (97) only if the following principle is also assumed:

(100) Case marking is obligatory

That is, if Case marking were optional, then the trace would not necessarily be Case marked, with the result that (97) would not necessarily be violated. Thus, for (97) to apply with any effect, (100) must be assumed. But the assumption that Case marking is obligatory is a problematic one, since it is redundant in light of the Case filter, a filter that we have argued to be an independent principle of grammar, not reducible to Theta theory. To see this, consider, for example:

(101) $[_{S'} [_S$ Bill AGR left]]

Under (100), the N″ "Bill" is obligatorily assigned Nominative Case by AGR (the only Case-assigning category occurring in (101)). But the obligatory assignment of Case is unnecessary. If Case assignment were optional, and AGR failed to assign Nominative Case to the N″ "Bill," the resulting structure would be excluded by the Case filter.

In what follows, we will present evidence that (97) is, in fact, inadequate and must be supplanted with a slightly stronger principle that will be motivated later. Under the incorporation of this principle, (100) is eliminable and can be replaced with the following principle of Case assignment, preferable to (100) in that it creates no redundancy with the Case filter:

(102) Case marking is optional

To begin, consider again the following violation of the Local Binding Condition discussed in Lasnik (1985):

(103) $[_{S'} [_S$ John$_i$ is believed $[_{S'}$ that$[_S$ he$_i$ likes $t_i]]]]$

As Lasnik notes, one conceivable yet inelegant approach to excluding such structures is by appeal to both (97) and the undesirable assumption (100). But as he notes, this approach is not only inelegant but also inadequate, because it fails to exclude examples of the following kind

(104) $[_{S'}[_S$ John$_i$ is believed $[_{S'}$ that $[_S$ he$_i$ is proud $t_i]]]]$

Since adjectives such as "proud" are not Case assigners, the NP-trace in (104) is not Case marked. As a result, (97) is satisfied. However, Chomsky (1986a) proposes a Case-theoretic means by which to exclude examples like (104). Chomsky proposes that adjectives, as well as nouns and prepositions, do assign Case, what is called "inherent Case." In addition, he proposes the following condition constraining the assignment of this kind of Case:

(105) The Uniformity Condition: If A is an inherent Case-marker, then A Case-marks NP if A Theta-marks the chain headed by NP (Chomsky, 1986a, p. 194)

As Chomsky (1986a, p. 194) notes, this condition "amounts to the requirement that inherent Case must be realized on NP under government by the category that theta-marks NP at D-structure." The Uniformity Condition excludes example (104); "proud" theta-marks the trace yet fails to govern the head of the chain "John." Thus, Chomsky (1986a) provides a Case-theoretic analysis of local binding violations like (103) as well as those like (104): The former (displaying no inherent Case assignment) can be excluded by adopting both (97) and (100), whereas the latter can be excluded by (105). However, Barss (1987) reveals an inadequacy of this approach to local binding violations. First, he considers a local binding violation of the following kind:

(106) $[_{S'}[_S$ John$_i$ seems $[_{S'}$that $[_S$ he$_i$ believes $[_S t_i$ to be nice]]]]]

This structure is excluded under (97) and (100); the verb "believe" obligatorily Case-marks the NP-trace, thereby creating a violation of (97). But, as Barss notes, the following structure he provides is permitted by (97) and (100):

(107) (= Barss' (26))
$[_{S'}[_S$ John$_i$ seems $[_{S'}$that $[_S$ he$_i$ believes yesterday$[_S t_i$ to be nice]]]]]

In (107) the trace is not Case marked. Under the Adjacency Constraint on Case assignment, the verb "believe" is unable to assign Case to the trace, since these two categories are not adjacent. Consequently, the NP-trace is not Case marked and (97) is satisfied (as is (105), which is inapplicable). As Barss discusses, one might conjecture that (107) is ill formed as a result of the fact that "believe" is unable to assign its Case feature. But, as he notes, the presence of a Case assigner that fails to assign its Case feature cannot be the source of the ill-formedness, since there are well-formed structures containing such categories. Consider again

(108) $[_{S'}$ Who$_i[_S$ do you believe sincerely $[_S t_i$ to be intelligent]]]

In the well-formed (108), as in the ill-formed (107), "believe" cannot assign its Case feature under the Case Adjacency Principle. From examples like (107), Barss concludes that the Local Binding Condition is an independent principle, not reducible to Case requirements on chains.

We now return to the structures with which we began this section. Consider again, for example:

(98) $[_{S'}[_S$ John$_i$ strikes $t_i[_{S'}$ that $[_S$ he won]]]]

As was noted, under the unwelcome assumption (100) (= Case marking is obligatory), this example can be excluded by (97) (= the requirement that NP-trace must not be Case marked). But, employing Barss' methods, notice that (97) is rendered inapplicable if an adverb were to occur between the Case assigner and the NP-trace, as in the following example:

(109) $[_{S'}[_S$ John$_i$ strikes clearly $t_i[_{S'}$ that $[_S$ he won]]]]

Since (97) is inapplicable, we now require some principle to exclude such structures. We propose that such structures are prohibited by the following principle:

(110) NP-trace cannot be governed by a Case assigner

This principle subsumes (97); it excludes any structure like (98), containing a Case-marked NP-trace, but, unlike (97), it correctly excludes examples like (109).

Notice that there is a certain symmetry with respect to the Case requirements we have proposed for wh-trace and NP-trace. Instead of requiring that wh-trace be Case assigned, we have proposed the slightly weaker requirement that "wh-trace must be governed by a Case assigner." And instead of the requirement that NP-trace cannot be Case assigned, we have proposed the slightly stronger requirement that "NP-trace cannot be governed by a Case assigner."[11]

Given (110), it is no longer necessary to appeal to (100) (= Case marking is obligatory) to exclude examples such as (98) (i.e., to exclude such structures we no longer need to force assignment of Case to an NP-trace). Rather, regardless of whether or not Case is actually assigned to an NP-trace, the structure is excluded by (110), since the NP-trace is governed by a Case assigner. Thus, the undesirable principle (100) (which creates a redundancy with the Case filter) can be eliminated and the following preferable Case assignment algorithm can be assumed[12]:

(111) Case marking is optional

Notes

1. See, for example, Chomsky (1980a) and (1980b) and Jaeggli (1980) for discussion.

2. Notice, in contrast to (17), the following is grammatical:

(i) I think there is usually a man outside

Lasnik (1989) postulates an S-structure roughly like

(ii) I think there is$_i$ usually t_i a man outside

Following Lasnik (1981), the verb "be" has undergone raising in the derivation of (ii). Since the lexical N″ "a man" is adjacent to the verb-trace, it can be Case assigned, provided the verb trace is assumed to be a Case assigner (see Torrego [1984] for evidence that verb traces do assign Case in Spanish). Since verb raising is prohibited in infinitivals, no comparable analysis is possible for (17). Hence, the contrast in grammaticality is explained.

3. If (5) excludes (48) and (49) because "who" lacks Case, it might also exclude the well-formed (46) for the same reason. This may indicate that the Case filter applies only to A-positions. If so, I leave open for further research why this should be so. Notice in this regard that we cannot simply claim that A′-positions are ignored at S-structure, since, for example, both g-assignment and parasitic gap licensure are sensitive to the status of A′-positions at this level.

4. Adjacency is, in fact, not a sufficient condition for contraction to apply. In addition, government is required.

5. Notice, however, that the exclusion of adjunct traces at S-structure does not follow from (67) if it is true that (Case-assigning) INFL governs an adjoined trace at S-structure (which depends on the exact definition of "government" and on the precise location of adjunct traces). For the sake of argument, suppose INFL does govern an adjoined trace at S-structure. If so, then when INFL is a Case assigner, an adjunct trace is allowed at S-structure under (67). Consequently, it seems that we cannot derive (68) from (67). One possible solution to this problem is to assume that a Case-assigning INFL cannot simultaneously license a subject (by Case-assigning it) while also licensing an adjunct trace with respect to (the Case-theoretic) (67). This restriction can be expressed as follows:

(i) Licensing is unique; that is, if X licenses Y, then there is no Z such that X licenses Z

We interpret (i) as applying within modules (i.e., if a licensor L licenses a category C with respect to Case theory, then L licenses no other category with respect to Case theory, but L might license another category with respect to Theta theory). Thus, for example, an Exceptional Case marker (ECM) licenses one category by Case-marking it while licensing another by Theta-marking it. This is consistent with (i), since the ECM licenses only one category with respect to Case theory and only one category with respect to Theta theory.

Principle (i) allows us to derive (68) from (67); that is, INFL cannot license both the subject (via Case assignment) and the adjunct trace (by virtue of being a governing Case assigner). Since Case-assigning INFL must Case-assign the subject (as required by the Case filter) the adjunct trace is not licensed. Hence, it must be absent, precisely the result we desire.

Notice that principle (i) may be extremely general, accounting for, among other things, the uniqueness of theta assignment (as specified by the Theta Criterion), as well as the uniqueness of Case assignment. The adequacy of this principle, and whether it can be extended to establish a biunique relation between licensors and licensees, awaits further research.

6. Kayne, n. 14, notes that either the subject trace is a Caseless variable or the objective Case-marked trace in Comp is the variable.

7. The contrast in grammaticality between sentences (72) and (73) holds also in Italian (hence, this language too apparently allows Case marking into Comp). However, as Rizzi (1982, n. 18) observes, if Case marking into Comp is allowed, infinitival indirect questions of the following form are incorrectly generated:

(i) *Non so $[_{S'}[_{Comp}$ chi$_i]$ $[_S$ t_i venire]]
     "I don't know $[_{S'}[_{Comp}$ who$_i][_S$ t_i to come]]"

If Case marking into Comp occurs, "chi" (= "who") can be Case marked, thereby satisfying the Case filter. To exclude such structures, Rizzi tentatively assumes that indirect questions are NPs; that is, the structure is

(ii) $V[_{N''}[_{S'}[_{Comp}$ Wh] S]]

In (ii) the embedded Comp is not governed by V because of the presence of N". Hence, (i) is correctly excluded, because it violates the Case filter; that is, the NP "chi" is Caseless.

8. Kayne (1980) excludes such examples by the Nominative Island Condition (NIC), which he formulates as

(i) NIC: A Nominative anaphor cannot be Case free in S'

In so doing, Kayne proposes that "the NIC be strengthened to require not simply a "proper binder" but a Case-marked "proper binder." Under the assumption that the trace of wh-movement is an anaphor, (i) excludes structures like (94) as well as "that"–trace configurations. Kayne argues that this principle is also responsible for the ungrammaticality of nominative extraction from the complement of a non–Case assigner, as in

(ii) *$[_{S'}[_S[_{N''}$the only person] $[_{S'}$ who$_i$ $[_S$ it is not
      essential $[_{S'}$ t_i $[_S$ t_i talk to her]]]]]] is Bill]]]]

Since the trace in Comp cannot be assigned Case by the adjective "essential," the subject trace is "Case free in S'," thereby violating the NIC. By contrast, similar extraction from the complement of a Case assigner is allowed. See Kayne for further discussion and also Chomsky (1981) for a reinterpretation of this kind of data and potential problems with this analysis.

9. See, for example, Chomsky (1981, 1986a), Davis (1984), May (1981), Sportiche (1983), and Belletti (1986). Within the framework of Chomsky (1986a), the requirement on NP-trace is expressed by the following condition on chains:

(i) If C = $(a_1, \ldots, a_n)$ is a maximal CHAIN, then a_n occupies its unique theta-position and a_1 its unique Case-marked position (Chomsky, 1986a, p. 137)

See also Chomsky (1986a, pp. 144/199) for an alternative, binding theoretic way of enforcing the requirement that NP-trace be Caseless.

10. The works cited in the previous footnote provide evidence for (97) not involving Psych-Predicates. We are using Psych-Predicate constructions only to avoid certain complexities surrounding other forms of evidence. It should,

however, be noted that the structure of Psych-Predicate constructions is controversial. See Belletti and Rizzi (1986) for a recent analysis.

11. Under the recognition of inherent Case, the requirements are not absolutely symmetrical. That is, since NP-trace can in fact be governed by an inherent Case assigner (as in, e.g., "Rome's$_i$ destruction t_i") the requirement on this category must be that it cannot be governed by a structural Case assigner. By contrast, the requirement on wh-trace is simply that it must be governed by a Case assigner, where government by either a structural or inherent Case assigner suffices.

12. As Andy Barss observes, double-object constructions such as the following are a potential problem for the Case requirements on traces we have proposed

(i) $[_{S'}$ what$_j$ $[_S$ was John$_i$ given t_i t_j]]

If we make the standard assumption that the passive participle "given" is not a (structural) Case assigner, then the NP-trace conforms to the requirement that it must not be governed by a Case assigner. But now how can the wh-trace be governed by a Case assigner, as required? Suppose that the verb and the first object form a constituent in a double object construction. (See Barss and Lasnik [1986] [and the references cited] for discussion.) Assuming that this constituent is a Case assigner, it Case-assigns the second object (under adjacency). Under this analysis, then, the wh-trace would be governed by a Case assigner, while the NP-trace would not (i.e., the structure would be generable, as desired).

Bibliography

Aoun, J. 1983. Logical forms. *Linguistic Inquiry* 14:325–332.

———. 1985. *A Grammar of Anaphora.* Cambridge, Mass: MIT Press.

Aoun, J., and R. Clark. 1984. On non-overt operators. ms. USC/UCLA.

Aoun, J., N. Hornstein, and D. Sportiche. 1981. Some aspects of wide scope quantification. *Journal of Linguistic Research* 1:69–95.

Baker, C. L. 1970. Notes on the description of English questions: The role of an abstract question morpheme. *Foundations of Language* 6:197–219.

Baker, M., K. Johnson, and I. Roberts. 1987. Passive arguments raised. ms. McGill/UC Irvine/University of Geneva.

Barss, A. 1985. Adjunction and reflexive hierarchical relations. ms. MIT.

———. 1987. Case and the local binding condition. ms. University of Connecticut.

Barss, A., and H. Lasnik, 1986. A note on anaphora and double objects. *Linguistic Inquiry* 17:347–354.

Belletti, A. 1986. Unaccusatives as Case-assigners. Lexicon Project Working Paper 8, Lexicon Project, Center for Cognitive Science, MIT.

Belletti, A., and L. Rizzi. 1981. The syntax of "ne": some theoretical implications. *The Linguistic Review* 1:117–154.

———. 1986. Psych-Verbs and Th-Theory. Lexicon Working Paper 13. Lexicon Project, Center for Cognitive Science, MIT.

Borer, H. 1981. On the definition of variable. *Journal of Linguistic Research* 1:17–40.

Brody, M. 1984. On contextual definitions and the role of chains. *Linguistic Inquiry* 15:355–381.

Browning, M. 1987. Null operator constructions. ms. MIT.

Chomsky, N. 1973. Conditions on transformations. S. Anderson and P. Kiparsky (eds.), *A Festschrift for Morris Halle*. New York: Holt, Rinehart, and Winston.

———. 1977. On wh-movement, in P. Culicover, T. Wasow, and A. Akmajian (eds.), *Formal Syntax*. New York: Academic Press.

———. 1980a. *Rules and Representations*. New York: Columbia University Press.

———. 1980b. On binding. *Linguistic Inquiry* 11:1–46.

———. 1981. *Lectures on Government and Binding*. Dordrecht: Foris.

———. 1982. *Some Concepts and Consequences of the Theory of Government and Binding*. Cambridge, Mass.: MIT Press.

———. 1986a. *Knowledge of Language: Its Nature, Origin and Use*. New York: Praeger.

———. 1986b. *Barriers*. Cambridge, Mass.: MIT Press.

Chomsky, N., and H. Lasnik. 1977. Filters and control. *Linguistic Inquiry* 8:425–504.

Contreras, H. 1984. A note on parasitic gaps. *Linguistic Inquiry* 15:704–713.

Davis, L. 1982. Argument binding and control. *Journal of Linguistic Research* 2:89–113.

———. 1984. *Arguments and Expletives: Thematic and Nonthematic Noun Phrases*, PhD dissertation, University of Connecticut.

———. 1986. Remarks on the Θ Criterion and case. *Linguistic Inquiry* 17:564–568.

Epstein, S. 1983. Topicalization, left dislocation and relativization. ms. University of Connecticut.

———. 1984. A note on functional determination and strong crossover. *The Linguistic Review* 3:299–305.

———. 1986a. The local binding condition and LF chains. *Linguistic Inquiry* 17:187–205.

———. 1986b. On lexical proper government. ms. University of Connecticut.

———. 1987. *Empty Categories and Their Antecedents*, PhD dissertation, University of Connecticut.

———. 1989. On adjunction and pronominal variable binding. *Linguistic Inquiry* 20:307–319.

Freidin, R., and H. Lasnik. 1981a. Core grammar, case theory, and markedness. *Proceedings of the 1979 GLOW Conference*, Scuola Normale Superiore di Pisa.

———. 1981b. Disjoint reference and wh-trace. *Linguistic Inquiry* 12:39–55.

Fukui, N. 1987. LF extraction of "naze" why: Some theoretical implications. ms. MIT.

Groos, A., and H. van Riemsdijk. 1979. Matching effects in free relatives. ms. University of Amsterdam.

Higginbotham, J. 1980. Pronouns and bound variables. *Linguistic Inquiry* 11:679–708.

———. 1981. Anaphora and GB. *Cahiers Linguistiques d'Ottawa* 9. Université d'Ottawa.

Huang, J. 1982a. *Logical Relations in Chinese and the Theory of Grammar*. PhD dissertation, MIT.

———. 1982b. Move WH in a language without WH movement. *The Linguistic Review* 1:369–416.

Jaeggli, O. 1980. Remarks on to-contraction. *Linguistic Inquiry* 11:239–246.

———. 1986. Passive. *Linguistic Inquiry* 17:587–622.

Kayne, R. 1980. Extensions of binding and case-marking. *Linguistic Inquiry* 11:75–96.

———. 1981. On certain differences between French and English. *Linguistic Inquiry* 12:349–371.

———. 1983. *Connectedness and Binary Branching*. Dordrecht: Foris.

Koopman, H., and D. Sportiche. 1982. Variables and the Bijection Principle. *The Linguistic Review* 2:139–160.

Lasnik, H. 1981. Restricting the theory of transformations: A case study. N. Hornstein and D. Lightfoot (eds.), *Explanations in Linguistics*. New York: Longman Press.

———. 1985. Illicit NP movement: Locality conditions on chains? *Linguistic Inquiry* 16:481–490.

———. 1989. Case and expletives: Notes toward a parametric account. Paper presented at the 1989 Princeton Workshop on Comparative Syntax.

Lasnik, H., and M. Saito. 1984. On the nature of proper government. *Linguistic Inquiry* 15: 235–289.

———. (forthcoming). *Move Alpha*. Cambridge, Mass.: MIT Press.

Lasnik, H., and J. Uriagereka. 1988. *A Course in GB Syntax: Lectures on Binding and Empty Categories*. Cambridge, Mass.: MIT Press.

Lebeaux, D. 1983. A distributional difference between reciprocals and reflexives. *Linguistic Inquiry* 14:723–730.

May, R. 1977. *The Grammar of Quantification*. PhD dissertation, MIT.

———. 1979. Must Comp-to-Comp movement be stipulated? *Linguistic Inquiry* 10:719–725.

———. 1981. Movement and binding. *Linguistic Inquiry* 12:215–243.

———. 1985. *Logical Form: Its Structure and Derivation*. Cambridge, Mass.: MIT Press.

McNulty, E. 1984. Determining syntactic arguments. ms. University of Connecticut.

———. 1988. *The Syntax of Adjunct Predicates*. PhD dissertation, University of Connecticut.

Pesetsky, D. 1982. *Paths and Categories*. PhD dissertation, MIT.

Pollock, J.-Y. 1981. On case and impersonal constructions, in R. May and J. Gueron (eds.), *Levels of Syntactic Representation*. Dordrecht: Foris.

Reinhart, T. 1979. Syntactic domain for semantic rules, in F. Guenther and S. Schmidt (eds.), *Formal Semantics and Pragmatics*. Dordrecht: D. Reidel.

Rizzi, L. 1982a. Lexical subjects in infinitives: government, case and binding. In *Issues in Italian Syntax*. Dordrecht: Foris.

———. 1982b. On chain formation. ms. Università della Calabria, Cosenza.

———. 1986. Null objects in Italian and the theory of pro. *Linguistic Inquiry* 17:501–558.

———. 1990. *Relativized Minimality*. Cambridge, Mass.: MIT Press.

Sportiche, D. 1983. *Structural Invariance and Symmetry in Syntax*. PhD dissertation, MIT.

———. 1985. Remarks on crossover. *Linguistic Inquiry* 16:460–470.

Stowell, T. 1981. *Origins of Phrase Structure*. PhD dissertation, MIT.

Tiedeman, R. 1987. WH-questions, parametric variation, and the ECP. ms. University of Connecticut.

Torrego, E. 1984. On inversion in Spanish and some of its effects. *Linguistic Inquiry* 15:103–131.